Eliot Ness
THE REAL STORY

Second Edition, Revised & Expanded

Paul W. Heimel

CUMBERLAND HOUSE

NASHVILLE, TENNESSEE

Published by
CUMBERLAND HOUSE PUBLISHING, INC.
431 Harding Industrial Drive
Nashville, Tennessee 37211
www.CumberlandHouse.com

Cover design by Unlikely Suburban Design, Nashville, Tennessee

Library of Congress Cataloging-in-Publication Data

Heimel, Paul.
    Eliot Ness : the real story / Paul W. Heimel.—2nd ed., rev. and expanded
        p.   cm.
    Includes bibliographical references and index.
    ISBN 1-58182-139-5 (pbk. : alk. paper)
    1. Ness, Eliot. 2. Detectives—United States—Biography. 3. United States.
Federal Bureau of Investigation. I. Title.
HV7911.N45 H45 2000
363.2'092—dc21
    [B]   00-043086

Printed in the United States of America

1 2 3 4 5 6 7 8—04 03 02 01 00

To honest cops everywhere

Acknowledgments

Most of what has been written and said about Eliot Ness is exaggerated, distorted, sensationalized, or fabricated. Many of those who could have helped to fill the gaps are deceased. Others who were acquainted with Ness, or have information about him, acknowledge gaps in their recollections. Separating fact from fiction or speculation has been a major challenge, made possible only by the interest, support, and encouragement of others who care about the truth.

Dialogue, in those limited instances where it is used, is re-created to the best knowledge of the sources who, during interviews, quoted Eliot Ness as best they could recall.

This book is the product of exhaustive research, countless interviews, and rewrites, each involving the elimination of information or episodes that could not be substantiated or reasonably assumed.

Eliot Ness: The Real Story never would have been completed without the help of many people who shared my sense of mission. With apologies to anyone whose name has been inadvertently omitted, they are: Louis Abraham, John Adduci, Fred Anderson, William Ayers, Dr. James Badal, John Binder, William Bogart, Doug Bretz, Karl Bretz, D. Bruce Cahilly, James Cloonan, Max Allen Collins, Robert Currin, Larry Del Grosso, Alan Dickerson, Jack Dorfeld, Katharine Dorfeld, Leslie Easton, Bill Grabe, John Graves, Sue Gunn, Joseph and Barbara Heimel, Lugene Heimel, Paul Joseph Heimel, Steve Heimel, John Herrington, Rodney Heymann, Christina Hice, Robert Hooftallen, Michael Husain, Whiz Iiames, George E. Q. Johnson Jr., John O. Jones, Virginia Kallenborn, Shirlee Leete, David Kerr, Raymond Koontz, Mark Lehman, Jeannette Libonati, Carl Lindahl, the Reverend Robert Loughborough, Fred McGunagle, Mildred Mackey,

Matthew Mangino, Rebecca McFarland, the Reverend Robert B. Merten, Jane Metzger, Gerri Miller, Dan T. Moore, Dr. George Mosch, Paul Newey, William Olson, William Pekarski, Joe Phelps Jr., Rick Porrello, John Rigas, Piet Sawvel, B. Mark Schmerling, Michael Schneider, Viktor Schreckengost, Lynne Skinner, Robert Stack, Al Sutton, Steve Talkington, Mary Taylor, Gerry Wallerstein, Lewis Wilkinson, Al Wolff, Gus Zukie.

Introduction

WE AMERICANS LOVE A hero; we're fascinated by a villain. Stories pitting good against evil captivate us. That could explain our fascination with Eliot Ness.

Who was Eliot Ness?

The purpose of this book is to explore that question with a degree of thoroughness never before attempted by dozens of journalists, authors, historians, and other researchers who have pondered it over a span of more than a half-century.

Most of those who have studied Ness in the hopes of sharing their findings with wide audiences have turned back in frustration, concluding that the public is more interested in the sensationalized accounts than in the truth.

The past five years of my life have been largely devoted to sharing my findings on the life and times of Eliot Ness while, at the same time, gathering additional information. My greatest regret was rushing a self-published book into print before I had the full story—or at least as complete a story as a researcher can reasonably expect to compile.

The elevation of Ness to celebrity status was irresistible and perhaps inevitable. Yet people have a distorted view of the man who bashed the breweries of Al Capone in Chicago, fearlessly battled organized crime and official corruption in Cleveland, served his nation during World War II, and through it all refused to compromise his principles, even when to resist temptation meant certain personal sacrifice.

Though the familiar character presented on the television screen and movie reel is distorted, Ness's actual accomplishments were legitimate. He deserves his image as a champion of law and order—a symbol of honesty, integrity, and bravery.

This book is an attempt to separate the man from the legend. It is a story of good versus evil that is complex and uniquely American.

Eliot Ness

PART ONE

Chicago

CHAPTER ONE

"Bye-Bye, Snorky"

HUNDREDS OF CURIOUS CHICAGOANS gathered at the city's Dearborn Street Station on a cool spring night in 1932, hoping to catch a glimpse of an American celebrity—not Eliot Ness, but his archenemy of the Prohibition Era, Alphonse "Scarface" Capone. After four years, the federal law enforcement machinery had finally toppled Capone from his seat atop one of the most brutal, efficient, and lucrative organizations in the history of American crime.

Crooked cops, politicians, and judges had looked the other way while gang wars strewed Chicago's streets with corpses. These officers were not about to stand in Capone's way; they were on his payroll. Capone had become a combination public enemy–folk hero. But now, this mastermind and former muscle boy of a criminal empire built on bootlegging, prostitution, gambling, and racketeering was on his way to prison.

Handcuffed and linked to another inmate by a three-foot-long chain, Capone awkwardly climbed out of the U.S. marshal's car, his ragged gray topcoat sweeping the ground as he tried to bury his face in his left shoulder. He and his prison mate huddled behind a phalanx of police officers, detectives, and deputies who bulled their way toward the loading platform. Cameramen protested as the circle of officers pushed past them. Capone looked up briefly then squinted from the glare of photographers' flashbulbs.

"Damn it, come on!" he barked to the other inmate, who stumbled as he tried to keep up. "Let's get the hell out of this!"

Capone then directed his ire at the newspaper reporters. "Go to hell, you lousy rats!"

Among the group of onlookers were many friends and family members who gathered to bid him a silent farewell. The officers stopped at the foot of a stairway leading to the passenger car entrance. Capone stood silently, looking downward, as a dozen federal officers scampered up the steps and fanned out for a quick inspection of the Dixie Flyer, a Pullman train bound for the federal penitentiary in Atlanta.

Once the signal went out that all was clear, Capone and the other prisoner were led up the steps and through the doorway. The crowd pushed forward for one last look at "Public Enemy Number One" as the group moved down the center aisles to the second car from the end. Photographers flashed away as Capone frowned and again buried his face in his shoulder, concealing the deep scar— the ugly aftereffect of a New York street fight when he was in his teens—that gave him the nickname he detested.

Federal guards poured into the cars on either end. Their leader, Eliot Ness, watched through the doorway as a uniformed officer helped Capone remove his overcoat and lit the prisoner's cigar before locking him into leg irons. Capone leaned back and closed his eyes, no longer concerned that his left profile was fully exposed to the photographers on the platform outside. At long last, he was resigned to his fate.

Ness slipped between the guards and watched in silence as Capone forced a slight smile for the half-dozen reporters who began firing questions at him.

"I don't know much about Atlanta," Capone said, his voice barely audible. "I guess, for one thing, it's gonna be hot. I figure I'll lose some weight, maybe play on the prison baseball team. Hey, I'm a pretty good pitcher and first baseman, you know."

Federal marshals ordered the reporters out, but Ness remained in the doorway, waiting for Capone to acknowledge his presence. Finally, Capone looked up at the man who had worked so hard to cripple his lucrative bootlegging business. This may have been their only face-to-face encounter, and it's possible that Capone didn't recognize Ness.

"Well, I'm on my way to do eleven years," he said flatly, peering out the window into the early evening sky. "I've got to do it. I'm not sore at anybody. Some people are lucky. I wasn't." He paused. "There was too much overhead in my business anyhow, paying off all the time and replacing trucks and breweries. They ought to make it legitimate."

"That's a strange idea coming from you," Ness retorted. "If it was legitimate, you certainly wouldn't want anything to do with it."

Capone glared at his young antagonist but said nothing. Ness backed away, feeling triumphant, and the door slammed shut. By the time Capone regained his freedom, the former crime boss would be a mere shell of the dynamic force that ruled Chicago with an iron fist. Syphilis, already eating away at his central nervous system, would force him to spend his final years as a bloated paranoiac who could recall nothing of his Chicago days and sometimes failed to recognize his own wife and son.

President Herbert Hoover and law enforcement personnel nationwide celebrated the downfall of Al Capone. Equally elated were rival gang leaders who were positioned to pick up the spoils of the Chicago crime wars and continue Capone's self-proclaimed mission of "giving the public what the public wants."

Eliot Ness was in no mood to celebrate. He stood rigidly on the dock, raising his shoulders to shield his neck from the cold wind as he tucked his hands into the deep pockets of his overcoat. A long, piercing whistle silenced the crowd. "Bye-bye, Snorky," Ness whispered to no one in particular.

Thick, gray coal smoke poured into the air as the wheels began to turn. The engine's chug became a loud roar, quickly dispersing the crowd. Ness quietly walked to his car then turned back toward the station, just in time to see a pair of red lights from the back of the Dixie Flyer glowing like rubies as the train disappeared into the night.

Ness's team of federal agents had saved a case of Capone's finest bootleg whiskey, confiscated in a raid, in anticipation of celebrating the occasion, but their leader declined the invitation.

"You guys go ahead," he told them. "I've got some work to do."

CHAPTER TWO

"Elegant Mess"

HARD WORK CAME NATURALLY to Eliot Ness. By the time he was nine, he was cleaning the floors and doing other odd jobs at his father's bakery in suburban Chicago, always eager to please.

Peter and Emma Ness were among the thousands of Norwegians who came to America in the late 1800s, seeking a better life in a land where economic opportunities were said to be limitless. Their arrival at Ellis Island coincided with the assassination of President James Garfield, not that either of the immigrants realized it at the time. "I knew that something big was going on," Peter Ness said of his first few days in America. "But I didn't speak English and nobody around me spoke Norwegian, so I didn't know what."

A master baker, Peter opened a modest bakery in Kensington, a cohesive Scandinavian ethnic conclave on Chicago's South Side. Emma, the daughter of a Norwegian dressmaker and an English engineer, split her time between tending to their two sons and helping her husband manage his business. Effie, their oldest daughter, was working on a teaching degree at Northwestern University. The other daughters, Nora and Clara, soon married and left home. Eliot's only brother, Charles, eyed a business career after graduating from high school.

The Ness bakery served a growing number of customers in the Chicago Scandinavian community. Eventually, Peter Ness opened a second retail outlet; a third and fourth would follow. The Nesses were never wealthy, but they were not poor by neighborhood standards. Eliot once told a newspaper reporter, "I'm so proud to be the son of two people who built a successful business and raised a large family while never cheating anyone out of a nickel."

Peter and Emma's first son, Charles, was born in 1890. Eliot did not arrive until thirteen years later, on April 19, 1903. The fact that they named him after George Eliot, the British novelist, suggests that his parents were not aware that they had bestowed on their youngest child the pen name of Mary Ann Evans.

Peter Ness was often away from home, tending to his bakeries, so the responsibility for raising Eliot fell to Emma. This close, dependent relationship with his mother helped to shape Ness's gentle personality in early adulthood. She sometimes behaved as if her son could do no wrong and instilled the same attitude in him.

"He was so terribly good that he never got a spanking," she recalled in a newspaper interview conducted during the peak of her son's prominence as a crimefighter in the 1930s. "I never saw a baby like him."

As close as he was to his mother, Eliot respected his father and craved his attention.

"What I now appreciate most about my father is the way he took the time to give me quiet lectures separating right from wrong," Ness told one interviewer. "He made sure I recognized the importance of hard work, honesty, and compassion. He never had a lot to say, but when he did speak, I knew it was something worth listening to. I always took it to heart because I didn't see him all that much. . . . I just wish I had gotten to know him better before he died."

Exhausted by their daily routines, Eliot's aging parents too often gave in to their youngest son's demands. A freckle-faced lad with a winning smile and quiet manner, Eliot spent much of his early childhood with neighborhood pals, gathering at the Palmer Park playground or visiting the nearby soda fountain for ice-cream sundaes and penny candy.

Eliot had an independent streak, even early in his life—"a mind and a will all his own," his mother said.

"We used to tease him for playing with girls, but he didn't seem to mind," said William Olson, who grew up two doors down from the Nesses. "We'd play army, or baseball, or other games that were just for boys. We'd invite him to play, too, and he would just look away and say, 'Naw, no thanks.' He seemed uncomfortable; nervous, I guess. After a while, we quit asking him."

One of Ness's closest companions was Wallace Jamie, the son of Eliot's sister Clara and her husband, Alexander Jamie, an investigator with the U.S. Justice Department. The two ended up spending a great deal of time together, with Wallace Jamie telling interviewers that he looked up to his uncle Eliot as a big brother figure.

"Self-reliant" was Jamie's description of Ness, who taught him how to defend himself with his fists against neighborhood bullies. The two shared a strong interest in "cops and robbers," fueled at least in part by the tales that Alexander Jamie would share with them from his law enforcement career.

Eliot was a bright and attentive student at Pullman Elementary School, but he was reluctant to speak out in class unless encouraged by his teachers. He could sometimes be found reading detective novels or comic books off in a corner by himself while classmates played nearby. After school and during the summer, Eliot pedaled his bicycle around to the stops on his newspaper route then hurried over to his father's bakery and begged to help. He particularly enjoyed riding along on delivery routes, pocketing tips for later use at the soda fountain.

J. A. Strom, who married Eliot's sister Nora, said that Ness took care of himself, talked little, and "was a good listener to older members of the family." He was also impressed with Eliot's sense of humor.

Childhood acquaintances recall how Ness attacked every task, no matter how menial, with determination and total commitment, often at the expense of personal friendships.

"We used to call him 'Elegant Mess,' which was really a put-down," recalled Jeannette Libonati, a classmate of Ness's at Fenger High School. The nickname stemmed from Eliot's often-spotless appearance and his inability, or unwillingness, to fit in with any of the high school cliques.

"It seemed like he always had something on his mind," Libonati said. "I guess he was daydreaming, or nervous. Some people considered him arrogant, like he thought he was better than everybody else, but I think he was just uneasy in social settings. Once you started talking to him, he loosened right up and was fine. He just didn't ever take the first step."

Among the many ironies of Eliot Ness's life is the fact that Jeannette, his classmate, became the wife of Roland Libonati, one of Al Capone's closest associates and a Chicago politician of some renown.

The compulsory military training at both Calumet Junior High and later Fenger High School did not appeal to Ness, yet he excelled at it. By the time he reached his senior year at Fenger, Eliot had matured from a gangly adolescent to a strong, square-shouldered young adult. He seemed taller than his six feet because he was so slender, but that slimness belied his powerful arms and shoulders. His brown hair, neatly parted in the middle, and his soft gray eyes offset a slight pug nose. A fashionable, well-fitting wardrobe complemented this natural attractiveness. The former Elegant Mess, now considered a "catch" by his female classmates, found it easy to socialize with girls, more so than his male classmates, though he was more interested in friendships than romance.

Graduating near the top of his class, Ness had his choice of colleges, but he instead went to work for a Chicago South Side auto plant. Within a matter of weeks, he grew tired of dipping radiators and accepted a job as a real estate office clerk. He also worked briefly at the West Pullman munitions plant.

His mother urged Eliot to continue his education, but it was only after Peter Ness took his son aside for a heart-to-heart conversation about his future that Eliot agreed to enroll at the University of Chicago.

"He said he hadn't worked day and night so that his youngest child would be a failure and have to work just as hard," Ness would relate many years later. "Failure" was a harsh judgment by the elder Ness, who by all accounts was well liked, active in community affairs, and successful in his business.

His mother was delighted that Eliot decided to continue his education. "One day, Eliot came home from work with a new suit and a briefcase," she told a newspaper reporter. "He announced that he already enrolled in the University of Chicago because he didn't want to get into a rut without a higher education. The enrollment first and announcement later was typical of Eliot."

After declaring multiple majors in pre-law, commerce, and political science, Eliot switched to accounting. In the classroom, he dressed in stylish sport coats. Women were naturally attracted to this quiet, handsome Norwegian, intrigued perhaps by an inner sadness that lurked beneath his pleasant exterior.

As Ness began to seek out more intimate feminine companionship, he developed an interest in Edna Staley, the daughter of a Chicago factory worker. Edna was an attractive young woman whose dark hair, light blue eyes, and heart-shaped face reflected her Scandinavian heritage. She and Eliot met in elementary school but attended separate high schools and barely knew each other as children. Ness had seen Edna in passing while visiting the office of Alexander Jamie, where she worked as a secretary, and finally summoned the courage to ask her for a date. From that moment on, Edna once said, she knew that Eliot Ness was the man with whom she wanted to spend the rest of her life.

Ness pledged the Sigma Alpha Epsilon fraternity, much to the chagrin of his parents, but was never active in the group's affairs. More often than not, he declined invitations to attend beer parties. Instead, Ness concentrated on tennis, which he played with such intensity that some schoolmates considered him a showoff. What he lacked in physical coordination, he made up for with technique, strategy, and endurance. Those same qualities also made him practically unbeatable in table tennis.

Ness also began studying martial arts. Three nights a week he attended classes in jujitsu, developing a strong passion for both the sport and the mental discipline that it required.

Eliot was filled with boundless energy. Despite the demands of his studies—at which he excelled with seemingly little effort—his involvement with women, his affinity for tennis and martial arts, and his fraternity connections, he still worked part time at his father's bakery.

During his final year of college, Ness became more comfortable participating in classroom discussions and impressed his teachers with his emerging leadership qualities and persuasive manner. He remained a compulsive reader, immersing himself in every mystery novel or American history book he could find. He also liked to write, often going far beyond the required word count for an essay or term paper. He signed his name in a clear, confident manner, stretching the final *s* with a long upward flight, which handwriting experts say is often the mark of a person who takes pride in finishing a job.

In 1925, Ness was awarded a bachelor's degree in business administration and political science. With industrial development all around him, numerous business firms courted the twenty-two-year-old Ness. He flirted with the idea of enrolling in law school. Instead, Ness became a field officer for the Retail Credit Company, an Atlanta-based firm that investigated people who applied for insurance coverage.

The "investigation" work he had been promised consisted of checking credit ratings and verifying the legitimacy of insurance claims. If nothing else, the two-year stint with Retail Credit showed Ness what he didn't want to do for a living. Eliot's days were spent in the field, while his nights were devoted to paperwork, all for a salary that would not even allow him to rent a modest apartment. He continued to spend what little spare time he had with Edna or with Alexander Jamie.

By that time, Jamie had been promoted to chief investigator for the Justice Department's Prohibition Bureau. He had already made a name for himself as a key figure in the federal government's enforcement of Prohibition laws throughout the greater Chicago area. Jamie not only collected evidence of conspiracies between the producers and sellers of the illicit alcoholic beverages, he also headed a secret task force charged with investigating corruption within the Prohibition Bureau itself.

As their relationship evolved, Ness, although not on the government's payroll, began working hand in hand with Jamie. Ness persuaded his brother-in-law to take him along during a variety of surveillance missions and undercover operations. After regular lessons at the U.S. Coast Guard firing range, Eliot became a crack shot with a pistol. This growing interest in law enforcement prompted him to enroll in a criminology course at the University of Chicago, studying under August Vollmer, a noted expert in the field.

In August 1926, with those credits added to his résumé, Ness was hired as a trainee with the U.S. Treasury Department's Chicago Division. Just a few weeks later, Jamie used his influence to have his nephew transferred to the Prohibition Enforcement Unit for the Treasury Department. Eliot Ness thus became one of some three hundred agents charged with the impossible task of drying up Chicago.

The Prohibition agent was held in wide and profound contempt by the average wet citizen, who disliked his function and indiscriminate toughness, and by the bootlegger, who saw him as a dishonest and expensive nuisance. With no civil service requirements in place for Prohibition agents, the bureau rapidly filled with incompetents, political appointees, and even gangsters. Enough agents lived far above their fifty-dollar-a-week means to support the widely held assumption that they were on the take; most of them were.

In a speech he delivered several years after his service in Chicago, Ness recalled how disturbed his mother was when she learned her son would be associated with such a group:

"So many of them are dishonest men," she said, protesting with a searching look at him.

"Not me," Eliot soothed her. "If there's anything you taught me, Mother, it's to be honest."

Peter Ness intervened. Pulling his wife close, he said, "A man needs a set of values and an education, and then he has to set his own course."

Emma nodded her agreement and never again protested her son's choice of a career.

CHAPTER THREE

Big Jim, Little John, and "Tommy Gun"

INDIVIDUAL STATES HAD BEEN outlawing alcoholic beverages since the middle of the nineteenth century. Not satisfied by this crazy quilt of liquor control measures, politically powerful groups such as the Women's Christian Temperance Union and the Anti-Saloon League of America pressed their case that alcohol was, if not the root of all evil, at least responsible for the vast majority of the nation's social ills.

In 1919 the necessary three-fourths of the states ratified a congressional resolution that became the Eighteenth Amendment to the Constitution. The measure, known as the Volstead Act, was named for a Republican representative from Minnesota who proclaimed that one of the main functions of government was to legislate morality.

President Woodrow Wilson opposed Volstead, but Congress overrode his veto. Thus, effective January 17, 1920, the federal government was in the business of enforcing Prohibition. The vice lords of New York, Chicago, and other major U.S. cities couldn't have been happier. When alcohol was legal and its production regulated, quality standards had to be met, while market forces kept a close check on profits. With these barriers removed, the underworld could dictate the quality, price, and distribution of alcoholic beverages throughout the nation.

No sooner had the ink dried on the federal legislation than the crime organizations began turning out millions of gallons of illicit beer and a variety of liquors. They also opened routes to funnel high-quality Canadian alcohol into the domestic distribution network.

Larger breweries—Anheuser-Busch in Saint Louis among them—converted to production of high-grade glucose for the confectionery, baking, and canning trades. Smaller brewers had three options, short of shutting down: They could convert to the manufacture of legal "near beer," first brewing the standard product with its alcohol content of 3 to 4 percent, and then de-alcoholizing it to 0.5 percent; they could lease or sell their breweries for legitimate enterprises; or they could continue producing beer in defiance of the law, under the management and protection of gangsters.

The "Great Social Experiment" of Prohibition was disregarded and flouted by most Americans, many of whom resorted to producing their own home brew. Flavoring extracts, bay rum, and medicinal preparations were widely used for beverage purposes, often with harmful consequences.

In most cities, anyone who wanted liquor could get it delivered to his doorstep by a bootlegger. For anything from a quiet drink with friends to a wild night on the town, he could take his pick from a variety of speakeasies that operated with little interference from law enforcement authorities. The finer hotels gave their guests mixers such as club soda and ginger ale, then insisted that their patrons sign an affidavit stating that they would not use the beverages for highballs.

In less-populated areas, most of which were already "dry" by local ordinance or custom, many a farmer continued distilling whiskey solely for his own family and neighbors—the traditional "still on the hill." Drugstore and café owners sold alcohol under the counter for "medicinal purposes." On college campuses, fraternity brothers—Eliot Ness sometimes included—found great adventure in imbibing.

As the illegal liquor trade flourished, it gave rise to its own vocabulary. The term "moonshine," used since the eighteenth century to describe the phantom presence of spirits distilled at night, hidden from inquisitive eyes, became a part of everyday parlance. Anyone who produced and peddled moonshine was labeled a "bootlegger," a term that originally referred to drinkers' tendency to hide their spirits in the upper part of the boot. Far from the sinister figures these labels might suggest, the moonshiners and bootleggers of the 1920s enjoyed widespread popularity, if not respect, from a thirsty populace.

Class distinctions developed, as described at the time by Federal Prohibition administrator Maurice Campbell:

> First we have the night club and extravagant "private clubs" patronized by visitors bent on seeing night life. Next in order is the bar patronized by the businessman. Often he thinks it is clever to drink his cocktail in defiance of the law. I am sorry to say that a considerable section of the business community likes a sly drink. Then we have the bohemian place in the cellar or the garret, supposedly patronized by artists or people who would like to be. After them there is a great gap in the social order of the speakeasy. Finally there is the criminal gathering of the lowest order. In these places it is possible to buy any kind of drink, occasionally genuine but generally diluted or poisonous. No matter who says it "just came from the boat," it usually just came from some nearby still or bathtub.

Each of these was regarded by its patrons as somewhat of a private club, not wide open to the public, but not very hard to enter, either. Welding everyone together into a common brotherhood was the knowledge that all present were engaged in a conspiracy to violate a very unpopular law.

Prohibition agents were not prepared for the danger and drama that their job entailed. Officers could make more money and avoid the hazards by accepting bribes. Many men who took the jobs had no intention of enforcing the law. It was not unusual for a Prohibition agent to leave his job for a more lucrative business—bootlegging. Local law enforcement officials were of little help. Most of them opposed Prohibition, and many regularly violated the law themselves.

Enforcement efforts, such as they were, focused more on international smuggling. Newspapers occasionally carried stories of rumrunners who were shot dead at sea or on land, purportedly for pulling a weapon on federal officers when, more likely, their arrest would be too much of a bother to the enforcers. For every incident that was reported, there were likely a half-dozen or more that were not. This played right into the hands of the crime lords, because it protected their elaborate system of production and distribution. Defended by the Coast Guard and border patrols from the importation of alcoholic beverages, they could amass huge profits from their domestic production. Whiskey and other beverages that did get past the enforcers would often be "cut" with various substances, repackaged, and sold at highly inflated prices.

Widespread public defiance of Prohibition provided the underworld with money in amounts and continuity never known before in crime history. As racketeers' fortunes increased, the criminal outfits expanded their operations, muscling into the control of gambling casinos, brothels, numbers games, slot machines, horse books, and phony labor unions. Dry laws also stripped the state and federal governments of a huge source of tax revenue.

The Eighteenth Amendment sparked a brutal turf war among gangsters across the country to meet the demand for alcohol. Of even deeper concern to many law enforcement officials and government policymakers was the growing sentiment among Americans that the law of the land was misguided and, therefore, could be ignored.

Nowhere in the nation was the violation of Prohibition laws and the spread of corruption more evident than in Chicago.

Ske-kag-ong, or "wild onion place," was the name given by the Ojibwa Indians to the river that branches out from Lake Michigan and divides into two parts about one mile inland. By the time of the American Revolution, both the river and the surrounding settlement were firmly established as Chicago.

Separate monolithic ethnic neighborhoods developed, few of them overlapping. About five hundred thousand Poles settled in neighborhoods on the sprawling South Side. Southern Italian immigrants were concentrated in two areas, the crowded "Little Italy" section and Chicago Heights, a separate city about one hour south of Chicago. The wealthy congregated in the relatively compact North Side, while Chicago's industries sprang up on the West Side.

These regions all intersected at the "Loop," the city's central business district. The seamier side of Chicago was the "Levee District," between Clark Street and Wabash Avenue, where brothels and speakeasies were everywhere, and where youth gangs and pickpockets roamed the streets.

By the beginning of the twentieth century, Chicago, known as the "Queen of the Lake," had become the hussy of America. Its open display of raw vice and spectacular mayhem was appalling to outsiders and to many of its own inhabitants. The colorful names of the South Side neighborhoods—Satan's Mile, Dead Man's Alley, and Hell's Half-Acre—spoke volumes. The red-light district stretched for block after block, lined with prostitutes, pimps, pickpockets, and hoodlums.

Chicago replaced New York as the nation's nerve center for bootlegging and organized crime. By the late 1920s, an estimated twenty thousand speakeasies were flourishing in the Windy City. The city came to symbolize the Roaring Twenties, a violent, colorful decade in which people lived fast, thumbing their noses at authority and openly enjoying those vices that formed the foundation of criminal syndicates.

Among the major crime figures learning their trade in Chicago was James "Big Jim" Colosimo. The son of an immigrant from Consenza, Italy, Colosimo spent his early adulthood as a pimp, extortionist, and precinct captain on the South Side. His big break came in 1902, when he married brothel keeper Victoria Moresco and assumed control of many bordellos and ancillary saloons throughout Chicago.

Before Prohibition, Colosimo had built his trade with prostitutes and young "white slaves." His nightclub, the popular Colosimo's Café at 2128 South Wabash Avenue, became the unofficial headquarters of the Chicago underworld. Celebrities, policemen, and politicians all rubbed shoulders with gangsters at Big Jim's, which was adorned with green velvet walls, gold and crystal chandeliers, and an immense mahogany-and-glass bar. Expensive tapestries and murals depicting tropical vistas hung on the walls. Beautiful chorus girls performed on a stage controlled by hydraulic lifts. The bar was stocked with the largest selection of illicit beverages in all of Chicago.

Upstairs, customers could find gambling tables of almost unlimited stakes as well as a wide variety of female companions. Colosimo's Café would rock until dawn or beyond, with Big Jim himself in the midst of it all, complete with massive diamonds and other symbols flaunting his considerable wealth.

It was inevitable that he would receive a visit from the Black Hand, a Sicilian society that specialized in extortion. The Black Handers insisted that the generosity he regularly showed to aldermen and cops also be extended to his fellow Italian Americans. Colosimo caved in to the demands for some time but then stubbornly resisted. Further pressured, he turned to a powerful New York crime boss, Johnny Torrio, for protection and business advice.

Behind the gentle manner and diminutive appearance of "Little John" Torrio lurked a ruthless villain who exercised near-total control of the New York rackets. In his 1930 book *Al Capone: The Biography of a Self-Made Man,* Chicago journalist Fred D. Pasley wrote:

> Torrio was one of the elder fuglemen of the powerful New York Five Points gang. The Five Pointers are dark fellows—cosmopolites of crime. He who rises to leadership with them is no ordinary ruffian, and Torrio rated a vice-presidency. He had executive ability, business sagacity, and a practical imagination. He was skilled in the duplicity of politics, proficient in the civilities, smooth of tongue and adroit of manner. He had a plausible front and he was young—only 29 and ambitious.

Torrio saw Chicago as a fertile field for his criminal enterprises. After arranging for the extermination of three Black Handers who had attempted to extort money from Colosimo, Torrio joined forces with Big Jim to consolidate Chicago's prostitution, gambling, and alcohol rackets.

This coincided with the Chicago voters' elevation of the bombastic William Hale Thompson Jr. to the mayor's office in 1915. Thompson was a husky former athlete who rose through the Republican ranks by bullying those around him and exploiting the prejudices of ethnic and national groups. Despite promises to rid Chicago of crime and corruption, Thompson sent word that he was eager to play ball with the underworld. Naturally, Colosimo and Torrio turned their forces loose to assure that Thompson was elected.

It did not take Torrio long to decide that Colosimo lacked the administrative skills and self-discipline necessary to manage the rackets effectively. In 1918, Torrio acquired a four-story brick building in the Levee District at 2222 South Wabash Avenue, just a block from Colosimo's, and turned it into his own headquarters, which became known as the Four Deuces. On the ground floor was a nightclub with a long mahogany bar where local whiskey sold for a quarter. Canadian whiskey and rum imported from the Bahamas cost 75 cents. The upper floors contained Torrio's business offices; a posh gambling hall where roulette, poker, faro, and blackjack were featured; a horse-betting parlor; and a brothel that was a cut above the typical flophouses that dotted the South Side.

The Four Deuces became a huge melting pot of criminals from the Windy City. Among the clientele were the soft-spoken, smiling florist Dion O'Banion; "Little Hymie" Weiss; the trigger-happy Genna brothers; the blustering Colorado Cowboy, Louis Alterie; and any number of lesser-known gangsters of Italian, Sicilian, Irish, Polish, and Jewish descent.

In 1921 Torrio returned to New York to encourage some of his former colleagues to become part of the action in Chicago. Among those who agreed to join him was Al Capone.

No one symbolized the wanton disregard for the law more than Capone. One of nine children born to Neapolitan immigrants, Alphonse often bristled when his Italian connections were mentioned. "I'm no Italian," he would snap. "I was born in Brooklyn."

Big and strong for his age, Capone was quick to anger. When he was fourteen, he dropped out of school after assaulting a teacher. This was his first formal rebuff from an American institution and, by extension, the mainstream of American life.

While kicking around the streets of New York, Capone fell in with several adolescent neighborhood gangs and became well versed in turf warfare, random mischief, and professional crime. As the American establishment rejected them, many immigrant children, Alphonse Capone included, found refuge and a sense of identity in the gangs. He was arrested at least three times as a teenager, twice on suspicion of murder and once for disorderly conduct, but none of the charges stuck.

Brooklyn's famous Calabrian gangster, Francesco Ioele, alias Frankie Yale, installed Capone as a bouncer and bartender at the Harvard Inn, a modest Coney Island dance hall and underworld hangout. Effective with his huge fists or with a club, the hulking, hard-knuckled eighteen-year-old kept peace and gained immediate favor with Yale. He perfected "the look," a gangster's gaze designed to strike mortal fear in the hearts of men.

Capone did not always come out on top. One night, while tending bar, he poured drinks for a smalltime criminal, Frank Galluccio, and Galluccio's sister. When Capone made a remark that Galluccio took as an insult to the woman, he pulled a switchblade from his pocket, vaulted the bar, and slashed at Capone's face. The attack left a wound near Capone's left ear and another down his cheek, earning him the nickname he detested: "Scarface." Ironically, Galluccio went to work for Capone many years later in Chicago for one hundred dollars a week as a bodyguard. Many others who crossed Al Capone's path were not so fortunate.

The syphilis that shortened Capone's life was probably contracted while he was under Yale's employ. One of the job's fringe benefits was the service of prostitutes, which Capone frequently enjoyed. He curbed many of his promiscuous activities when he became romantically involved with Mary "Mae" Coughlin, an Irish woman Capone met at a Brooklyn cellar club. Their only child, Albert "Sonny" Francis Capone, was born on December 4, 1918, about a month before Al and Mae were married.

In 1919 Capone moved his family to Baltimore where he worked as a clerk for a construction firm. He became familiar with accounting procedures and learned to read balance sheets—skills he would use later. The money he craved to pamper his wife and son eluded him, however. Capone accepted the invitation from Torrio to join him in Chicago.

There he served as a bartender, pimp, chauffeur, and bodyguard, steadily rising in an organization that was rapidly expanding its domain. Journalist Courtney Ryley painted this picture of Capone in the book *Capone: The Life and World of Al Capone* by John Kobler: "I saw him in front of the Four Deuces a dozen times, coat collar turned up on winter nights, hands deep in his pockets as he fell in step with a passerby and mumbled, 'Got some nice-looking girls inside.'"

Capone summoned other family members to join him at the fifteen-room red-brick house he bought on the South Side. He turned the building into a fortress, with armed guards at each entrance and iron bars on the windows.

With Prohibition sweetening the pot for the best-run criminal organizations, Big Jim Colosimo became the victim of his own success. On the afternoon of May 11, 1920, he arrived at his café shortly before four o'clock, chatted briefly with his secretary, and walked to a hallway next to the cloakroom. Two shots rang out. The secretary rushed over to discover Colosimo's body lying facedown on the porcelain floor, blood streaming from a bullet wound behind his right ear.

Police never made an arrest for this "piece of work," but the evidence pointed to Frankie Yale as the killer. Historians who have studied the evolution of organized crime in Chicago believe Yale was hoping to move in on the city's lucrative vice trade by knocking off Colosimo. If that was the case, his strategy backfired. Big Jim's death consolidated Torrio's organization, effectively locking Yale out of Chicago.

Torrio expanded the bootlegging operations and established trade agreements that guaranteed territorial sovereignty. Rivals warmed to Torrio's plan to eliminate wasteful hostilities. The frightening prophecy of Chicago Crime Commission director Henry Barrett Chamberlin was coming true: "Modern crime, like modern business, is tending toward centralization, organization, and commercialization. The men and women of evil have formed trusts."

Torrio recognized that beer was the beverage of choice for the Chicago working class, a big moneymaker even at small profit margins, and what better place to produce it than a brewery that was already up and running? Brewers in Chicago, believing that Prohibition would probably be repealed in a year or two, were not inclined to sell their properties. A few tried to meet the government's regulations for "near beer," but the public was not interested in this substitute brew. Torrio cornered the lion's share of the beer business by making the manufacturers offers they could not refuse. His gangsters would front as company officials, making the payoffs to police officers and Prohibition agents, and fight hijackers or territorial invaders. They would also take the fall in the unlikely event of a raid. In return, brewers furnished the equipment, technical skills, and administrative expertise.

Under agreements with Chicago's leading gangs, nearly every speakeasy, brothel, and cabaret in the metropolitan area was forced to buy its supplies from mob sources. For hard liquor, they turned to Dion O'Banion, chief of an organization that controlled the "Gold Coast," where townhouses and apartments of the city's wealthy and fashionable overlooked Lake Michigan. Reared in poverty as an Irish plasterer's son, O'Banion became a skilled florist. His round face wore a habitual grin, but under the tailored clothes on his small frame he carried an assortment of revolvers. "Dino" filled orders at his flower shop on State Street, while his operatives ran Canadian whiskey into Chicago, cut it with cheap diluents, and shipped it off to retailers at highly inflated prices.

The Genna gang reigned supreme in Little Italy, thanks in large part to a government license they had secured to handle industrial alcohol. Most of this was redistilled, colored, and then flavored to imitate whiskey, brandy, or other forbidden beverages. The Gennas' legal plant could not begin to supply the demand, so they persuaded hundreds of tenement dwellers and shopkeepers to let them install portable copper stills in kitchens.

Al Capone observed these developments from his new position in Chicago's dominant crime syndicate: manager of the Four Deuces. He also summoned his brother, Ralph "Bottles" Capone, from New York to join the organization.

For three years there was peace in gangland as the power of Torrio's organization swelled. Resistance from policemen or politicians was overcome by bribery, intimidation, or a combination of the two. Once Torrio was convinced Al Capone could handle more authority, he elevated his young recruit to a full partnership and assigned Ralph Capone to manage the Four Deuces.

It was only a matter of time before rivals would seek a greater share of the action. The most brazen of these was the O'Donnell gang from Chicago's Far South Side, who began running beer into territories that were supposed to be the exclusive domains of the Torrio-Capone organization. Fortified by hired guns imported from New York City, the O'Donnells strong-armed speakeasy owners and began hijacking the Torrio-Capone delivery trucks.

In September 1923 the O'Donnell gang felt the first sting of retaliation. Hours after a half-dozen gang members went on a violent spree, assaulting uncooperative tavern owners and smashing furniture, the group was reposing at one of its own outposts, a saloon on South Lincoln Street. Suddenly, three avengers burst through the doors. They wrestled one of the O'Donnell gang members, Jerry O'Connor, to the ground. Then they marched him out onto the sidewalk, where one of the avengers put a sawed-off shotgun to O'Connor's temple and pulled the trigger.

This was the opening shot of Chicago's bloody "beer wars," during which the O'Donnell forces—and all other challengers, for that matter—were no match for the Torrio-Capone machine. As the body count rose, witnesses placed Capone at the scene of several slayings. None of them, however, would repeat these observations under oath.

Battle tactics were changing as a new weapon, the Thompson submachine gun, or "tommy gun," arrived in Chicago. This high-powered military weapon, capable of firing eight hundred rounds per minute, commanded a price of two thousand dollars on the black market. Once the gangsters acquired tommy guns, Chicago-area policemen had no choice but to follow suit.

By the mid-1920s, Chicago was paying a stiff price for its gang violence and political corruption. The city was no longer being considered as a site for manufacturing plants and corporate headquarters. Reports of rampant gang murders were also scaring away tourists. The street warfare shocked most Chicagoans, but many took solace in the notion that "they're only killing each other." They greeted spicy newspaper reports more with curiosity than with outrage.

The public became fascinated with the gangsters' vocabulary. A $5 bill was a fin; the $10, a sawbuck; and the $100 a C-note. One thousand dollars was a gran'. A man shadowed was tailed or cased. A hoodlum was a hood (the "oo" pronounced like mood). An indictment or complaint was a rap; a pretty woman, a broad; a revolver, a heater; and a cop was the law.

One who talked too frequently was a squawker. If a criminal confessed, he sang. There wasn't much singing, since most gangsters obeyed *Omerta,* a sacred Sicilian code of confidentiality translated as "silence beyond death."

Stopping the wars in the streets was one thing, and much of the Chicago populace rallied behind that cause, but shutting off the flow of alcohol did not have nearly as much public support. Federal agents fell into disfavor for their overzealous enforcement of Prohibition laws, which included raids of private residences and high-profile arrests for possession of as little as a single bottle of liquor.

Chicago voters finally sickened of the bootleggers' best friend, Mayor Bill Thompson, and elected a reform-minded municipal judge, William Dever, to replace him. Torrio and Capone took their cue from the election and moved across the city border to the community of Cicero, thirty minutes west of the Loop and a safe distance from city police jurisdiction. About 80 percent of Cicero's forty thousand inhabitants were from Bohemia in Central Europe, or their parents were. They were quiet, submissive folks who wanted their daily beer, a heavy, robust brew. The residents of Cicero resented Prohibition and all but ignored it.

After plotting the ambush of Cicero, Torrio left for an extended vacation in Europe. Unleashed, Capone struck with a vengeance. He and his oldest brother, Frank Capone, opened dozens of speakeasies and nightclubs while taking over most of those already in operation.

Challengers from Cicero who emerged to take on the corrupt incumbents in the 1924 election never stood a chance. The Capones recruited about two hundred thugs to patrol each voting district and ensure success for compliant officeholders.

Author John Kobler described the election day tactics as follows:

> As a voter waited in line to cast his ballot, a menacing, slouch-hatted figure would sidle up to him and ask how he intended to vote. If the reply was unsatisfactory, the hooligan would snatch the ballot, mark it himself, hand it back, and stand by, fingering the revolver in his coat pocket until the voter had dropped the ballot into the box. Defiant voters were slugged, honest poll

watchers and election officials kidnapped and held captive until the polls closed.

Capone's forces also seized ballot boxes and replaced votes that were not cast in favor of the preferred candidates.

Law enforcement officials mounted an eleventh-hour counter-offensive. More than one hundred specially deputized Chicago police officers and detectives were dispatched to Cicero to restore order. A squad of four officers and a detective pulled up at the corner of Twenty-second Street and Cicero Avenue, where the Capone brothers and another man were intimidating voters. The trio apparently mistook the officers for rival gangsters. Frank Capone reached for his gun, but before he could pull it out of his pocket, two of the officers blasted him with both barrels of their shotguns. He fell dead on the sidewalk.

His brother's death was a turning point for Al Capone. He would, from that day forward, be a dedicated outlaw.

CHAPTER FOUR

"It Was His Funeral"

NOT SURPRISINGLY, A SLATE of politicians sympathetic to organized crime was swept into office in Cicero. Within six months, more than 150 gambling establishments and 100 speakeasies were running round-the-clock. A new state-of-the-art gambling house, the Hawthorne Smoke Shop, offered handbook play totaling as much as $50,000 a day. Capone also took control of the Hawthorne Race Track, which presented more fixed horse races than legitimate ones.

Despite Mayor Dever's best intentions, most of Chicago's rackets continued unabated, although less visible. With the Four Deuces temporarily padlocked, Capone opened a new Chicago outpost at 2146 South Michigan Avenue. He hung a doctor's shingle, reading "A. Brown, M.D.," above the door. A casual visitor entering the building would have no reason to suspect he was anywhere other than in the reception room of a physician's suite. Farther inside, however, the medicine dispensed by "Dr. Brown" was actually a sampling of moonshine Capone could offer retailers.

Off to the side of this bogus "examination room" was a small office occupied by bookkeeper Jack Guzik, now a figure of considerable influence in the Torrio-Capone organization. A short and pudgy man, the pale-complected Guzik had jowls that spilled over his collar and quivered when he spoke. He was never seen without his tortoiseshell glasses and broad-brimmed hat. One of eleven children born to an Orthodox Jewish family, Guzik had worked in the vice trade for many years, mostly as a pimp, before Torrio recruited him as a financial adviser and bookkeeper.

Guzik became known as "Greasy Thumb," which may have been a reference to his culinary habits or his success in greasing the palms of police officers and politicians. It was a moniker that those who had dealings with him did not use, any more than Al Capone was known as "Scarface" to his cronies. Capone's more acceptable nickname was "Snorky," which in its Italian derivation means "elegant."

Torrio and Capone entrusted Guzik with all of their financial records. His accounting procedures were thorough and revealing, as federal investigators would gleefully discover. Separate binders neatly arranged in his office contained ledgers, indexes, memoranda accounts, and day books involving more than two hundred buyers of illicit beverages. Guzik's records also included truck and boat routes for transporting liquor from Canada and the Caribbean to Chicago. More important, they reflected which police officers, politicians, and Prohibition officers were on the take.

In early 1924 Chicago police raided Dr. Brown's office and came away with boxloads of records. "We've got the goods now," beamed Mayor Dever. From these books, officials estimated the Torrio-Capone organization's annual gross income at $70 million, give or take a few million, making it one of the Midwest's most profitable business enterprises. Capone posted a huge reward for the return of the books. Days later, a municipal judge ordered the records impounded and returned to their rightful owners.

Capone survived another close call on May 8, 1924. Hearing that a low-level gangster named Joe Howard had roughed up Jack Guzik during a barroom argument, Capone hunted down the assailant at a South Wabash Avenue saloon. According to eyewitnesses, as Capone swung through the door, Howard turned and called to him, "Hello, Al."

"What's the idea of pushing Guzik around?" Capone shouted.

"Listen, you dago pimp. Why don't you run along and take care of your broads?" Howard retorted.

Capone, deeply insulted by any reference to his involvement with prostitution, emptied a revolver into Howard's head and shoulders as three customers and a bartender looked on in shock. The witnesses told police what had happened, prompting a warrant to be issued for Capone's arrest, but he was nowhere to be found. By the time Capone walked into a Chicago police station four weeks later to turn himself in, the witnesses were stricken with "Chicago amnesia." No indictment was ever brought in the murder of Joe Howard.

Word soon reached federal investigators that Capone had established his official headquarters at the Hawthorne Inn in Cicero, next to the numbers action at the Hawthorne Smoke Shop. Lawmen also learned that Capone now controlled the Hawthorne Kennel Club's dog tracks, where four hundred greyhounds chased electric rabbits. The dogs were either overfed or starved to assure that they rewarded the preferred bettors.

Many Chicago and Cook County officials felt comfortable mingling with the gangsters at the Hawthorne Inn, since they were beyond the reach of Chicago's law enforcement authorities. Upstairs, Capone relaxed to his phonograph's sounds of opera music. A biographer, Laurence Bergreen, believes Capone was regularly using cocaine during this period of his life. Others doubt or even contest Bergreen's conclusion.

Back in Chicago, the uneasy alliance of the rival gangs was unraveling. Dion O'Banion brazenly started marketing his beer in Chicago and Cicero. The Genna brothers were cutting into whiskey sales previously controlled by O'Banion's forces on the North Side. Bloodshed was inevitable.

O'Banion was the first to fall, not long after he duped Johnny Torrio into visiting a North Side brewery and tipped off police. Arrested on the spot for bootlegging and conspiracy, Torrio produced a wad of bills from his pocket and peeled off twelve thousand dollars to cover his bail.

On November 10, 1924, O'Banion was busily filling flower orders for another gangster's funeral when a dark blue Jewett sedan eased into a parking space on State Street, in front of the Gothic Holy Name Cathedral. Three men exited the car and strode to the flower shop.

"Hello, boys. Have you come for the flowers?" O'Banion inquired as he approached the trio, his right hand extended for a greeting. One of the assailants, Mike Genna, grabbed the outstretched hand and pulled O'Banion forward, off-balance, while the other men, John Scalise and Albert Anselmi, riddled the florist's body with six bullets. A final shot was fired into his left cheek as O'Banion lay sprawled among his flowers.

"Deany was all right and he was getting along better than he had a right to," Capone told one newspaper reporter. "But, like everybody else, his head got away from his hat. . . . He decided to be the boss of the booze racket in Chicago. It was his funeral."

O'Banion's gang was swiftly reorganized under the leadership of Earl Wajciechowski, better known as Hymie Weiss. A devout Catholic, Weiss was somehow able to reconcile his savage instincts with his spiritual inclinations. He vowed swift and brutal revenge for O'Banion's murder.

Racketeers and bootleggers were growing far too disorganized and combative for Johnny Torrio. Shifting allegiances made him uneasy, so he and his wife embarked on a southern cruise, hoping that tensions would ease. Weiss's gunmen were only a day or two behind.

Capone was also a marked man. On January 12, 1925, he stepped out of his chauffeur-driven car and entered a restaurant at the corner of State and Fifty-fifth Streets. Seconds later, a limousine pulled up and three occupants raked Capone's vehicle from stem to stern with gunfire, injuring his driver. Capone soon learned that the assailants were Hymie Weiss and two accomplices, "Schemer" Drucci and Bugs Moran. Drucci was a midlevel gangster who derived his nickname from his propensity for concocting far-fetched hits and heists. George "Bugs" Moran was more violent, less stable, and unquestionably jealous of the Torrio-Capone organization's success.

Capone promptly ordered a custom-built Cadillac from General Motors, complete with a steel armor-plated body, double panes of bulletproof glass, a gun compartment, and movable window. Bullets would splatter off this seven-ton portable fort as harmlessly as raindrops off a tin roof. It had a special combination lock designed to prevent Capone's enemies from jimmying a door to plant a bomb.

The Cadillac and accompanying bodyguard, exceeding that of the president of the United States, became a familiar sight in Chicago.

Torrio eventually came back to face charges stemming from the brewery raid. On the evening of January 24, as he stepped out of his Lincoln sedan, Weiss and Moran emerged from a blue Cadillac and opened fire with a sawed-off shotgun and pistol. Two shots connected with Torrio's jaw and chest, sending him to the pavement, and two more bullets entered his arm and groin.

Weiss and Moran were shocked to read in the morning newspaper that Torrio was still clinging to life in a hospital bed. A grief-stricken Al Capone stood by as a sentinel. Within days, Torrio was interviewed by police. "Sure, I know who they are," he whispered from his bed. "But it's my business. I've got nothing to tell you." *Omerta.*

A few weeks later, a frail and bandaged Torrio limped into court and was sentenced to nine months in the Lake County Jail. His treaties broken and his profile much too high for his liking, Torrio transferred all of his holdings in breweries, brothels, gambling halls, and speakeasies to the Capone family. With that, Al Capone had arrived at the top.

Capone established lavish new headquarters in a suite at the Hotel Metropole, 2300 South Michigan Avenue, just around the corner from the Four Deuces. The hotel lobby became a beehive of activity. Prominent criminal lawyers and high officials of the police department joined politicians and speakeasy owners waiting their turn to consult with Mr. Capone. Police officers in uniform streamed in and out. Upstairs, gambling went on openly and prostitutes visited at all hours of the day and night.

The new crime lord showed himself to be as adaptable as he was invincible. When the police or Prohibition agents zeroed in on his breweries, Capone was forewarned and hastily converted the targeted facilities to production of near beer. This legal brew would then be injected with a mixture of alcohol and ginger ale to become the "needle beer" that was a staple of speakeasies serviced by Capone.

Vice President Charles Dawes decried what he considered Chicago's "secession from the United States" to escape the Volstead Act. In a February 1926 speech, Dawes spoke with alarm of:

the moonshiners and bootleggers, many of them immigrant stock trained and tempered in European wars, running their own government, enforcing contracts, making and breaking politicians and seeing men of their choosing appointed to the bench and other positions. A colony of unnaturalized persons, feudists, blackhanders and members of the Mafia, aided by gangs of American citizens . . . have formed a super government of their own in Chicago. Many of these outlaws have become fabulously rich as rumrunners and bootleggers. They are working in collusion with the police and other officials building up a monopoly in the unlawful liquor business and dividing the territory among themselves under penalty of death to all intruding competitors.

Police continued to find corpses in alleys behind speakeasies, in trash heaps, and in vacant lots. Business operators who resisted the extortionists found their stores blasted by "pineapples," the slang term for everything from high-powered dynamite to crude, homemade bombs.

Public tolerance of the gangland slayings began to run out on April 27, 1926, after William H. McSwiggin, a young assistant state's attorney of Cook County, was gunned down. The son of Sgt. Anthony McSwiggin, a highly decorated detective of the Chicago Police Department, "Billy" had been friends with the O'Donnell gang ever since childhood. On the night of his murder, he and two of the O'Donnell brothers joined three cohorts and visited several speakeasies. They settled in at the Pony Inn, one of the saloons that had switched from Capone to the O'Donnells for beer supplies.

Capone assembled five cars and about a dozen men to post themselves outside. When the group emerged, the motorcade moved into position and opened fire, mortally wounding McSwiggin and two of the gang members.

The police investigation of these slayings went nowhere. A grand jury blamed a conspiracy of silence in the underworld: "There is an element of fear involved, because anyone who does aid the public officials by giving facts is very likely to be 'taken for a ride.' Silence and sealed lips of gangsters make the solution of this crime, like many others, thus far impossible."

The consensus of police, private detectives, and newspaper reporters was that McSwiggin was not an intended target of the assassins. Nevertheless, the public perception—"they only kill each other"—was changing. Perhaps, at long last, Chicago had been roused from its sodden lethargy.

Responding to a public outcry and pressure from Sergeant McSwiggin and his influential friends, police swept through dozens of Capone-controlled speakeasies and gambling houses, destroying equipment and sending customers scurrying. They gathered evidence of Prohibition violations, and from the Hawthorne Smoke Shop they came away with another batch of financial records documenting Capone's illegal business activities.

No one at the time realized the important role these ledgers would play in the government's case against several key figures in the Capone organization. Wrapped in plain brown paper, tied with a string, and buried in an obscure cabinet at police headquarters, these documents contained breakdowns of gambling profits during an eighteen-month period. Every few pages, Guzik had divided a balance between "A" for Al Capone, "R" for Ralph Capone, and "J" for Jack Guzik.

Capone fled to Lansing, Michigan, accompanied by two of his bodyguards, "Machine Gun Jack" McGurn and Frank Nitti. He considered turning over the rackets to his brother Ralph and Guzik and finding a more secure way to make a living. With these thoughts in mind, as well as a desire to clear his name, Capone agreed to appear before the grand jury convened to probe the Cicero murders.

"I've been convicted without a hearing of all the crimes on the calendar, but I'm innocent and it won't take long to prove it," Capone declared as he reemerged and spoke with newspaper reporters. "I trust my attorneys to see that I'm treated like a human being and not pushed around by a lot of coppers with axes to grind. Of course I didn't kill McSwiggin. Why should I? I liked the kid." Capone then stunned all of Chicago by announcing that even the young prosecutor was on the mob's payroll. "I paid McSwiggin. I paid him plenty and I got what I was paying for." Independent investigations confirmed Capone's shocking revelation.

News of this payoff was plastered throughout the nation, drama-tizing the cozy relationship between the Chicago underworld and those officials who were supposed to be enforcing the law. Even the *Chicago Tribune,* a "wet" newspaper, appealed to President Calvin Coolidge to "place the full weight of his administration and the vast power of the federal government behind the move to rid Chicago of the gangs of alien gunmen who are terrorizing the community."

Hymie Weiss and the other O'Banion forces, still intent on avenging the florist's murder, orchestrated their own show of strength. On September 20, 1926, they dispatched eight touring cars to Cicero and peppered Capone's Hawthorne headquarters with gunfire. More than one thousand shots were fired during the first of the high-profile "motorcade-style" attacks that would become commonplace in Chicago.

Three weeks later, Weiss and four of his associates parked in front of the Gothic Holy Name Cathedral, in the same space Dion O'Banion's killers had occupied. Bullets poured from the windows of a boarding house as the men reached the middle of the street. Weiss dropped to the pavement, his body fatally riddled with ten bullet holes. His bodyguard and beer-runner, Patrick "Paddy" Murray, fell dead beside him.

Capone was strongly suspected of being behind the killings, but he steadfastly denied any involvement: "That was butchery. Hymie was a good kid. He could have got out a long time ago and taken his beer and been alive today. They began to get nasty. We sent 'em word to stay in their own backyard. But they had the swelled head and thought they were bigger than we were. Then O'Banion got killed. Right after Torrio was shot—and Johnny knew who shot him—I had a talk with Weiss. 'What do you want to do, get your-self killed before you're thirty? You better get some sense while a few of us are still alive.' He could still have got along with me, but he wouldn't listen to me. There's enough business for all of us with-out killing each other like animals in the street. I don't want to end up in the gutter, punctured by machine gun slugs."

His words did little to assuage the national dismay over the growing lawlessness. The escalating violence in Chicago went on unabated, reaching a feverish pitch. Pressure for a federal crackdown intensified. On April Fools' Day, 1927, the Treasury Department elevated its Prohibition Unit to bureau status and announced plans to more strictly enforce the dry law.

Into this setting came a young, idealistic, and untested Prohibition agent named Eliot Ness.

CHAPTER FIVE

What the Public Wants

NESS'S FIRST ASSIGNMENT GAVE him a taste of the frustration he would face in his new job. Ted Kuhn, a veteran Chicago Prohibition agent who worked with Ness during his first week, recalled how excited his partner was to find a still.

"He couldn't wait to make an arrest," Kuhn said. "He thought it would have some kind of domino effect and scare away all of the other moonshiners. I said, 'You've got a lot to learn, kid. Did you tell anybody about what you found?' And he said, 'Just a couple of guys in the department.' I knew right then that we'd never be arresting anyone in that case, but I figured it would be a good lesson for Eliot.

"I told him, 'You better get an arrest warrant right away.' He nodded and filled out the paperwork. By the time we got to the home, the still was gone and the couple who lived there pleaded ignorance. Eliot vowed to act more swiftly and confidentially the next time. I'll say this for him, he was a fast learner."

Ness, who carried a .38 Colt snub-nosed pistol in a shoulder holster, was soon teamed with another young officer, Dan Koken. They were dispatched to Chicago Heights, about thirty miles south of Chicago, late in 1927 for an undercover operation devised to gather evidence of Sicilian bootlegging activity and payoffs. Koken had already become familiar with the Chicago Heights scene by posing as a crooked Prohibition agent and accepting a payoff. He and Ness hit it off right from the start. They shared a passion for adventure, and each took pride in the fact that he was a designated "special agent," as opposed to a run-of-the-mill "prohibition agent."

The duo were sometimes joined by a third officer, a Greek known as A. M. "Nine-Toed" Nabors. A native of Georgia, Nabors had lost part of a foot during World War I. He spoke in a southern drawl and frequently flashed a winning smile, accented by light, wavy hair that made him, in the words of Ness, "the handsomest man I ever saw."

Chicago Heights was a hotbed of bootlegging, laced with stills supplying buyers in Iowa, Wisconsin, Kentucky, and Tennessee, as well as speakeasies much closer to home. Organized crime had a stranglehold on virtually all of the commerce and law enforcement, but turf battles were escalating. Alexander Jamie sent his special unit of Prohibition agents, his brother-in-law included, to Chicago Heights to investigate.

Ness, Koken, and Nabors made one minor raid, seizing about $500 worth of liquor from a speakeasy, and were promptly approached by a Sicilian who suggested that, for $250 a week, Ness and his partners might be persuaded to look the other way. This was precisely the opportunity they had hoped for.

After they accepted the money, the three agents were welcomed at the Cozy Corners, a Chicago Heights saloon frequented by underworld figures. They rode in a large black Cadillac that the government had seized during a raid many months earlier. The group's chauffeur, Frank Basile, spoke Italian and assisted the agents in interpreting some of the dialogue they heard. Basile knew more than the Italian language—he had been arrested on boot-legging charges himself and had turned state's evidence, testifying against a Capone crony, Lorenzo Juliano. An excited Ness believed he was on a trail of criminal activity that would lead him directly to Al Capone. In reality, Capone's rivals controlled the Chicago Heights area where he was working.

Ness and his partners enjoyed rubbing shoulders with the boot-leggers, gathering evidence all the while. The fact that Chicago

Heights police officers, in uniform, were among patrons at the bar was both revealing and disconcerting. "Rum-runners from Iowa, southern Illinois, Saint Louis and as far away as Kansas City would come," Ness wrote of the Cozy Corners in a short manuscript that would become the basis for the book *The Untouchables*. "They would leave their cars, loaded with liquor, with the bartenders and the cars would be driven away by members of the Chicago Heights alcohol mob. The drivers from out of town would stay at the bar, drinking, or avail themselves of what the brothel on the second and third floors had to offer. That was one of their rewards for delivering the booze."

Some of the beverages peddled at the Chicago Heights speakeasies were produced much closer to home. Ness's team found one neighborhood where "alky-cooking" was so common that a foul-smelling odor enveloped the entire area. Law enforcement tended to ignore these and thousands more tenement dwellers who converted corn sugar into ethanol. The technique provided income to needy families who, by their sheer numbers, could not be raided wholesale because local politicians understood such a move would end any possibility of reelection.

Ness ignored the political implications in his zeal to enforce the law and, in his eyes at least, chip away at Capone's empire. His group cruised the area for two nights and discovered that two Cadillacs with three occupants each were tailing them. The next night, they changed cars and took a back route into Chicago Heights, escaping notice. The agents went house to house, compiling a list of those homes where they detected the telltale odor of fermenting mash.

Armed with the list of alky-cookers, Ness sought a meeting at the Cozy Corners with purported gang leader Joe Martino to demand additional money in return for the agents' silence. Martino, a short, smooth-faced, dark-complected man with wavy dark hair, was the lone survivor of a once-powerful Chicago Heights gang. His day had pretty much passed by this time, but Martino did serve occasional ceremonial functions as a representative of the Unione Siciliana. He may also have been a decoy for the real heavyweights of organized crime in Chicago Heights, Jimmy Emery and Dominic Ruberto.

Ness wrote in the original draft of his memoirs:

> We had quite an argument about the amount to be paid. I was the
> main objector and the hungry one. We brought up questions
> about how much they paid other law enforcement officials and
> who, but they were careful not to bite too hard on these leads. At
> this meeting, in the same room, but sitting apart from the group,
> we noticed a swarthy, silk-shirted Italian who apparently did not
> understand a word of English nor did he speak any English. We
> agreed on a weekly sum, which I think was in the neighborhood
> of $500. As the meeting broke up, Frank Basile [Ness actually
> used the pseudonym Burt Napoli] turned white and, pulling me
> aside, said, "The silk-shirted Italian has just asked whether or not
> he should let you have a knife in the back."

As with many incidents recounted in Ness's original manuscript
and the book that followed, it is difficult to determine where the
truth leaves off and the sensationalizing begins. In *The Untouchables,* readers are informed that Nabors pulled a sawed-off shotgun
from his coat and held the Sicilians at bay while Ness and the other
agents left the Cozy Corners with five hundred dollars in cash and
an assurance that the bribes would be doubled.

Following the meeting with Martino, Ness decided it was time
to strike, even at the expense of blowing the agents' cover. They
obtained eighteen warrants and swept through the alky-cooking
neighborhood, arresting more than two dozen suspects, destroying
equipment, and seizing moonshine.

Days later, on December 11, 1928, the lifeless body of Frank
Basile was found brutally beaten and shot, dumped in a Chicago
Heights ditch. This may have been an act to avenge Basile's testimony against Lorenzo Juliano, or a response to the Ness team's activities. Eliot Ness assumed the latter.

"I had expected it, I suppose," Ness wrote. "You think that nothing can disturb you and that your nerves are impregnable. Yet, looking down at that familiar face, different somehow in its last repose, I
realized that death is something to which we never become calloused
if the person is someone close."

A suspect arrested for Basile's murder hanged himself in his
prison cell before investigators could get a statement. "The evidence

on him was positive enough to make us feel that the person who had gotten Frank had been brought to justice," Ness wrote.

Ness and his partners went after the Chicago Heights villains with a vengeance. A longtime resident of Chicago Heights and acquaintance of Al Capone told author Laurence Bergreen, "One time two truckloads of merchandise were coming in. Ness and his men stopped the truck, grabbed the drivers, squeezed their balls and beat the s— out of them. Hit them with clubs. It looked as though the shipment would never be delivered, but then money changed hands and the truck got through." Unlike many officers in the Prohibition Bureau, Ness and his partners dutifully reported these bribes and all others to their superiors.

The team was joined by Martin Lahart, a smiling Irishman and physical fitness buff who was not reluctant to use force when warranted. At Lahart's urging, the team stormed into the Cozy Corners and arrested everyone in sight, from bartenders to prostitutes.

Ness's memoirs detailed a telephone call he received at his parents' home, where he was still living, immediately after the raid. A rough voice on the other end of the line warned: "I got a message for you. You've had your last chance to be smart. Just keep in mind that sometime soon you're going to be found layin' in a ditch with a hole in your head and your wang slashed off. We'll keep reminding you so you won't forget to remember."

Although frightened, Ness took the call as evidence he was making a difference. He immediately had his parents' home placed under twenty-four-hour police guard and quietly moved into an apartment with Agent Nabors. On many occasions, Ness slept over and ate his meals at his office in Chicago, afraid to be seen on the streets. Although his relationship with Edna Staley remained strong, he told her that because of the danger and secretive nature of his work it would be better if they stopped seeing each other for a while.

In the meantime, Chicago had not heard the last of Big Bill Thompson. Capitalizing on public opposition to Prohibition and using his own bombastic campaign style, Thompson announced, "I'm wetter than the middle of the Atlantic Ocean. We'll put police back traveling beats instead of sniffing around for a little home brew or frisking pantries for a hip flask."

His campaign coffers swelled with underworld contributions. Thompson rolled over Dever in the mayoral election and promptly filled many key positions with officials who were sympathetic to the bootleggers. Police officers, politicians, and magistrates were once again lining up for payoffs from Al Capone, who bragged that his organization was spending upward of $30 million a year to buy cooperation.

Capone's charisma was undeniable, and he played upon the "folk hero" image. "He has concentration and executive ability beyond the ordinary," wrote Chicago columnist Russell A. Johnson. "He is utterly fearless except when it is sensible to be afraid. I have never known a person who wasted fewer words in reaching the heart of a problem. Yet Capone, despite his intelligence, loses all perspective when it comes to a discussion of his rights under Prohibition. He sincerely believes that he has every right to supply booze to 'nice people' who seem eager to welcome his wares. 'Some of the biggest drys in the country buy from me and have for years,' he says, 'so let's stop kidding ourselves.' His attitude toward Prohibition may be his Achilles' heel."

Capone was seen in public more than ever, but he remained an elusive target for his rivals. Joseph Aiello, head of an extended crime family that succeeded the Genna brothers as Little Italy's boot-legging kingpins, joined forces with Bugs Moran and other O'Ban-ion disciples in an effort to unseat Capone. Four professional hitmen, lured to Chicago by a fifty-thousand-dollar bounty his rivals placed on Capone's head, left in caskets. Each was found with a nickel in his palm, the signature of Capone's top gun, Jack McGurn.

"I'm the boss," Capone declared to reporters in response to the Aiello-Moran offensive. "I'm going to continue to run things. Don't let anybody kid you into thinking that I can be run out of town. I haven't run yet and I'm not going to. When we get through with Aiello, Moran, and their guys, there won't be any opposition and I'll still be doing business."

Soon afterward, the crime boss was singing a different tune. The 1928 presidential election attracted the attention of the indomitable Bill Thompson, who knew he could never build a national con-stituency if he were allied with the man who was recently declared

America's "Public Enemy Number One." Capone, a symbol of wealth and indulgence in a time of nationwide economic gloom, had grown too big for Thompson to explain away. The mayor proclaimed that the days of leniency and hand-holding were over. A series of well-publicized, albeit insignificant, raids on some of Capone's businesses created the desired illusion.

Capone played along, announcing that he was giving up the rackets and exiting Chicago. Leaning back in his huge chair, smoke curling from his fat Havana cigar, he told reporters:

> Let the worthy citizens of Chicago get their liquor the best way they can. I'm sick of the job. It's a thankless one and full of grief. I give the public what the public wants. I never had to send out high-pressure salesmen. I could never meet the demand! Sure, I violate the Prohibition law. Who doesn't? The only difference is I take more chances than the man who drinks a cocktail before dinner and a flock of highballs after it, but he is just as much a violator as I am. Ninety percent of the people of Cook County drink and gamble, and my offense has been to furnish them with those amusements. Whatever else they may say, my booze has been good and my games have been on the square. Well, tell the folks I'm going away now. I guess murder will stop. There won't be any more booze. You won't be able to find a craps game.

Chicagoans greeted Capone's news conference with everything from skepticism to celebration. Among those able to read between the lines was Eliot Ness. While his colleagues chuckled at the quotation from Capone in the morning papers, Ness did not crack a smile; Al Capone ran counter to all that he believed in.

Excitable and unsure of himself during his first few months with the Prohibition Unit, the boyish-looking Ness, now twenty-six, was beginning to exhibit maturity beyond his years. With dogged determination, he worked many hours beyond what was expected for his modest salary. He complained openly to his superiors about the widespread corruption he observed within the organization, and he didn't care whose toes he stepped on.

In June 1928 Ness received his long-awaited promotion to "special agent" within the Treasury Department's Prohibition Bureau–Chicago

Division, along with a four-hundred-dollar raise, making his annual salary twenty-nine hundred dollars. An evaluator wrote that Ness had come from a "good family, keeps good company, [and is] always a gentleman." He was further described as "courageous, reliable in every respect, [a] clean young man, morally a fine fellow."

Although he did not say so publicly, Ness was personally opposed to the Volstead Act and recognized the difficulty in enforcing it. In fact, he was an occasional violator himself. At the same time, he saw the dry law as a valuable tool to use in the attack against the more serious criminal acts of graft, extortion, and murder, as well as a means of attacking Al Capone's financial foundation.

Thompson became the laughingstock of the 1928 presidential campaign and withdrew from the race. The Chicago electorate spoke with a voice that was loud and clear. Nearly every candidate connected with the Thompson administration was resoundingly defeated. The *Chicago Tribune* called the election results "the work of an outraged citizenship resolved to end the corruption, the machine gunning, and pineappling, and the plundering which have made the state and the city a reproach throughout the civilized world."

The *New York Times* reported, "The political revolution in Chicago came as a surprise to most political observers. They had thought that the city was disgraced, but not ashamed."

"The election brought results that are gratifying to the entire country," the *Washington Post* added. "It was a mighty blow for the restoration of law and order in Chicago. The voters seem to have been aroused from their apathy."

To make matters worse for Capone, Herbert Hoover defeated Al Smith in the presidential election and announced plans for an all-out offensive against the organized crime networks symbolized by Capone. At the same time, the Supreme Court gave federal law enforcement officials a powerful, though sophisticated, weapon.

The case involved Manley Sullivan, a bootlegger, who filed no tax return on the grounds that income from illegal sources was not taxable and to declare such income would be self-incriminatory. The high court ruled against Sullivan, finding no reason that a business that was unlawful should be exempt from paying taxes. As for the argument against self-incrimination, the ruling stated, "It would be an extreme if not extravagant application of the Fifth Amendment to say that it authorized a man to refuse to state the amount of his income because it had been made in crime."

His impending departure from the Chicago scene notwithstanding, federal officials kept Al Capone in their crosshairs. Capone did move with his wife and son to a lavish estate at Palm Island in Biscayne Bay, Florida, just outside of Miami. He also shifted his Chicago operations to the massive Lexington Hotel on Twenty-second Street and South Michigan Avenue. Scarface Al then set out to eliminate his competition.

The first to fall was Frankie Yale, who had hooked up with the Aiello gang to hijack trucks delivering liquor from New York to warehouses under Capone's control in Chicago. A half-dozen Capone soldiers tracked down Yale on Forty-fourth Street in New York, forced his car into a curb, and pummeled his body with lead from sawed-off shotguns, revolvers, and a tommy gun.

Undaunted, the Aiellos teamed with another familiar Capone nemesis, Bugs Moran, to establish hundreds of home alky-cooking stills in immigrant Italian neighborhoods. They marketed the synthetic liquor they produced to those speakeasy operators who were brave enough to buy it.

Moran even taunted Capone. "The beast uses his muscle men to peddle rot-gut alcohol and green beer," he told one reporter. "I'm a legitimate salesman of good beer and pure whiskey. He trusts nobody and suspects everybody. He always has his guards. I travel around with a couple of pals. The behemoth can't sleep nights. If you ask me, he's on dope. Me, I don't ever need an aspirin."

At least seven casualties—four on the Aiello side and three on Capone's—could be counted during a series of ambushes that followed Frankie Yale's murder. The single event that came to symbolize the savagery and lawlessness of Chicago took place on February 14, 1929. The night before, Bugs Moran had received a phone call informing him that a truckload of prime whiskey, hijacked as it left Detroit bound for Capone's warehouse, was available at a cost of fifty-seven dollars per case. Moran told the caller to deliver the goods to a brick warehouse behind the offices of SMC Cartage Company, at 2122 North Clark Street.

A light snow was falling and the temperature was well below zero the next morning as a black Cadillac, looking very much like a police car, pulled in front of the warehouse. Two uniformed men and two others dressed in civilian clothes hurried into the building. Moments later, Moran and two associates turned the corner onto North Clark Street. Believing the sedan was a patrol car, the trio fled. Suddenly, gunfire erupted like a furious drumbeat, and a dog barked in desperation. Two deeper blasts followed.

Neighbors looked on as two men in plain clothes emerged from the warehouse, their arms raised in the air, while the uniformed men, holding pistols, ordered their captives to walk toward the car. They drove south and turned onto Ogden Avenue. Many of the neighbors went about their business, assuming that they had just witnessed the arrest of two North Siders caught in the act of bootlegging—a fairly routine occurrence except for the large amount of gunfire.

Troubled by the ceaseless barking of the dog from inside the building, one nearby resident went to investigate. He discovered a scene of carnage nearly beyond description. It eventually became known as the Saint Valentine's Day Massacre.

The seven men sent by Moran to unload the whiskey had been ordered to line up against the rear wall. Then the executioners opened fire with systematic efficiency, swinging their machine guns back and forth three times—at the victims' heads, chests, and stomachs. Along the wall where the seven had stood, blood splashed down the yellowish bricks. Blood from their bodies continued to streak across the oily surface of the stone floor as police arrived. Two of the victims had survived the initial assault, as evidenced by the fact that their faces were blown away by shotgun blasts.

Despite being hit with fourteen bullets, one of Moran's men, Frank Gusenberg, was still breathing when police finally arrived. He regained consciousness long enough to tell a detective posted at his hospital bedside, "Nobody shot me . . . I ain't no copper." Then he died. *Omerta.*

"Only Capone kills like that," was Moran's angry reaction. He vowed to punish the assassins with "all the tortures of the Spanish Inquisition."

Capone had an alibi; he was in Florida when the massacre took place. Phone records, however, revealed several conversations in the days leading up to the killings between Capone, Jack Guzik, and some of the syndicate's other Chicago operatives. Police also learned that Machine Gun Jack McGurn had visited Capone then returned to Chicago just before Valentine's Day.

Circumstantial evidence linked the killings to Capone's organization, but no arrests were ever made. When the warehouse was demolished in 1967, dozens of Chicago residents rushed to the scene to scoop up souvenir bricks.

CHAPTER SIX

Only a Matter of Time

T HE SAINT VALENTINE'S DAY MASSACRE was a wake-up call to the nation that things in Chicago had gotten out of hand. Congress debated—but never passed—a proposal to double or even triple the $14 million being spent annually on Prohibition enforcement. Instead, lawmakers hastily passed the "Five and Ten" Bill, imposing a five-year prison term and ten-thousand-dollar fine for violation of certain provisions of the National Prohibition Act.

President Herbert Hoover, sworn into office on March 4, 1929, vowed to pick up where Coolidge had left off in using federal resources to clean up the Windy City. Hoover honored his campaign promise by launching an all-out offensive to enforce Prohibition laws and collect evidence of income tax evasion by Capone and his colleagues. As a symbolic gesture, he hosted a delegation from the Women's Christian Temperance Union for a photograph with him on the White House lawn. *Time* magazine called him the "dry hope."

Hoover vowed to work "week by week, year by year, as rapidly as possible to build up the enforcement of the laws of the United States, whether they relate to Prohibition, or narcotics, or any other subject." Behind the scenes, Hoover was plotting how best to marshal the federal forces to tackle the wanton lawlessness symbolized by Capone. He and his advisers recognized this would take far more than enforcement of the unpopular Prohibition law. They began by dispatching investigators to Chicago on a top-secret mission to determine which judges were corrupt and which local police officers could be trusted.

After a meeting on March 19, 1929, with Walter Strong, publisher of the *Chicago Daily News*, and Judge Frank Loesch of the Chicago Crime Commission, Hoover wrote in his memoirs that the duo had convinced him "that Chicago was in the hands of gangsters, that the police and magistrates were completely under their control, that the governor of the state was futile, that the federal government was the only force by which the city's ability to govern itself could be restored." This was to be accomplished at once, without publicity and regardless of expenses.

No matter how much his associates urged him to keep a low profile, Al Capone flaunted his wealth. In the wake of the Supreme Court's decision in the Manley Sullivan case, that was a mistake. His purchase of the Florida property and expensive furnishings confirmed his bloated income.

The mission of verifying Capone's income fell to Elmer L. Irey, head of the Internal Revenue Service's Intelligence Unit. Irey, thirty-one, was a former post office stenographer who occupied a small Treasury Department office on the third floor of 1111 Constitution Avenue in Washington, D.C., directly across the street from that of his rival, J. Edgar Hoover, in the Justice Department Building. Irey's Intelligence Unit operated almost anonymously in the shadow of Hoover's Federal Bureau of Investigation.

A prickly, self-effacing public servant, Irey initially argued that his agency did not have the resources to investigate Capone. Irey never had a chance against J. Edgar Hoover, who maintained that the Sullivan case shifted primary responsibility for the attack on Capone to the Treasury Department. The real reasons behind Hoover's refusal to unleash the forces of the FBI against Capone will probably remain a mystery forever. The director's hands-off approach was the source of considerable resentment in 1929.

Under the scenario announced by Treasury Secretary Andrew Mellon, the Treasury Department would gather the evidence and the Justice Department would prosecute. Irey, in his book, *The Tax Dodgers*, wrote, "It all became clear. Justice was willing to prosecute (by law nobody else could) but in case of failure Treasury would have to take the blame, although Justice had its own investigative agents, the famous FBI. Sounds silly, but that's government. Anyway, Mellon was my boss. Ergo, 'Yes Mr. Mellon. We'll get right on it.'"

For assistance, Irey recruited Frank J. Wilson, a former real estate salesman from Buffalo, New York, who had already established solid credentials by uncovering financial chicanery of lesser bootleggers as an investigator for the American Food Administration. Wilson, forty, looked to be in his mid-fifties with his bald head and sunken eyes framed by wire-rimmed glasses, accented by a cigar that constantly dangled from his lips. He was a man of unquestionable integrity, known for his gritty determination and thoroughness.

Irey and Wilson had their work cut out for them. Not only were the Capones expert money launderers, they also had taken advantage of a 1923 Illinois law prohibiting branch banking in the state. The small, independent banks that sprang up in suburbs such as Cicero were perfect repositories for deposits under aliases.

On the Justice Department side, U.S. attorney George Emmerson Q. Johnson joined the team. Johnson, fifty-three, was a tall, wiry Swede with unruly hair parted in the middle and round wire-framed glasses. The *Q* in his name did not stand for anything; he only inserted it to differentiate himself from other George E. Johnsons. His mission was to close down Capone's enormous bootlegging operations and to collect evidence of crimes, including but not limited to Volstead violations.

Capone took solace in the fact that his gambling and bootlegging operations were cash-only. He did all of his business transactions through front men and third parties, avoiding any direct personal link to income sources. Nevertheless, Capone underestimated his opponents. Irey and his colleagues were hot on his tail. At the same time, a new breed of Prohibition agent, symbolized by Eliot Ness, was arriving on the scene.

With the death of Frank Basile still fresh in his mind, Ness eagerly accepted an assignment to help with a massive raid in Chicago Heights in early 1929. Through a cooperative effort of the federal government and a handful of honest local law enforcement authorities, Johnson sent almost one hundred federal agents and Chicago police detectives into the community. They invaded the haunts of every known gangster in the region, breaking into breweries and alky-cooking homes, shutting down speakeasies, seizing gambling equipment and weapons, handcuffing prostitutes, and gathering ledgers that tied many of these criminal activities to Al Capone.

The most bizarre aspect of the raid was the arrest of the entire Chicago Heights police force. Once these officers were behind bars in their own jail, unable to warn the other lawbreakers, the raiders rounded up their quarry. Ness and Lahart were given the honor of nabbing Joe Martino. "We read the warrant to him and he went to the closet to pick up a topcoat," Ness wrote. "At the same time, he threw a weapon on the floor. He became deathly sick and we had trouble getting him to the station."

Martino, at age forty-five, had survived the gang wars longer than most. No sooner was he freed on bail than the real powers of the Chicago crime scene silenced him forever. As Martino stood quietly in front of his saloon on East Sixteenth Street one afternoon, a large motorcar occupied by four men drew up and paused long enough for the gunmen to deliver twelve shots to Martino's body.

"His hands were still clasped in the pockets of his working trousers," wrote a reporter for the *Chicago Heights Star*, one of the first people to reach the scene. "The slaying was accomplished in the usual gangland manner."

Only after Martino's murder was Ness informed that the gangster was Capone's adversary, rather than a partner. He learned an important lesson from the Martino affair. After the initial shock and embarrassment faded, Ness became more cautious in his investigative work. Chicago newspapers made little mention of the young, aggressive crimefighter, and when his name did appear in print it was invariably spelled "Elliott."

Trying to make a name for himself, Ness teamed with Marty Lahart once again to pull off an eye-opening sting operation right inside the Shakespeare Avenue police station. Lahart dressed as a skid row derelict and had himself arrested, under an assumed name, for vagrancy and public drunkenness. Taken to the station, he was approached by a uniformed officer carrying two pints of whiskey and invited to make an offer.

Lahart produced two dollar bills from his pocket and exchanged them for one bottle. "If you need any more, come back around here any night after midnight and ask for me," the officer told him. "But keep this to yourself. If you tell anyone, I'll have your ass back in here in a minute."

The agent's subsequent report on the experience prompted the firing of two policemen and the transfer of two others who had known about the private bootlegging operation but kept silent.

Even this bizarre episode drew little press attention. Reporters, however, did take note when a federal grand jury returned eighty-one indictments against members of the multimillion-dollar bootlegging and gambling rackets in Chicago Heights. Particularly noteworthy was that Capone ignored a subpoena to appear before the grand jury for questioning. When a Florida physician claimed Capone was too ill to make the trip to Chicago, a dozen federal agents were dispatched to Miami to gather evidence contradicting his claim.

Weeks later, Capone "recovered" from his ailments and slipped back into Chicago to address some even more pressing challenges to his reign. The Chicago Heights raid had been troublesome, but of even greater concern to Capone were the Treasury Department agents who had begun shaking down his lieutenants and demanding information about financial transactions and income sources. Now he learned from a Sicilian insider that the Aiello gang was acting up again, and there was an even more concerted effort to kill Capone.

Acting through an intermediary, triggerman Frankie Rio, Capone invited a couple of Aiello's better-connected soldiers, John Scalise and Albert Anselmi, to a dinner at the Hawthorne Inn. Unknown to the duo, Capone and Rio had concocted a scheme to test their guests' loyalty. They staged an argument that culminated with Rio slapping Capone in the face and storming out. The following day, hoping to capitalize on the rift, Scalise and Anselmi approached Rio with a plot to kill Capone and seize control of his rackets.

On May 7, Capone summoned Scalise, Anselmi, and Joseph "Hop Toad" Guinta, new head of the Unione Siciliana, to a dinner.

Feasting and toasting by dozens of Capone's closest allies lasted long into the night, finally interrupted when Capone pounded a spoon against his glass and called for silence.

"This is the way we deal with traitors!" he said angrily as he reached for a baseball bat and slowly approached the trio. Capone proceeded to batter each of them to within an inch of his life. Then several gunmen appeared to finish the job. The next morning, the bodies of Scalise, Anselmi, and Guinta were found along a remote road near Wolf Lake, Indiana.

The brutal attack was stark evidence of Capone's rapidly deteriorating physical and mental condition. Now, not only was the federal government zeroing in on Capone, many members of his own organization were questioning his judgment. The crime bosses eagerly accepted an invitation to participate in a "peace conference" at Atlantic City, New Jersey. Little John Torrio, a free man again, was brought in to put his organizational skills to use.

About thirty delegates, cutting across all ethnic and national divisions, signed a pact that established geographical boundaries. Under the agreement, the assassination of rival gang members would cease. Some of the smaller enclaves were given incentives to disband and affiliate themselves with the larger, more powerful organizations. Among the notable absentees was Bugs Moran, who continued to argue that Capone must be eliminated as revenge for the Saint Valentine's Day Massacre.

Capone was a participant but left the impression that he had no intention of adhering to the rules. Worried that his life was in danger, and seeking a safe haven, Capone arranged to have himself arrested in Philadelphia for carrying a concealed weapon. He entered a guilty plea, assuming that he would be sent to the Philadelphia County Jail for a few weeks. But Judge John E. Walsh imposed the maximum sentence: one year behind bars at Pennsylvania's Eastern State Penitentiary.

If President Hoover needed any confirmation that his approach was long overdue, the Atlantic City conference was it. This meeting raised the ugly specter of a national crime organization that, if effectively operated, could render the federal law enforcement machinery impotent.

Prohibition enforcement alone was clearly not the answer. Even the *Wall Street Journal,* in an editorial published June 21, 1929, ridiculed the law: "Without realizing its consequences, we have permitted our lawmakers to make a felony of that which, in its nature, is not a heinous crime . . . the root of the whole trouble is in the law itself—a law at which a respectable portion of the people rebel."

During the fiscal year ending June 30, 1929, some 750 Chicago saloons, speakeasies, and breweries were padlocked, flooding the courts with two Prohibition-related matters for every nonrelated offense. Prison populations rose by 50 percent during the period from June 1927 to June 1929. Government popularity was fast ebbing to below that of gang members.

With Al Capone out of the picture, it was time to strike at Ralph Capone and the others tending to his criminal enterprises. Ralph had already passed up one opportunity to get the IRS off his back. He had signed returns for 1922 through 1925 admitting to a tax liability of $4,065 on earnings of $55,000, but he failed to pay what he owed. Ralph was now considered the closest domino to Scarface Al.

Financial assistance came from the Chicago Association of Commerce, which formed a group of underground saboteurs known as the Citizens' Committee for the Prevention and Punishment of Crime. This organization consisted of six business leaders who, fearing retribution, insisted on anonymity. Among them were *Chicago Tribune* publisher Col. Robert McCormick and Sears, Roebuck and Company president Julius Rosenwald. When the chairman, prominent businessman Col. Robert Isham Randolph, refused to name the other members, the press dubbed them the Secret Six.

"There is not a business, not an industry in Chicago that is not paying tribute, directly or indirectly, to racketeers and gangsters," Randolph declared. "The problem of corruption runs deeper than most people realize. The men who take money from bootleggers for overlooking violations of the Volstead Act are incapacitated for arresting them for any other crime."

With the concurrence of President Hoover, Alexander Jamie was appointed as chief investigator for the Secret Six. Earlier in his career, Jamie had been an investigator for the Justice Department. When Prohibition took effect, Jamie was named chief investigator for special intelligence in the Chicago area. He was largely responsible for determining which Volstead Act violations were worthy of investigation due to their links to organized crime and which might better be ignored because they represented no more than an appetite for alcohol.

Jamie had distinguished himself as an effective administrator during the crackdown on organized crime in Chicago Heights. His new role was announced with great fanfare in the *Chicago Herald and Examiner:*

> Alexander G. Jamie, courageous federal operative, will assume the directorship of the criminal investigations begun by the Chicago Association of Commerce to shatter the alliance of crime, police and politics. Yesterday, his forty-eighth birthday, Jamie concluded 14 years of service with the government and was already in the first of his investigations for the Secret Six. . . . Jamie is reticent to discuss the possibilities in his new position. In the past he has been known as the quiet conductor of some of the major investigations of the local Prohibition Administration. "This office will not seek publicity," he said. "We will cooperate with the constituted authorities in obtaining the conviction of criminals. The police will make arrests and the courts convict— but we will merely assist in investigation." Mr. Jamie is known in his Prohibition work to have refused huge bribes and government officials speak of him as a man of high intelligence and integrity.

Jamie, appalled and disillusioned by the corruption and inefficiency in the Prohibition Bureau, welcomed the opportunity to coordinate the Secret Six's involvement with the Justice and Treasury Departments while still retaining his federal authority. Working with George Johnson and Johnson's new assistant, William Froelich, Jamie was instructed to establish a special squad of federal agents that would attack the Capone outfit's most lucrative source of income—bootlegging. As his revenue decreased, Capone would be less effective in bribing police officers and politicians or otherwise buying influence.

Each member would be carefully screened to ensure that the team consisted only of agents who were trustworthy, competent, and incorruptible. When the conversation turned to leadership, Jamie enthusiastically recommended his young brother-in-law, whose personnel file reflected just those qualities. Finding honest men among the corruption-ridden Prohibition Bureau was no easy task. Ness, it seemed, was one of the very few agents who had earned a reputation for reliability and honesty.

These records showed that Ness served the Prohibition Bureau with "coolness, aggressiveness, and fearlessness in raids"; that he had "far more than the average number of arrests"; and that he had "spoken out about the Prohibition Bureau's holding back in its fight against the mob, rather than cleaning house." On the other hand, these same files contained notes suggesting that Ness's superiors were concerned about his "tendency to want to make a name for himself."

Summoning Ness for an interview, Wilson and Johnson asked only a handful of questions before agreeing that he was well suited to head the Justice Department's special Capone Squad. Eliot eagerly accepted their offer.

Impressed with his heightened status, Ness telephoned Edna Staley, who had all but given up hope in their relationship, and asked her for a dinner date. She eagerly accepted.

Ness's selection did not sit well with everyone, especially contemporaries who considered him too eager to strike and too young and inexperienced to be put in charge of a campaign against a target as sly and well connected as Al Capone.

CHAPTER SEVEN

Sending a Message

T HE CAPONE SQUAD'S MISSION was easily summarized: track
down and destroy the mob's breweries and distilleries, thus
drying up Capone's major source of income while collecting evidence of Prohibition and tax law violations.

Ness was directed to assemble a squad of up to a dozen men,
using a list of candidates believed to be trustworthy, effective, and
unlikely to shrink from dangerous assignments.

"This was like a dream come true," Ness wrote of his assignment. "It was something I had hoped for from the first day I became
involved with the Prohibition Bureau. I knew that the only way to
really go after Capone was to start fresh with officers who were not
already corrupted. I couldn't wait to get started."

He settled into an office at the Transportation Building in
Chicago and began to study Justice Department personnel files. He
sought single men from across the country who were excellent
marksmen with physical stamina and courage. The job would also
require skills in surveillance, disguise, evasive driving, and self-
defense. Ness also considered factors such as ethnic background and
drinking habits before finally deciding on five agents:

- Martin J. Lahart, a Chicagoan who had already teamed with Ness for the Cozy Corners raid and the Shakespeare Avenue police station undercover work. Ness was well aware of Lahart's abilities and his commitment to the job, so he designated him as his chief lieutenant.

- Thomas Friel, a wiry, medium-sized recruit who was tempered as hard as the anthracite in his native Scranton, Pennsylvania. A former state police trooper, Friel thirsted for undercover work.

- Samuel M. Seager, a former guard on death row at Sing Sing. Seager's quiet, confident manner and hard, expressionless facial features, combined with his six-foot-two, two-hundred-pound frame, commanded instant respect, plus he knew how to handle hardened criminals.

- Bernard V. "Barney" Cloonan, a broad-shouldered Irishman from Chicago with black hair and a ruddy complexion. Another of Ness's Prohibition Bureau acquaintances, the soft-spoken Cloonan had fought as a marine in France and longed for an opportunity to leave a desk job he found too confining.

- Lyle Chapman, a tall, lean, scholarly looking former collegiate football player brought in from Detroit. Chapman's analytical mind had been focused on criminology since his early teens. A war veteran and graduate of Colgate University, Chapman brought a scholar's insight to unraveling the bootleggers' paper trail.

Ness also needed technical experts. Justice Department files yielded many possibilities from both inside and outside Chicago. Ness reviewed the credentials of about three dozen agents before he settled on:

- Paul W. Robsky, a wiretap specialist and native Chicagoan working out of the New Jersey division. The diminutive, easy-mannered Robsky served as an aerial photographer during World War I and spent a year rooting out moonshiners in South Carolina. He wore an old, oversized hat that came down over his forehead and nearly obscured his eyes.

- William Gardner, an expert at undercover work. Gardner, a solid, 240-pound Native American, had been a college football star. He was working out of the Prohibition Bureau's Los Angeles district when Ness summoned him. In his mid-forties, Gardner was the "old man" of the squad. He had been sent from his Chippewa tribal home on the western plains to the Indian Industrial School in Carlisle, Pennsylvania, to be taught the "white man's ways." He went on to earn a law degree from Dickinson College.

- Michael King, a crafty disguise artist from the Virginia Prohibition Bureau, had an excellent memory and an innate ability to blend into a crowd and tail a suspect.

- Joseph Leeson, a thirty-year-old agent from Cincinnati, possessed excellent driving skills. He stood six feet two inches tall and was as solid as a rock, with a jutting chin and granite-hard eyes.

- Jim Seeley, a twenty-seven-year-old Chicago native, had worked as a private detective and cultivated many sources within the city's criminal gangs.

Another member of the group, who managed to keep his affiliation a secret for several years, was Al "Wallpaper" Wolff. Raised on Chicago's West Side, the tall, beefy Wolff had been closing down open-air stills in the Kentucky hills when he was transferred to Chicago shortly after the Saint Valentine's Day Massacre.

Among other agents mentioned as having at least brief affiliations with Ness's team were Robert D. Sterling, Warren E. Stutzman, George Steelman, and Dan Vaccarelli. For years, rumors have persisted that one or more of the officers selected by Ness didn't turn out to be as honest or as loyal as had been expected, and they may have been quietly removed from the squad. If so, there is no documentation of such action.

William Froelich, Johnson's well-groomed and enthusiastic assistant, was chosen to address the group during an initial meeting. Froelich's direct tone of voice commanded instant attention.

"You'll have no hours and I'll back you up to the limit," he told the team. "The important thing is results. We want to dry up Chicago. I mean bone dry. I want every brewery and every still found and destroyed. Any records you get will be invaluable. I'll turn them over to Treasury for processing. They'll handle all the paperwork. What I want from you men is action."

"If anybody wants out, now is the time to say so," Ness inter-jected. "Some of us may not get out of this alive. Keep that in mind before you get into this too deeply. This is your last chance to walk away from it."

One by one, the recruits reaffirmed their commitment.

Ness's team was initially aided by contacts with leaders of rival gangs who had a particular interest in seeing Capone's influence diminished. Additional information came from Secret Six investi-gators who established a bogus speakeasy that accepted beer ship-ments from Capone. "Bartenders" on the payroll of the Secret Six fed numerous tips overheard from patrons and delivery men to government agents.

An unofficial inventory gave Ness an indication of the scope of Capone's bootlegging operations: at least twenty breweries, each producing hundreds of barrels of beer per day. In addition, investi-gators were aware that Capone's organization was buying huge quantities of whiskey, gin, and other liquor from underworld sources. Jamie estimated that as much as one-third of the alcohol and a substantial quantity of the Capone outfit's income were being paid out in graft and protection.

Ness had serious reservations he did not share with his fellow agents. In *The Untouchables*, he wrote:

Doubts raced through my mind as I considered the feasibility of enforcing a law that the majority of honest citizens didn't seem to want. I felt a chill foreboding for my men as I envisioned the vio-lent reaction we would produce in the criminal octopus hovering over Chicago, its tentacles of terror reaching out all over the nation. We had undertaken what might be a suicidal mission. . . . Unquestionably, it was going to be highly dangerous, yet I felt it was quite natural to jump at the task. After all, if you don't like action and excitement, you don't go into police work. And what the hell, I figured, nobody lives forever!

Intelligence reports suggested that Capone had ordered the exe-cutions of as many as three hundred people, most of them from rival organizations. Gangsters rarely assaulted federal officers, due to the harsh repercussions they would face if caught. They also observed an unwritten code protecting from harm all women, children, and other family members not directly involved in the business enterprises. Ness wondered how long that policy would remain in effect once his group began to pound away at Capone's economic lifeblood.

Despite the laissez-faire approach of law enforcement officials to this point, Capone had taken certain measures to conceal his operations. Employees manned the breweries for only short periods of time, all that was required by the beer-making and packaging process. Because there was no overt activity during the daytime hours, and little at night, finding these facilities was not easy. Barrels of mothballs masked the usual brewery odors. Doors and windows were covered with black paint, cloth, and other padding to prevent light leaks.

Ness began by breaking his team into pairs and directing these agents to trace the routes from the retailers back to warehouses or, better yet, to the breweries themselves. This involved posting his men at several speakeasies and surreptitiously following the trucks that drove off with empty barrels.

It did not take long for the Capone Squad to pick up a scent. Seeley and Leeson positioned themselves outside Colosimo's Café at about two o'clock one morning just before a large truck drove up. Its two passengers loaded several empty barrels onto the back. The agents tailed the truck through the South Side, observing several more pickups, and then followed it to an abandoned factory at the corner of Shields Avenue and Thirty-eighth Street, near Comiskey Park.

They rented a small apartment about a block away and summoned Ness, who arrived in less than an hour. Seeley and Leeson agreed to take turns on a round-the-clock watch of the factory. Later that same day, King and Cloonan arrived early at the Transportation Building to report that they too had tailed a truck that collected empty barrels from several establishments and delivered them to the same building.

After observing more than a dozen trucks pulling in and out before sunrise, curiosity got the better of Seeley. Donning some old clothes he found in a closet at the apartment house, he disguised himself as a vagrant and sneaked over to the plant. Climbing on the roof, Seeley peered down through a skylight and spotted about a dozen men busily spraying and scrubbing beer barrels. Another six workers wiped the barrels dry and stocked them on wooden skids. This was no brewery; it was a barrel processing plant and it gave the investigators a hint of how massive Capone's bootlegging operation had grown.

Ness called his team back to the Transportation Building to discuss how to best use the information without blowing their cover. He directed Leeson and Seeley to follow some of the trucks coming out of the warehouse and pinpoint breweries where the clean barrels were being refilled. The group was interrupted by the late arrival of Robsky and Friel, who were out of breath and obviously excited by their discovery of an apparent brewery. The agents wanted to organize a raid for the same day, but Ness was against it until he had an opportunity to personally visit the site.

That afternoon he joined Robsky and Friel for a trip to 2271 Lumber Street. The large, wooden-front building was amid a row of industrial warehouses. A sign reading "Singer Storage Company" was an obvious cover. Ness eased the big Cadillac into a parking lot about one-half block away and sat quietly, studying the warehouse and pondering how to attack it. Large double doors on both the front and back of the building would allow the officers to mount their attack from opposite directions.

Ness laid out a plan by which Friel and Robsky would break through the rear doors, their revolvers raised, at the same time Ness, Leeson, and Gardner were crashing through the double doors in the front. Returning to headquarters, he summoned the others to go over the plans. That night, two cars loaded with shotguns, axes, and crowbars pulled into the dark corner of a parking lot near the brewery. After Ness and Robsky synchronized their watches, Robsky and Friel drove off and parked on an adjacent street, where they had a clear view of the rear doors.

A few minutes after ten o'clock, they observed a large truck pulling into the driveway and up to the back doors. Three loud honks of the horn caught the attention of somebody inside and the doors opened just wide enough to allow the truck to pass through. A second truck followed the same routine, using three short horn blasts to gain entry. Ness loaded a pair of shells into his sawed-off shotgun and motioned for the trio to advance.

Nervously, they moved into position. As the second hand on Ness's watch passed the twelve mark at exactly 10:15, he raised an ax behind his head and pounded it hard against the lock securing the double doors. The wood cracked, allowing Gardner to slip a crowbar under the lock, splitting it in an instant. Yet rather than gaining immediate entrance to the warehouse, the three came face-to-face with a solid steel door.

Ness's pulse quickened and sweat formed on his brow as he made several feeble attempts to penetrate the door with his ax. More than a minute had passed, and they were still on the outside, making a lot of noise and jeopardizing the safety of their fellow agents.

Now desperate, Ness pulled a .38 Colt from his shoulder harness and fired a shot point-blank into the lock. The door still would not budge. He took aim and fired again. This time, a large section broke loose and fell to the pavement. Gardner jammed his hulking shoulder into the double doors and one of them gave way, allowing the three men to rush into the building. Weapons raised, the agents were prepared for the worst, but there were no workers to be seen. Robsky and Friel were also missing.

Lining one of the side walls in the large, well-lighted room were numerous wooden vats, each standing eight feet tall. Two shiny trucks, half-filled with beer barrels, occupied the center of the concrete floor. A half-burned cigarette on a corner table sent swirls of smoke into the air. The stench of sour mash was almost overwhelming as Ness, Gardner, and Leeson eased their way farther into the warehouse. A hard pounding from the back of the building answered their questions about the whereabouts of Robsky and Friel. They had also been stalled by the heavier-than-expected security measures.

Ness was scoping the tightly boarded windows, gripping the .38 in his right hand, when he spotted a flight of wooden stairs leading to a trap door in the ceiling. The mystery was solved. A fire escape on the side of the building had allowed the brewery workers to slip off into the darkness.

"Damn it!" roared Seager, grabbing an ax from Gardner's hand and savagely whacking a hole in the side of a vat. A stream of beer cascaded onto the floor and formed a stream flowing into a drain.

Although the raid netted no suspects, Ness and his partners did seize 19 vats, each with a capacity of 1,500 gallons. They also confiscated 150 barrels of beer, sealed and ready for delivery to Chicago area speakeasies, and tons of mash. If nothing else, the Capone Squad had sent a message, and the man at the top was sure to hear it.

Eastern State Penitentiary, a massive structure built in 1829 under the premise that isolation and rigid discipline reformed criminals, had never before been so accommodating. Capone used his influence to acquire a large console radio, carpeting, wall hangings, a desk, an easy chair, and alcoholic beverages. He regularly entertained visitors and enjoyed privileges unheard of for an inmate. Privacy and access to, among others, his brother Ralph allowed Capone to continue calling the shots for his outfit.

CHAPTER EIGHT

Inside Connections

D URING THE EARLY DAYS of the Ness team, there were several other raids on breweries and distilleries—unpublicized, poorly documented, and producing few arrests. Often, the leads came from anonymous phone calls, some of them from rival gangsters. As the weather grew colder, a visual inspection of a building's exterior was all that Ness needed to confirm that it was a brewery or distillery. Yellow-stained icicles hung from the bricks like frozen urine, colored by the steam and fumes that seeped through the walls.

Capone's people responded by having stool pigeons feed Ness misinformation, recalled Al "Wallpaper" Wolff. "We'd go in blazing, like real gangbusters, and come up with dry holes," he recalled. "This went on for several weeks. Finally, we learned to distinguish between the real leads and phony ones. Then we really went to town. The experience toughened Eliot. He still talked quietly, but with authority."

Occasionally, crooked cops would intercept the Capone Squad during surveillance missions or otherwise interfere. Froelich solved this by obtaining deputy lieutenants' badges for each squad member.

By charting delivery stops and piecing together reports from federal investigators and a handful of reliable city policemen, Lyle Chapman produced a profile showing the breadth and diversity of Capone's empire—from its bootlegging operations to the brothels, gambling houses, and hundreds of speakeasies scattered throughout an ever-growing circle around Chicago. Using Chapman's charts, Ness posted a huge wall map and stuck colored pins in it to correspond with the locations of speakeasies, breweries, barrel-cleaning plants, warehouses, and delivery routes.

During his off-hours, Ness's romance with Edna Staley continued to blossom. When he was with her, Eliot was reluctant to discuss his work, which was fine with Edna. As Alexander Jamie's secretary, she recognized the complexities and confidential nature of the Prohibition Bureau's work, as well as its danger.

One summer night at a fashionable Chicago restaurant where Eliot had taken Edna to celebrate her twenty-third birthday, he proposed to her and she eagerly accepted. Within a month, they were married in a quiet civil ceremony. The Nesses moved into a small apartment above a clothing store on the South Side, not far from Eliot's childhood home.

Meanwhile, the government's attack soon took on a sense of urgency, as news arrived that Capone would probably be released from jail sooner than expected. For technical expertise, Ness turned to Paul Robsky. The two spent long hours discussing the possibility of running wiretaps on some of the telephone lines being used by Capone's men. Federal investigators had already tapped the phones of the Wabash Hotel, a South Side building where Jack Guzik tended to administrative duties. Conversations loaded with specifics on criminal activities and financial information were transcribed for future use in tax evasion cases.

During Capone's absence, his brother Ralph had been far too careless in the way he bought and sold illicit beverages. With George Johnson's blessings, Ness and Robsky worked out an elaborate, albeit risky, plan to run a tap on Ralph Capone's personal telephone at the Montmartre Café, a shabby hotel and sandwich shop in Cicero where Ralph conducted much of his business.

The plan presented logistical problems from the start. Every room at the Montmartre had its own telephone, which was patched into a single exchange high on a pole next to the building. Suspicious activity at the junction box was sure to arouse the attention of "the men in the pearl gray hats." Even if he could reach the junction box,

Robsky wouldn't know what lines to tap. There was only one solution: create a cover for Robsky and get someone inside the building.

The first part was less challenging than the second. Ness contacted a childhood pal who was an executive with the telephone company and civic leader. The friend gladly supplied a fully equipped telephone repair truck, complete with overalls and company hats.

Next, Ness had to decide which of his agents stood the best chance of infiltrating the mob as a member of the "in crowd" at the Montmartre. He finally settled on Marty Lahart, a natural extrovert who could easily make friends, and Tom Friel, the most experienced undercover man.

By that time, at least some members of the Capone Squad had noticed suspicious-looking vehicles following them whenever they cruised city streets. To counter this, Ness directed some of his reliable contacts in the police department to spread the word that Lahart and Friel had been reassigned to the Prohibition Bureau's New York district. Considering the cozy alliance between some police officers and the underworld, news of the two agents' "transfer" was sure to reach Capone's organization.

Lahart and Friel then dropped out of sight, holing up in a seedy Cicero hotel. They allowed their beards to grow, acquired new wardrobes, and were welcomed into the Montmartre. A few days later, Lahart reported to Ness, tongue-in-cheek, that the duo had consumed more beer at government expense than the Capone Squad had seized during its raids.

Ralph Capone conducted most of his telephone conversations from an alcove behind the bar. He frequently let patrons use the same telephone for personal calls. The utility pole that contained the terminal box for all fifty of the Montmartre phones was in an area kept under round-the-clock guard. The only way Robsky would know which line to tap would be to hear a familiar voice.

"What are your chances of using Capone's phone?" Ness asked Friel the next time the agent checked in.

"I don't think my chances are too good, but Marty's got a good shot. He's gotten in pretty good with the big boys. And as long as we're spending money, these guys think we're great."

"That's good," Ness replied. "Tell him to find an excuse to use that phone and then see how they react. If they don't like the idea, tell him to back off. It's not worth getting killed over."

A week later, Lahart reported that he had used Capone's phone a half-dozen times. He had taken the plan one step further, supplying a Prohibition Bureau secretary with the phone number and receiving calls on the same telephone. His "friends" at the café were convinced that the calls were coming from a nagging wife.

The following afternoon, the team arranged for the secretary to place her call to the Montmartre at 4 P.M. By that time, Robsky was to be in place atop the pole, checking each junction until he detected the one to Ralph Capone's telephone.

The guards posed a major obstacle. In the wake of the Lumber Street brewery raid and other recent activities, Capone's people were more suspicious than ever. There was no certainty they would fall for the phone company disguises. Ness called in Leeson, Seager, Cloonan, and Gardner to go over a plan to divert the guards' attention. "They've been tailing my car, so they should know it when they see it," he told the agents. "I want you to take my car and drive it past that hellhole a couple of times, real slow. You know, look like you're checkin' the place out. They'll start following. Just keep 'em busy while Paul does his work."

Time passed all too slowly for the squad that day. Ness, somber-eyed, studied the latest transcripts from Guzik's telephone conversations at the Wabash. He stuck a pin on his wall map to identify another suspected brewery. The agents took turns reading the morning newspaper, where they learned that a judge, as expected, had granted Al Capone's petition for early release. He would be back in Chicago in a couple of weeks.

Much of the group's future activity hinged on whether the wiretap plan, a dangerous long shot, would succeed. Robsky had no way of knowing how many lines he would have to check before he found the right one, and there was always the chance that the truck would arouse suspicion, leading to a bloody confrontation. What if the telephone in Ralph Capone's office was unavailable? What if the guards came back before Robsky made the connections? What if Lahart and Friel were exposed then tortured until they told all they knew?

Ness tried to erase those fears from his mind as he and Robsky drove to the telephone company warehouse where a truck and two uniforms awaited them. About fifteen minutes before the secretary was supposed to place the call, Ness drove the service vehicle past two rough-looking men leaning on a railing in front of the Montmartre and pulled into an alley, just a few feet from the utility pole. The guards casually looked at the truck and then continued their conversation. Soon a third man joined the others. After they spoke for a moment, the trio hurried over to a black Ford and drove off, tires squealing.

"I'll bet they saw my car," Ness said with a smile as Robsky adjusted the climbing spikes on the heels of his boots and strapped on an equipment belt. "I just have to wonder how long their little joy ride is going to last."

"I hope it lasts long enough," Robsky said, testing the texture of the pole with one of his spikes. Ness looked at his watch. He tried to picture Lahart sitting nervously at the bar, waiting for a phone call he might have to prolong for twenty minutes or more, if Capone's people would let him.

The spikes rasped into the wood as Robsky made his ascent. Ness leaned against the pole, hiding his face from the Montmartre entranceway. Though usually cool in the most intense situations, the young lawman found himself jumping at every sound and straining his eyes to detect any movement.

Robsky made quick work of the box cover and his fingers were soon flying over the terminals. Ness instinctively patted his rib cage to be sure his revolver was ready. After about five minutes elapsed, Robsky leaned back against the strong leather of his security belt and shook his head.

"Run over it again," Ness said in a loud whisper. Robsky nodded his approval. Suddenly, he stopped then flashed a thumbs-up. Robsky fidgeted with an assortment of screwdrivers, wire cutters, and pliers clipped to his belt. Within a matter of seconds, the tap was installed. He closed the metal box with a sharp click and hurried down the pole.

"You owe me a barrel of beer—some of Capone's finest," Robsky said, smiling.

"I'll give you your own brewery if this little stunt works," Ness replied, patting his partner on the back.

Back at headquarters, Leeson gleefully reported on the decoys' trip through the streets of Cicero. Capone's guards had tailed their every move before Leeson suddenly swerved Ness's Cadillac into a vacant lot and watched the pursuers cruise by.

"We kept the goons busy," said a beaming Leeson. "They're probably still scratchin' their heads, tryin' to figure out what we were doing and where we ended up. Maybe someday they'll figure it all out."

CHAPTER NINE

"Nobody's Legit"

AL CAPONE STAYED APPRISED of developments in Chicago through his attorneys, who served as intermediaries between the kingpin and his top commanders. Their reports confirmed that his bootlegging empire was coming apart at the seams. The average person had less money to spend on alcohol, and those who did have the cash were complaining that the usually reliable Capone was sometimes unable to meet their demands. This was one measure of the Ness team's success.

Capone had other problems as well. The Treasury Department, once dismissed as a minor annoyance, was scrutinizing his financial dealings as never before. Any doubt about the seriousness of that probe was removed on October 29, 1929, when a grand jury returned seven indictments against Ralph Capone.

The tax evasion charges stemmed from deposits Capone had made under several aliases with the Pinkert State Bank, which was across from the Hawthorne Hotel in Cicero. In one of the bank's safety-deposit boxes, government agents discovered Ralph Capone's $100,000 cache and records showing that, in 1927 and 1928, he deposited more than $974,000 in five different banks under as many names. Investigators also uncovered evidence that Al Capone had a financial interest in the highly profitable Arsonia Stables, including ownership of seven thoroughbreds.

Ralph Capone's legal plight would have commanded huge head-lines, but the public's attention was focused on another news develop-ment. On "Black Friday," October 29, 1929, more than sixteen million shares were tossed overboard on the New York Stock Exchange for whatever price could be obtained. The nation was smothered in eco-nomic gloom.

No major city suffered more from the Great Depression than did Chicago. The city government ran millions of dollars in the red, prompting private groups to pass the hat in a desperate effort to keep schools open. A midwestern drought inflicted further hardship. Homeless families slept in alleyways, while clusters of shacks made of packing cases, tarpaper, and cardboard formed "Hoovervilles" in the outlying parts of town.

The depression altered Chicagoans' views of hoodlums. Unem-ployment and other economic factors lent a sense of urgency to the government's efforts to stop the underworld from skimming so much tax-free money off the top. Ironically, the federal government could not afford to continue bankrolling such a comprehensive law enforcement effort in Chicago. The Secret Six came to the rescue by helping to pay the salaries of the Capone Squad and several IRS undercover agents.

A badly shaken Ralph Capone, still unaware of the Mont-martre wiretap, freely discussed his defense strategy by telephone with lawyers, family members, partners in crime, and anyone else who would listen. He seemed confident that threats and bribery would cause the government's case to crumble.

Ness decided he wanted to sample the conversations himself one afternoon. Arriving at the listening post in a rented hotel room, he found Chapman seated at a small table, reading a newspaper. A tele-phone headset rested by his elbow, next to a legal pad and several sharp pencils.

Ness heard scattered conversations but nothing significant. He did take note of one call Ralph Capone received from a woman in New Orleans, informing him that the fix was in for a horserace that day. Capone told her to bet fifteen thousand dollars on the prearranged winner and deposit the earnings in a bank account she was keeping for the syndicate in her own name. The remainder of the day's calls consisted of smalltime beer orders and plans for social activities.

Across town, Frank Wilson sat for eighteen hours a day sifting through the financial records seized from the Capone operations. "I know where Al gets his money, but it'll take a little proving," he said during a strategy session. "Ralph is going down. I can prove where Nitti gets his money, and how much. The same goes for Guzik. Nobody wants to say much about Al, so maybe if we put some heat on his buddies, these guys will be more inclined to talk, just to save their own hides."

On March 18, 1930, reporters, cameramen, and curiosity seekers assembled outside Eastern State Penitentiary at the announced time of Capone's release. Prison warden Herbert B. Smith had told the press that Capone would emerge from the prison gates and walk to a car that would whisk him to a local airstrip to fly home.

In reality, Capone had already been smuggled out the previous night in the warden's car. He was taken to Graterford, about twenty miles northwest of Philadelphia, and held in the prison there until friends arrived the next day to pick him up. By the time Smith emerged to greet the press, Capone was two hundred miles away.

"We stuck one in your eye," Smith said smugly. "The big guy's gone."

Among those taking the greatest offense was Jake Lingle, a *Chicago Tribune* crime reporter who enjoyed a cozy relationship with the underworld. Furious that he was not informed of the warden's ploy, Lingle phoned Ralph Capone. One of Ness's men was listening in.

"Where's Al?" asked an angry Lingle. "I've been looking all over for him, and nobody seems to know where he is."

"I don't know where he is, either, Jake," Ralph Capone insisted. "I haven't heard a word from him since he got out."

"Jesus, Ralph. This makes it very hard for me. I'm supposed to have my finger on these things. It makes it very embarrassing with my paper. Now get this: I want you to call me the minute you hear from him. Tell him I want to see him right away." Ralph promised he would.

Lingle called again later, infuriated that his plea had been ignored. "Listen, you guys ain't giving me the runaround, are you? Just remember, I wouldn't do that if I were you."

Ralph Capone knew full well where his brother was. Not twenty minutes before Lingle called, Ralph had received a phone call informing him that Al was celebrating his freedom with a night of drinking at the Western Hotel in Cicero. As the alcohol soaked into his brain, Capone flew into a violent rage.

"We're up in room 718 at the Western and Al is really getting out of hand," a frantic caller told Ralph. "He's in terrible shape. Will you come up? You're the only one who can handle him when he gets like this. We've sent for a lot of towels." A follow-up call informed Ralph that his services would not be necessary; his brother had passed out.

Sobering up the following morning, Capone slipped into his headquarters at the Hawthorne to huddle with some of his lieutenants. Their immediate focus was deputy police chief John Stege's bold declaration that he intended to "clap Capone in jail as soon as he sets foot in the city." City police, including the two dozen staking out Capone's Prairie Avenue home, had orders to detain him upon sight.

Capone's attorney, Thomas Nash, assured him that the police were powerless to act unless they first secured an indictment listing specific charges. Accompanied by Nash, a confident Capone marched into the Federal Building, a massive monument to civic dreariness at the corner of Dearborn and Adams, and demanded to see the indictment. He was met by deputy chief Stege and assistant state's attorney Harry Ditchburne.

"Al, what do you know about the Valentine's Day massacre of the seven Moran brothers?" Ditchburne asked.

"I was in Florida then," Capone snapped back.

"Yes, you were in Florida too, when Frank Yale was murdered?" Stege asked.

"I'm not as bad as I'm painted. If you sift through everything I was ever accused of, you'll find I didn't do it. I get blamed for everything that goes on here, but I had nothing to do with those things you're talking about."

"Personally, you don't commit the murders, but we're not far wrong, are we, in assuming that your gang is responsible?" said Stege.

"I'm not responsible for what others do," Capone insisted.

"You're not a very good citizen, Al," Stege continued. "If you were walking along the street with your brother and he was killed, wouldn't you come here and tell us who killed him?"

"Well, put yourself in my place and see what you'd do."

"There used to be a time when the police department wouldn't have a hundred murders in ten years. But since you gangsters have been at war, we've had three hundred murders in a year," said Stege, exaggerating the figures. "That's why we're driving you out of town."

"You, Mr. Ditchburne, as a lawyer, know the police can't do that," Nash interjected.

"I'm not here to tell the police what not to do," Ditchburne said. "I'm here to advise them what to do. I'm not interested in protecting Mr. Capone. If he feels he's being arrested wrongly, he has his remedy. He can sue for false arrest."

"I don't want to sue anybody," Capone said. "All I want is not to be arrested if I come downtown."

"You're out of luck," Stege told him. "Your day is done. How soon are you getting out of town?" Stege turned to Nash and said, "You'd better advise him to get out of Chicago."

"Lenin and Trotsky and others have rebelled against that kind of treatment," Nash retorted.

"I hope Capone goes to Russia!" said Stege in a parting shot as he rose from behind his desk and stormed out of the office.

Ditchburne conceded that the police had no grounds to detain Capone, pending the filing of criminal charges for his failure to appear before the grand jury in its bootlegging probe many months earlier. Meanwhile, some reporters had learned of Capone's whereabouts and were waiting when he and Nash emerged from the Federal Building.

"It's kind of hard trying to figure out who wants me," Capone chuckled, before he and Nash drove off.

Back at his big mahogany desk in the spacious offices at the Lexington Hotel, Capone agreed to be interviewed by Genevieve Forbes Herrick of the *Chicago Tribune*. Descending the hotel steps

with his patent leather hair shining in the bright overhead lights, he
was vintage Capone:

> Why should I be indicted? All I ever did was sell beer and
> whiskey to our best people. All I ever did was supply a demand
> that was pretty popular. Why, the very guys that make my trade
> good are the ones that yell the loudest about me. Some of the
> leading judges use the stuff. They talk about me not being on the
> legitimate. Why, lady, nobody's on the legit. You know that and
> so do they. Your father or your brother gets in a jam. What do you
> do? Do you sit back and let him go over the road, without trying
> to help him? You'd be a yellow dog if you did. Nobody's really on
> the legit, when it comes down to cases. You know that.

Capone pressed a buzzer to summon his wife, Mae, and his sister
Mafalda from an upstairs room. They came downstairs, nervously
shared small talk with Herrick for a couple of minutes, then returned
to their suite.

"Did you notice my wife's hair?" Capone said. "Those streaks of
gray—she's only twenty-eight and she's got gray hair worrying over
things here in Chicago." (Mae Capone was actually thirty-one at the
time, two years her husband's senior.)

The exclusive interview was page-one news in the *Tribune*. A
sidebar told of Capone's generosity in donating money to a soup
kitchen on the South Side, where thousands of people suffering
through the effects of the depression could get a warm meal. This
was the same Capone who had purchased hundreds of turkeys for the
poor people of the South Side the previous Thanksgiving.

Another story told of Capone's appearance at a horse racetrack in
Charleston, Indiana, where thousands stood and cheered when he
arrived with his bodyguards, waving his clasped hands above his head
like a prizefighter entering the ring. George E. Q. Johnson, who was
attending the races that day, bristled when the band broke into a rous-
ing rendition of "It's a Lonesome Town When You're Not Around"
while Capone, a sunburst in his yellow suit and yellow tie, took his seat.

Arriving at the Transportation Building to confer with Johnson,
Ness picked up a copy of the *Tribune* and scanned the front page as he
mounted the steps. "Have you seen this? Can you believe it?" he

exclaimed as he whisked through the doorway into Johnson's office, plopping the newspaper on his colleague's desk. "They turn this guy into a damned hero! He sits back in his silk pajamas, tells everyone what a wonderful guy he is, and she plays right along. How could that gal from the newspaper be so gullible?"

Johnson tried to calm him. "You know his days are numbered, Eliot. Everybody knows what he is, and he's no hero, that's for sure. It's just a matter of time 'til he's out of the picture. All of these guys are going down, eventually."

That assessment was reinforced by the treatment Capone received when he appeared at Dyche Stadium in Evanston, Illinois, to watch the college football game between Northwestern and Nebraska. He supplied dozens of Chicago-area Boy Scouts with complimentary tickets, and the boys initiated a cheer of "Yea, Al!" which echoed around the stadium. Before halftime, however, Capone and trigger-man Jack McGurn were subjected to merciless heckling. When they finally decided they could take no more and rose to leave in the third quarter, they were followed by about four hundred undergraduates who booed and hissed.

Ralph Capone came to trial on tax evasion charges in April 1930. Directing the prosecution was Frank J. Wilson, a rising star in the eyes of Elmer Irey and other federal officials carrying out President Hoover's directives.

"He fears nothing that walks," Irey wrote of Wilson. "He will sit quietly looking at books seven days a week, forever, if he wants to find something in those books. He is soft-spoken and unemotional. Only the endless stream of nickel cigars he massacres keeps him from being a paragon of virtue."

Wilson got what he was after. Ralph Capone was convicted on all counts and received a sentence of three years in prison, along with a ten-thousand-dollar fine. The fine would be no problem for Capone, but the prison time was something he vowed to fight to the highest courts. He was allowed to remain free, pending his appeal.

"You got caught because you weren't smart," Al Capone told his brother in a telephone conversation recorded by Ness's team. "You talked too much and you put too many things in writing. You gotta be smart, Ralph."

The trial and other developments at the federal level served as a wake-up call to many Chicago-area bootleggers. Recognizing that the 1927 Supreme Court decision in the Sullivan case could just as easily apply to them, dozens of gangsters from across the country hurried to the Federal Building to pay whatever back taxes the Internal Revenue Service determined they owed.

They may also have taken their cue from President Hoover's signing of an act in May 1930 that consolidated several Prohibition enforcement agencies under the Department of Justice. "The system of protection collapsed," wrote Kenneth Allsop in his 1961 book *The Bootleggers*. "Suddenly no one could tell to whom bribes could be safely paid—and if they were paid, if they would stick. Who was 'in'? Who was 'out'? No one knew for sure."

Although he spent much of his time with deskwork, Alexander Jamie was occasionally called upon to investigate the Capone outfit's activities firsthand. By strong-arming two men apprehended in a delivery truck, Jamie uncovered a plot to smuggle massive quantities of whiskey from Canada to service Chicago-area speakeasies. Two large-cabin airplanes were used to transport about seventy cases each from a loading field in Windsor to a small airstrip near Cicero. In return for a promise of immunity from prosecution, the deliverymen identified Ralph Capone as the leader of the operation.

Jamie calculated the profit of the smuggling ring at almost $1.5 million over eight months. Two high-profile raids led by Jamie on May 8, 1930, at the famous Cotton Club at 5240 Twenty-second Street and the Greyhound Inn produced corroborating evidence.

Many saw the government's pursuit of Ralph Capone as merely a trial run for the case that would be brought against his brother Al. Prosecutors were careful to focus only on the tax case, and not on Prohibition violations, since jurors would not be inclined to take Volstead Act enforcement as seriously.

The last thing Capone wanted was a long, messy trial that could expose his criminal empire. Seeing the four-foot-high stack of evidence against his brother, Capone retained the services of Lawrence P. Mattingly, a renowned Washington tax lawyer. Mattingly tried to negotiate a deal, but to no avail. He and Capone appeared before Frank Wilson and Ralph Herrick, the tax agent in charge of the Treasury Department's Chicago Enforcement Division, for a cat-and-mouse discussion of Capone's business activities and his tax obligations.

"What records have you of your income, Mr. Capone? Do you keep any records?" Herrick inquired.

"No, I never did," Capone replied in a low, respectful tone.

"Any checking accounts?"

"No sir."

"How long, Mr. Capone, have you enjoyed such a large income?"

"I never had much of an income."

"I will state it differently—an income that might be taxable."

"I would rather let my lawyer answer that question."

Mattingly interjected that he had reviewed the issue with another of his clients, Johnny Torrio, and determined that Capone's salary was nowhere near the threshold above which federal income taxes had to be paid.

Wilson asked Capone if he had ever tried to conceal his own financial dealings by purchasing real estate and depositing money under the name of his wife or any other relative.

"I would rather not answer that," was Capone's reply, repeated several times as the questions grew more specific.

One potential witness who could have shed some light on Capone's finances was *Chicago Tribune* crime reporter Jake Lingle. As the wiretapped conversation suggested, Lingle was well aware of many financial enterprises in which Al Capone had a direct interest. A Chicago West Side native, Lingle had prided himself on his ability to infiltrate the mob. He supplied facts to other *Tribune* staffers who fashioned articles based primarily on Lingle's information. For eighteen years, Lingle's work had given his newspaper countless exclusive stories from inside gangland. Although he enjoyed easy access to Capone, Lingle also was on good terms with the police.

But Jake Lingle was not all that he seemed. A heavy gambler, he often spent more money in one night of gambling than he made from his modest weekly salary. His clothing and his vehicles left no doubt that he enjoyed supplemental income. Faced with the threat of being exposed as a Capone operative, Lingle told prosecutors he was willing to talk. Wilson arranged to meet him at the Tribune Tower the following day.

A nervous Lingle decided to visit one of his familiar haunts, the Washington Park racetrack, for some early afternoon action. He hurried down the stairs into the long pedestrian tunnel passing under Michigan Avenue, trying to catch the next train out of a nearby Illinois Central Railroad station.

A tall, blond man in his early twenties was seen elbowing people aside, trying to catch up to Lingle. As the man drew even, he took a gun out of his pocket, leveled it to the back of Lingle's head, and fired a bullet into the reporter's brain. Lingle fell forward, the day's horse racing form still in his hand and a burning cigar clenched between his teeth. The assassin dropped his gun and ran off.

Eliot Ness wasn't camera shy, even in these early family photographs.

Eliot was much younger than his four siblings, three sisters and a brother. Nora was his second-oldest sister, and she is pictured with him below (*left*). A bundled Eliot was photographed with his mother during one of Chicago's colder moment (*below right*). "Whew, that face!" wrote Emma Ness in the family scrapbook next to this image of her youngest child.

In 1925, with a bachelor's degree in political science and business administration in hand, Ness (*left*) became a field officer for an Atlanta-based firm that investigated people who applied for insurance coverage.

In August 1926, Ness was hired as a trainee with the Chicago Division of the U.S. Treasury Department. A few weeks later, with the help of a brother-in-law, he joined the Prohibition unit. In 1927 he was issued the identification below.

THE UNITED STATES
TREASURY DEPARTMENT · BUREAU OF PROHIBITION
Washington, D.C.   MAY 20,   19 27
THESE PRESENTS WITNESS THAT

Eliot Ness

(whose photograph and signature under official seal are annexed), is regularly appointed and commissioned by the Bureau of Prohibition of the United States Treasury Department to enforce the laws and regulations relating to the manufacture, sale, transportation, control and taxation of alcohol and of intoxicating liquors, under the authority vested in the Bureau of Prohibition by the Congress of the United States and the Secretary of the Treasury.

J. M. Doran
Commissioner of Prohibition.

COUNTERSIGNED:

Assistant Commissioner--Prohibition.

○

This commission is void if autographed photograph of appointee does not bear the seal of the Treasury Department.

No. **557**

Eliot Ness

When Ness joined the Prohibition Unit, Chicago was under the thumb of Al Capone. The crime boss had been rough and tough as a teenager and had been a bouncer and a street enforcer in New York before joining his mentor, Johnny Torrio, in Chicago.

Despite his reputation as a brutal underworld leader, Capone enjoyed celebrity status. Below, Gabby Hartnett from the Chicago Cubs signs a baseball for Sonny Capone while city politician and Capone associate Roland Libonati looks on.

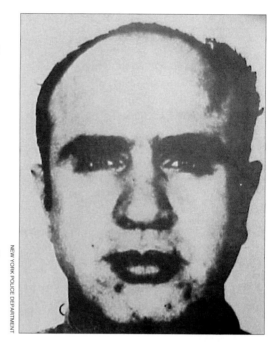

NEW YORK POLICE DEPARTMENT

CHICAGO TRIBUNE

The Saint Valentine's Day Massacre in 1929 claimed seven lives. Despite evidence linking the killings to Capone's outfit, no arrests were ever made. The sheer brutality of the murders, however, could not be ignored. In the U.S. Congress a proposal to double or even triple the $14 million being spent annually on Prohibition enforcement was debated but never passed.

To distance himself from such occurrences as the Saint Valentine's Day Massacre, Capone (*above right, after a workout with future heavyweight champion Jim Braddock*) spent much time in the Miami Beach, Florida, area. Chicago Mayor William "Big Bill" Thompson (*below left*) was one of Capone's best friends. Crime boss George "Bugs" Moran ruled Chicago's North Side (*below right*) and was one of a handful of gang leaders who would stand up to Capone.

COURTESY ALCOHOL, TOBACCO AND FIREARMS

Ness and his handpicked Capone Squad, known as the Untouchables, were given the task of gathering evidence for the government's prosecution of the Chicago crime czar. Above, Ness is in the driver's seat, Untouchable Al Wolff is in the back seat, and an unidentified colleague stands alongside.

The midday murder of newspaper reporter Jake Lingle on June 30, 1930, drew the public's attention again to the growing influence and brutality of organized crime in Chicago.

CHICAGO TRIBUNE

On the basis of a 1927 Supreme Court ruling known as the Sullivan decision, the criminals were vulnerable to prosecution for income tax evasion. To lay the groundwork for the case against Capone, the government moved first against Capone associate Frank Nitti (*above*), who probably grew this mustache in an attempt to hide his identity following his indictment.

In the photograph below, during his October 1931 tax evasion trial, Capone (*center*) confers with defense attorneys Michael Ahern (*left*) and Albert Fink.

Not long before their dissolution following the repeal of Prohibition in 1933, Ness (*back row, far right*) posed for this photo with Prohibition agents under his command.

When the Volstead Act was repealed, some of the Prohibition Bureau's tasks were delegated to a new Alcohol Tax Unit within the Bureau of Internal Revenue. Ness (*right*), now thirty years old, was part of this work, and his job focused on the accelerated growth of moonshining, particularly in the so-called Moonshine Mountains of Ohio, Kentucky, and Tennessee. In 1934 he was dispatched to the Cincinnati district. His assignment posed all the danger, possibly more, and offered none of the glory of his Chicago work.

Ness's work brought him to Cleveland, and his raids received newspaper coverage. In 1935 he left the Treasury Department for the position of public safety director of Cleveland.

This quaint cottage (*below left*) in Bay Village, with a view of the lake (*below right*), was the first home of Eliot and Edna Ness when they moved from Chicago.

The Cleveland Police Department earned respect after Ness instituted numerous reforms, including a new accident prevention squad that served as a model for others across the country and thirty new Harley-Davidson motorcycles equipped with two-way radios.

During the Great Lakes Exposition of 1936, Ness equipped police cars with "Voice of Safety" public address systems to help direct traffic and pedestrians.

During Ness's tenure as director of public safety, Cleveland was one of the first U.S. cities to install parking meters.

It was only appropriate that Ness represent the city of Cleveland for the presentation of the 1939 Safest City Award by National Safety Council president Col. John Stillwell (*right*). Just a few years before Ness's arrival, Cleveland had one of the nation's worst safety records.

Ness made sure that newspaper photographers were present when he handed over the results of an exhaustive investigation into police corruption to county prosecutor Frank Cullitan.

During the height of labor unrest, Ness (*right*) confers with investigator Henry Cowles and Police Lt. H. H. Moffitt at the site of one work stoppage.

A physical fitness buff, Ness played handball well into adulthood. He was also proficient in tennis. What he lacked in physical coordination, he made up for with technique, strategy, and endurance. Ness was a longtime student of jujitsu and self-defense and a hands-on instructor.

Evaline Ness, Eliot's second wife, was an artist and an illustrator. She enjoyed the good times with her husband, but as he became more involved in his work, she wanted more out of life. The Stouffer Boathouse at the mouth of Rocky River in Cleveland was their home. Evaline's studio was on the top floor.

During Ness's administration, one of the nation's first serial killers, the Mad Butcher (also known as the Kingsbury Run killer), began a short reign of terror. The killer was never identified despite a thorough investigation that included the circulation of "death masks" (*right*) by Ness and other law enforcement officials in Cleveland. Graphic newspaper coverage of the discovery of the killer's victims aroused the public to put considerable pressure on the frustrated investigators.

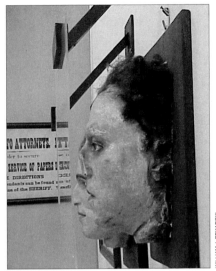

WILLIAM J. PEKARSKI

MERYLO COLLECTION, CLEVELAND POLICE HISTORICAL SOCIETY

Cuyahoga County sheriff Martin L. O'Donnell (*left*) points to the area where body parts from one of the Mad Butcher's victims were found.

Detective J. Peter Merylo (*left*) grills Todd Bartholomew, who reported to the police his gruesome discovery of the Mad Butcher's "Victim No. 12."

MERYLO COLLECTION, CLEVELAND POLICE HISTORICAL SOCIETY

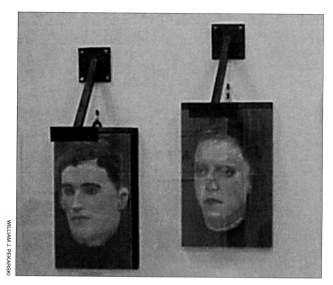

An exhibit at the Cleveland Police Historical Society preserves several death masks (*two of which appear above, side view at top of facing page*) of the Mad Butcher's victims. The outcry from the community led Ness, who noted that the killer preyed on transients, to order the fiery destruction of several "shantytowns" in the city (*below*). A newspaper caption described the police action, which curtailed the killer's activities, as "a descent into hell." Ness was roundly criticized for the assault.

Evaline created this sketch of her husband as he relaxed in bed and read a newspaper.

By the mid-1940s, the once youthful-looking Ness was showing the signs of stress related to both his job as public safety director and to problems in his personal life. In 1942 he resigned, albeit under a cloud, as Cleveland's safety director. After a night out with Evaline, Ness was involved in a car accident and failed to report it. It was also possible that his judgment had been impaired by alcohol. He took a position with the Federal Office of Defense as national director of the Federal Social Protection Program.

CHAPTER TEN

"The Whole Country Is Watching"

A L CAPONE'S CELEBRITY STATUS continued to eat away at Eliot Ness. He could not comprehend how the public tolerated a man who openly violated countless laws and was responsible for dozens of cold-blooded murders, all because of power and greed. In his writings, Ness made clear that he saw his job as a mission, as if he had been chosen to defend all that was good about America against all that was evil. If order was not soon restored, he believed, the entire nation could crumble.

"Acquiring the poise that comes with power, Capone has become even more dangerous," Ness wrote in a memo to his superiors. "Together with his ruthlessness, he has the qualities of a great businessman. Under that patent leather hair he has sound judgment, diplomatic shrewdness, and diamond-hard nerves of a gambler, all balanced by cold common sense."

With the wheels of justice grinding too slowly for his liking, Ness began battering away at the bootlegging business with renewed vigor.

"Eliot changed," Al Wolff noted. "The niceties of the law no longer meant all that much to him. He bent a few rules and even broke a few. We didn't always see eye-to-eye on that. Not that I'm criticizing him, but there were a couple of times when I refused to go and he understood. I will say this, though: any time Ness ignored the formalities or bent the rules, he had a darned good reason to do it."

Locating Capone's production facilities was sometimes easier than entering them. Besides falling for the occasional phony lead, too often Ness's team wasted precious time hacking through doorways with axes and battering them down with sledgehammers. This allowed those inside to destroy evidence or, as with the Lumber Street raid, to escape. Eventually, a frustrated Ness summoned Lyle Chapman to help him draw up blueprints for a sturdy vehicle that would enable the Capone Squad to enter the breweries more efficiently.

This ten-ton flatbed truck was equipped with a giant steel ram specially built for smashing through heavily reinforced doors. Handles were mounted in the cab so the raiders could steady themselves at the moment of impact. On each side of the truck were ladders, padded at the top to prevent noise when they were raised and positioned for access to roofs and fire escapes.

The truck was first used in a raid at 2108 South Wabash Avenue on June 13, 1930. Only scant details were recorded. Ness donned a leather football helmet and took his position in the passenger's seat as Chapman slipped behind the wheel. Four of the other agents spread out to cover the exits. As Chapman and Ness crashed through the front doors, five startled brewery employees darted for the back exit, running into the waiting arms of Gardner and King. This was the biggest arrest yet by the Capone Squad. Agents collected a variety of evidence—from trucks and vats to beer barrels and distilling equipment. They dumped hundreds of gallons of beer.

Despite the admonitions of his bosses and the advice of his fellow agents, Ness insisted on sharing news of the raid with reporters. Some colleagues considered him a glory-seeker, but Eliot shrugged off his critics, insisting that extensive publicity of his team's activities would tell the underworld that a new era had arrived. How better to demonstrate that, Ness argued, than to prove that no one—not even Al Capone—was above the law?

One of the unfortunate consequences of notifying the press in advance was that journalists sometimes either intentionally tipped off the operators to the impending raids, or they arrived at the suspected breweries before the agents. In one extreme case, mobsters spotted the reporters far enough in advance to move all of their equipment and beer supplies out. Ness and his crew ended up raiding a dry hole.

Privately, Ness recognized that publicity could make his team the target of retaliation. "We all realized we were sitting on a keg of dynamite with no means of determining the length of the fuse," he wrote in *The Untouchables*. This almost fatalistic approach to his work greatly disturbed Eliot's parents and Edna.

Ness's book also detailed a visit allegedly paid to him by a go-between he called "the Kid." According to Ness, this young visitor handed him an envelope containing twenty one-hundred-dollar bills and promised that weekly payments of the same amount would be delivered if the Capone Squad backed off.

"I could feel the anger rising in my chest," Ness wrote. "Fighting to get hold of myself, I walked around the desk and stood in front of him. Slowly, I reached down, pulled him out of the chair and, opening his jacket, stuffed the envelope back into his inner pocket. 'Listen, and listen carefully,' I told him. 'I may be only a poor baker's son, but I want you to take this envelope back to them and tell them that Eliot Ness can't be bought—not for two thousand a week, ten thousand, or a hundred thousand. Not for all the money they'll ever lay their scummy hands on.' With the boss back, the first step was bribery. What next?"

Capone's people didn't give up easily. A pair of them tried to buy cooperation by heaving a wad of one-hundred-dollar bills through the open window of a parked car occupied by Lahart and Seager. After a brief discussion with the hoodlums, Lahart tossed the money back at the men and drove away.

Ness called a press conference, inviting all of the influential Chicago-area reporters. With flashbulbs popping and pencils scribbling all around him, he recounted the two bribery attempts in dramatic fashion. Ness boldly repeated his team's determination to destroy Capone's bootlegging operations and to bolster the government's mounting case against the most powerful criminal organization in America.

"Probably it wasn't too important for the world to know that we couldn't be bought, but I did want Al Capone and every gangster in the city to realize that there were still a few law enforcement agents who couldn't be swerved from their duty," Ness recalled.

A writer from the *Chicago Tribune*, in the next day's edition, coined the phrase, "the Untouchables," to describe this small band of gangbusters. This was the first prominent mention of "Elliott" Ness in the Chicago newspapers, and he savored the recognition.

"Ness is new on the scene," said a newspaper profile introducing Chicago to the head of the Untouchables. "He is six feet tall, with a lean 180-pound frame, and slim waistline offset by broad shoulders, a boyishly-handsome face and a wave of freckles across the bridge of his nose. He has a pleasant smile, wavy brown hair parted in the middle, sleepy blue-gray eyes that can suddenly turn icy and piercing. He immediately strikes one as 'all business,' then smiles and winks, as if the fact that he is merely acting in a role is just between you and him. He is, in short, an enigma—but an enigma with lots of promise."

Capone eventually resorted to one of Ness's tricks. By bribing telephone workers, he was able to install sophisticated taps on the phone lines of Ness and others at the Transportation Building. Through these devices, Capone learned the identity of each agent and made sure that mobsters were tailing the investigators. When the phone conversations suggested a raid was imminent or when agents were spotted near one of his establishments, Capone ordered the brewery shut down for a "cooling-off period."

Capone's people also tried to discredit Ness in the eyes of his superiors and in the press by planting false information about his background and character. Then, perhaps just to irritate Ness, Capone's men stole his car, drove it into a ditch on the outskirts of the city, and left it there, a newspaper detailing the Untouchables' success draped over the steering wheel. Someone had drawn a target around Ness in the photograph that accompanied the story and had scrawled, "You're Dead," inside the target. Ness also received anonymous letters and telephone warnings intended to intimidate him. Still shaken by the murder of crime reporter Jake Lingle, Ness took the threats seriously, and he eagerly shared the information with reporters.

The government had an important ally in Judge John Lyle, the self-appointed scourge of gangsters. Lyle set bail so high that most of the brewery employees and other lawbreakers were forced to remain behind bars for weeks or even months awaiting legal proceedings. They were always presented with another alternative: telling what they knew of Capone's illegal operations in return for leniency.

Lyle also shrewdly invoked a little-used section of the Vagrancy Law to have Al Capone arrested. Questioned about such an untraditional application, the judge caustically replied that Capone fit the description of "vagrant," because he had no admitted source of income.

"If he tried to pay the fine, he would have to explain where the money had come from," Lyle reasoned. "Were he to recite the sources of his income, he would be opening the door to criminal charges. And any claim to legitimate employment would launch an investigation that could conceivably result in perjury charges. There was also the possibility that a vagrancy hearing would assist Treasury agents in their efforts to develop an income tax case against Capone."

Lyle's strategy resulted in a series of arrests and convictions, all overturned on appeal. If nothing else, the vagrancy crackdown kept Capone and several of his advisers busy while Ness, Wilson, Irey, and the others continued their work on the more serious charges.

Dark rumors continued to linger concerning Jake Lingle's affiliation with the mob. Evidence eventually surfaced to reveal that Lingle had served as a liaison between Capone's organization and City Hall, arranging for the protection of bootleggers and gamblers. In the process, he had cooperated with both Capone and Capone's rival, Bugs Moran—a dangerous practice.

Ralph Capone and others could be heard on the Montmartre telephone wiretap discussing Lingle's killing, but government investigators could not piece together enough incriminating evidence to directly link Al Capone to the crime. Ness's conclusion was that Capone either ordered the shooting or laid the groundwork by removing whatever protection he had previously maintained around Lingle.

Although dozens of witnesses got a good look at the assailant, no one would provide police with a useful description. Eventually, Leo Vincent Brothers, a labor union terrorist from Saint Louis, was charged with the murder. Despite promises of leniency, Brothers denied any involvement and was convicted by a jury.

Just three weeks after the trial, prosecutors received a letter from Mike de Pike Heitler, one of Capone's street enforcers, identifying eight of Capone's affiliates as conspirators in Lingle's killing. This chilling communication arrived days after Heitler's charred remains were found in the ruins of a house that had burned in Barrington, northwest of Chicago. Heitler had apparently sealed the letter and given it to his daughter, with strict instructions that it be placed in the mail if he died an unnatural death. Many, however, remain convinced that Bugs Moran ordered Lingle's death, anticipating that Capone would be blamed.

Revelations of Lingle's role in the Chicago crime scene caused immeasurable damage to public confidence in the press's ability to expose and combat crime and corruption. Harry T. Brundige, an old-style reporter with the *Saint Louis Star*, was granted an exclusive interview with Al Capone as part of his research for what would become a ten-part series exposing members of the Chicago press as blackmailers, bootleggers, bookmakers, influence peddlers, and close allies of the underworld.

"How many reporters do you have on the payroll?" Brundige asked.

"Plenty," Capone said. "You can't buck it, not even with the backing of your newspaper, because it's too big a proposition. No one will ever realize just how big it is."

The mounting evidence of crime and corruption only strengthened Ness's resolve during a visit to Frank Wilson's office to deliver the latest pile of transcripts from the wiretapped conversations at the Montmartre.

"We're gonna dry these bastards up pretty soon," Ness told him. "Here's some more ammunition for you guys. I've made a few notes in the border. It looks to me like Greasy Thumb Guzik is going to be running the show once Ralph is behind bars."

"Don't be so sure," Wilson replied, looking over the frames of his glasses. "We could take Guzik now if we wanted to, and probably Capone, too, for that matter. But I think we're better off letting them feed us more evidence. They're playing right into our hands."

"Well, my boys are getting impatient," Ness responded. "We've got ten times the evidence we need to nab these guys, and we're about ready to take out two more breweries. My men can't understand what you're waiting for."

"We're getting close, Eliot. I mean that. We've just got to make sure everything is in place. Hell, the whole country is watching this. We can't afford to make any mistakes." Ness nodded his head and turned to leave. "Keep up the good work," Wilson encouraged him.

"We're not giving up," Ness promised. "We'll do our job, as long as I can tell my men that something is going to come out of all their hard work."

What Wilson didn't share with Ness was the fact that federal officials were placing diminished importance on all of the evidence the Untouchables were gathering. With the income tax evasion case coming together so rapidly and so successfully, neither Wilson nor Johnson expected to prosecute Capone for Prohibition violations. Investigators in Florida had already gathered overwhelming evidence of Capone's lavish spending habits. These agents documented vehicle purchases, furniture and clothing orders, hotel bills, medical expenses, long-distance telephone charges, and other evidence of Capone's substantial income.

Back in Chicago, using cash payments and threats of incarceration, Wilson's men persuaded several prostitutes employed by Capone to sign affidavits incriminating their boss.

One of the Treasury Department agents, Michael F. Malone, was able to gain access to Capone's "fort" at the Lexington Hotel by posing as a Philadelphia gangster hiding out from the police. (Malone is referred to by the pseudonym "Patrick O'Rourke" in some accounts.) His charade included false criminal records bearing the seal of the Philadelphia Police Department. Malone also mailed letters to friends in Philadelphia and received responses, all bogus correspondence designed to further establish his false identity. Not only did Capone's people steam open these letters and inspect the contents, they also searched Malone's room, including an inspection of his clothing, which—luckily for him—bore Philadelphia labels.

Wilson, in his memoirs, called Malone "the greatest natural undercover worker the IRS ever had." Malone systematically gathered volumes of evidence covering Capone's baseball-bat assault of Scalise, Anselmi, and Guinta; numerous murders on Capone's behalf; and countless bootlegging, gambling, prostitution, and racketeering operations.

Among the agent's most startling discoveries was what may have been a plot by the Capone gang to murder Wilson at the Sheridan Plaza, where he and his wife had been staying under assumed names. Wilson was immediately assigned a bodyguard and moved to another hotel suite.

Pressured as never before by President Hoover to move in on Capone, Wilson pleaded in a memo for more time: "Important witnesses are either hostile to the government and ready to give perjured testimony in order to protect the leaders of their organization, or they are so filled with fear of the Capone organization that they evade, lie, leave town and do all in their power to prevent the government from using them as witnesses."

The president's impatience was understandable. Al Capone was an all-too-visible symbol of lawlessness and an embarrassment to the troubled Hoover administration. Moviegoers were introduced to a caricature of Capone in First National's *Little Caesar,* starring Edward G. Robinson, in early 1930. Warner Studios followed with *The Public Enemy,* featuring James Cagney, in 1931. Theater companies were also getting in on the act, including Broadway's *On the Spot,* which began in October 1930 and lasted for 167 performances. The Howard Hughes Studio also joined in, producing *Scarface,* starring Paul Muni.

After a meeting with President Hoover, Wilson decided to play his ace in the hole: an obscure Capone operative named Fred Ries. As cashier for Capone's gambling houses and racing enterprises, Ries would pile the earnings in a gunnysack and deposit them under aliases at Pinkert State Bank, where he was legitimately employed as a cashier. He converted the money to cashier's checks and turned them over to Jack Guzik and Al Capone.

A tall, stooped figure, nearly bald, Ries fled in fear for his life after initially being questioned. He was tracked down in Saint Louis and threatened with a long prison term if he continued to protect Capone. Ushered to Chicago to appear before a secretly convened grand jury, Ries nervously detailed how Capone's gambling house was pulling in profits of more than one hundred thousand dollars per night.

To lay further groundwork for the prosecution of Al Capone, the government moved forward against another of his key operatives, Frank "the Enforcer" Nitti. Mike Malone, who had become well acquainted with Nitti during his stays at the Lexington, learned that Nitti was making regular deposits on Capone's behalf at the Schiff Trust and Savings Bank. Grand jurors secretly returned an indictment against Nitti for failing to pay taxes on income of nearly $750,000 over a three-year period. Evidently, it wasn't secret enough, because Nitti promptly disappeared from Chicago.

Less than two weeks later, he was tracked down in the Chicago suburb of Berwyn. The Enforcer admitted responsibility for bank deposits of more than two hundred thousand dollars covering the profits of alcohol stills in Cicero, Little Italy, and the West Side of Chicago and from the Hawthorne Smoke Shop's gambling operations in Cicero. Nitti, good soldier that he was, insisted the money was his own, although the investigators knew better. His guilty plea to tax evasion charges brought a sentence of eighteen months at Leavenworth Penitentiary.

Combing evidence from a variety of sources, including the Untouchables' transcripts, prosecutors next persuaded a hastily convened grand jury to indict Jack Guzik for avoiding federal income taxes on almost $1 million in earnings over a three-year period. Everyone knew whose money Guzik was managing, but he was not about to admit it.

At Guzik's trial on November 19, 1930, Fred Ries appeared as a surprise witness to present damning evidence against not only Greasy Thumb Guzik, but also against Al Capone and others. Looking up at the prosecutor, Johnson, through thick, horn-rimmed glasses that partially obscured his face, Ries detailed the accounting system used for ledgers showing the Pinkert State Bank deposits on behalf of the Capone brothers, Guzik, and Nitti. Convicted of tax evasion and criminal conspiracy, the tightlipped Guzik was sentenced to a five-year jail term.

Ries, the greatest threat to Al Capone's freedom, was now a marked man. Chicago's Secret Six contributed ten thousand dollars to help federal officials protect their star witness by sequestering him in South America, under heavy security, while the crackdown continued.

From their cramped, windowless cubicle at the Federal Building, Wilson and two aides studied thousands of papers, from bank records and faded ledgers to handwritten notations and investigators' reports. Meanwhile, Capone returned to his retreat in Florida and sent back a settlement proposal to George Johnson and Frank Wilson. He promised to never again set foot in Chicago if the government would agree not to prosecute him for tax evasion or Prohibition violations.

Chief Judge John P. McGoorty was appalled: "Capone's most formidable competitors have been ruthlessly exterminated and his only obstacle towards undisputed sway is the law. Such a trade is unthinkable. The time has come when the public must choose between rule of the gangster and rule of the law."

Attorney Mattingly desperately wanted to avoid a full-scale trial, since a tax evasion conviction would mean almost certain jail time for his client. Perhaps in desperation, Mattingly committed a major tactical blunder, presenting the government with a document that would become the smoking gun prosecutors needed. It was a sworn affidavit from Al Capone estimating the crime boss's income at sixty-six thousand dollars for 1926–27 and two hundred thousand dollars for 1928–29.

These were mere fractions of the true figures. Mattingly gambled that prosecutors would accept the guilty plea in return for Capone's agreement to pay a substantial fine and leave Chicago forever. What he had actually provided to the government was, in effect, written admission of his client's guilt.

Capone was growing more irrational by the week. His bizarre behavior could probably be attributed to the effects that syphilis and perhaps substance abuse were having on his brain. The once-muscular Capone was a flabby 250 pounds and looked far beyond his years. He suddenly rejected his lawyer's strategy and tried to resort to his old way of settling disputes. Capone hired five professional hitmen from New York and gave them orders to murder Wilson, Johnson, and Irey. Through information supplied by Mike Malone and at least one other undercover agent, the targets of this plot were forewarned.

The federal officials summoned Mattingly and told him that they would hold both him and Capone personally responsible if there were any bloodshed. Capone agreed to call off the assassination plot, only to fall back on another of his tried-and-true methods of persuasion. He offered Irey a $1.5 million payoff if the IRS official could keep him out of jail. That proposition only strengthened Irey's resolve to put Capone behind bars for as long as the law would allow.

CHAPTER ELEVEN

Crumbling Empire

T O DIVERT ATTENTION FROM the tax evasion probe and gather
additional evidence of violations by Capone, George Johnson
and Alexander Jamie sent the Ness team out for its most aggressive
series of raids. The wall chart showed a clearly defined delivery
route from the barrel-cleaning plant at Shields and Thirty-eighth
to breweries and speakeasies across the metropolitan area. The
Montmartre wiretap also continued to provide a steady stream of
useful information.

The attack began at an abandoned factory at 1042 South Cicero
Avenue in Cicero. According to the plan, Lyle Chapman would
blast the truck through the front door while Ness rode in the passenger's seat. Martin Lahart was to ride on the back of the truck and
step off just before impact so he could cover the hole in the door.
They planned the attack for five o'clock the following morning.

At 4:47 Chapman turned the truck onto the cobbled surface of
South Cicero Avenue. He stopped about forty yards from the double
doors in the front so the men could quickly scan the area to determine if they had been detected. A squad car slipped behind the
truck. Paul Robsky, Thomas Friel, and William Gardner stepped out
and unhooked an extension ladder from the side of the truck, sliding
it up against the side of the building and climbing to the roof.

Chapman gunned the engine while Ness tightened his grip on the revolver he extended out the window. "Hit it!" he commanded. The truck charged forward, slamming hard into the doors with a ripping, rending crash and the shrill scream of tortured metal. The reinforced bumper scattered wood in every direction. The steel inner doors were no match for the truck.

A separate wooden wall, designed solely to conceal the activities behind it, had been erected about thirty feet inside the warehouse. "Hit it again!" Ness ordered, pointing to the wall. Chapman fired the gearshift into reverse, backed up, and plowed forward, collapsing the wall into a pile of splinters and dust. Ness counted five paralyzed, wide-eyed brewery workers as he leaped from the truck.

"Don't anybody move!" he shouted. "This is a federal raid."

Michael King, Joseph Leeson, and Barney Cloonan arrived from the other end of the building, having chopped their way through the back doors. Among the five men taken into custody was Steve Svoboda, one of Capone's most experienced brewmasters, and Frank Conta, a prominent member of the outfit. The suspects were handcuffed and loaded into squad cars for booking. After taking an inventory, the agents tore apart seven vats, each with a capacity of 320 gallons, and seized three new trucks.

Two weeks later, the Untouchables raided a smaller brewery and warehouse on Chicago's South Side. Four trucks were confiscated, along with alcohol supplies and equipment valued at approximately two hundred thousand dollars. Ness's group was led to the brewery by following a "drip can" that had been attached under the axle of a truck one of Capone's men was driving, leaving a dotted path leading right to the warehouse door.

Next on the hit list was a brewery at 3136 South Wabash Avenue that had only days earlier begun operating under the guise of the Old Reliable Trucking Company. Every day at dusk, a Cadillac with two men pulled into the corner of an adjacent lot. The occupants, armed with what appeared to be tommy guns, never left their posts. Trucks came and went from seven in the evening to about three in the morning, after which a half-dozen men departed on foot.

Once Ness became familiar with the routine, he ordered a raid for the early morning hours of April 11, 1931. A handful of reliable

Prohibition agents joined the Untouchables, increasing the force to fifteen men. As the truck's heavy bumper crashed through the double doors, it triggered an earsplitting clang of alarm bells. Ness whirled around in time to spot the black car with Capone's guards speeding past the brewery and out of sight. Anticipating that reinforcements were on the way, he knew his team had to move fast.

The truck barreled over the wreckage into a second set of doors, which fell with a loud thud. The brewery was in full operation. Three men scampered toward a dark hallway leading to the rear of the building, but Robsky and Friel were there to greet them at gunpoint. Two others who were tending to a huge vat raised their hands and surrendered without a struggle. As Ness stepped forward to handcuff the duo, he was shocked to discover that one of them was Svoboda, the brewmaster who had recently been freed on five thousand dollars' bail.

Among the items seized or destroyed were fourteen brewing tanks, each with a twenty-five-hundred-gallon capacity, along with five cooling tanks, modern electric pumps, and a huge air compressor. The finished beer alone was valued at one hundred thousand dollars. Had the brewery been permitted to operate unmolested for a year, it would have produced about $3.5 million in revenue.

Newspaper photographers captured Ness and Robsky thrusting axes into barrel after barrel of market-ready beer, pausing to watch the golden fluid gush out onto the floor. Other agents were photographed as they applied blowtorches to dismantle equipment. Ness filled several small vials with samples and then directed Robsky to open the valves on each fermenting tank. Hundreds of gallons poured out, overwhelming a floor drain with thick foam.

The inventory also included a barrel of fish skins, which were being used to improve the quality of the beer. Svoboda explained with pride how he would immerse the fish skins in each batch of brew, which helped to draw out the impurities and enhance the flavor.

Ness then turned the discovery of a tap on the phone line outside of the Transportation Building to his advantage as the series of raids continued. He explained in his memoirs: "I would let them think I was attending the theater or a sporting event on a certain evening, and would turn up seizing a beer truck or a brewery when they least expected it. They knew I loved to raid and that raids were rarely made without my being present."

Breweries were not the only targets of Ness's latest offensive. His Untouchables brazenly launched a series of raids on Capone's better-known speakeasies. Leading this attack was Al "Wallpaper" Wolff.

"I would go to a cabaret or a high-class tavern and carry a little tube where I'd put the whiskey and have it analyzed by a chemist," Wolff explained. "Then we'd get a warrant, go in and arrest them, call the trucks and move 'em out. We'd move everything but the wallpaper. That's why they gave me the nickname 'Wallpaper.' Capone himself came up with that one. He said I did a real clean job of takin' every-thing that wasn't attached."

Wolff recalled that the Capone Squad would sometimes knock off four or five speakeasies in a day, which made him unpopular in many neighborhoods. "People were hissing us because, you know, the Germans didn't like to lose their beer. But we had orders to dry Capone out. I wasn't out to be popular. I was just doing my job."

Because he spoke Yiddish, German, and Polish, Wolff could easily blend into crowds as either a businessman or a truck driver. He sometimes followed sugar trucks to the brewing plants and stills Ness would later target for raids.

"I always worked alone," Wolff said. "I seldom came into the office at the Transportation Building. I called Ness when it was time to go in and make a raid."

One of the transcripts from the Montmartre wiretap revealed a conversation between Ralph Capone, who was still free pending his appeal, and a mobster identified only as "Fusco." They were plotting a mission to recover some of the beer-making equipment that remained locked inside the South Wabash Avenue brewery that Ness's team had raided just a few weeks earlier.

Ness sent his men back and intercepted four men who arrived to load the material. The team waited until the quartet had hoisted a huge vat onto the back of a flatbed truck before apprehending them. A wild honking of horns by two drivers posted as sentinels warned the group of the raid, but it was too late. Among the suspects was another of Capone's top brewmasters and business associates, Bert Delaney, who was out on bail after being nabbed in an earlier raid.

The Ness team also took a swing through Chicago Heights, literally sniffing out three stills producing an estimated annual income of eight hundred thousand dollars for the Capone outfit. Five Sicilian men were taken into custody and eventually deported.

"We secured convictions against fifty-six men in this neighborhood last year, and we were just checking up today," Ness told a reporter. "I'll be back."

An editorial in the *Chicago Daily News*, entitled "Tale of a Telltale Nose," chided local police for failing to clean up the town:

> Young Mr. Ness employs a highly effective process. He drives around sniffing the breeze. When the penetrating odors of mash vats titillate his nostrils he follows his nose and raids the stills. Other officers of the law almost invariably are possessors of noses. However, when those useful organs catch intoxicating scents doubtless their possessors dream of rose gardens, or beds of violets drenched with dew, or of jasmine thickets and the songs of mockingbirds.

Capone's outfit responded to this latest assault on their facilities by bringing in Michael Picchi, a notorious hitman from Saint Louis. Picchi, a stringy, gaunt-cheeked veteran of the gang wars, was a stereotypical gangster, complete with cobra eyes and slicked-down hair. From a personal perspective, news of Picchi's arrival was the most important information that came to Ness through the wiretap at the Montmartre Café. It may have saved his life. By the time Picchi surfaced in Chicago, Ness had already taken precautions. He insisted that Edna move into a room at a large downtown hotel and assigned a round-the-clock guard outside her room. He also obtained a mug shot of the hired gun and distributed copies to those officers he knew to be reliable, asking them to be on the lookout.

"I was surprised that I didn't feel too perturbed about learning that I was marked for gangland execution," he wrote in *The Untouchables*. "Probably underneath I had been expecting just that for a long time."

Ness went on to present the following account of his one and only confrontation with Picchi. He was riding in the passenger seat of a car being driven by Marty Lahart on Chicago's South Side when Lahart caught sight of a suspicious driver behind them.

"We're being tailed—I can tell," he said, continuing to glance at the mirror. "That might be our boy. You better get down."

Ness slumped in his seat and slowly turned to his left to catch a glimpse of the driver. He could barely make out the silhouetted figure in a fedora, partially blocking the sunlight pouring through the car's back window. Lahart made a series of turns and the driver followed, closing the gap between the two cars. "You better get down and hold on," he cautioned Ness.

Lahart turned onto a side street in a residential section and followed it to an intersection, where he suddenly made a screeching U-turn. He steered the Cadillac straight in the direction of the other car and forced it up onto a sidewalk, then crashed into its rear bumper, jarring the driver forward. The two agents jumped out, guns drawn.

"Freeze, or you're a dead man!" Ness shouted. The instant he saw the driver's face, he knew it was Picchi. Reaching under Picchi's overcoat, Ness removed a revolver from its holster. The weapon turned out to be a "killer's gun," complete with a scratched-off serial number and a chamber full of dum-dum bullets. The agents loaded Picchi into their car and drove him to Kensington Police Station, where he was jailed on a charge of attempting to assault two federal officers.

Ness's next stop was his hotel room, where he found Edna pacing the floor, beside herself with worry. She tried to persuade Eliot to resign from the Prohibition Bureau and find a more secure career, but he was determined to complete the mission, as he saw it, of bringing Capone to justice.

Eliot did agree to move back into the couple's apartment after he arranged to have a second officer added to the twenty-four-hour guard detail. Edna still felt like a prisoner in her own home, keeping the shades pulled down day and night and never knowing when, or if, her husband would return.

CHAPTER TWELVE

A Marked Man

PAUL ROBSKY WAS ALL smiles as he burst into Eliot Ness's office, plopping a bulging stack of file folders on the desk. "Check this one out," he said, sliding a sheet across the desk to Ness. It detailed a conversation between a Cicero speakeasy owner and Jack Guzik, who was jail-bound in a week following the denial of his appeal. The bar owner demanded a shipment of liquor and threatened to turn to other sources if Capone could not deliver. Guzik lamented the organization's depleted supply and pleaded for patience.

Another transcript covered a dialogue between Guzik and one of Capone's street thugs, who demanded more money for bribing a couple of police officers.

"Listen, Hymie," Guzik told him. "Tell the boys they'll have to take a pass this month."

"They ain't gonna like it."

"Too bad, but we just ain't makin' the dough. And if we ain't got it, we can't pay it." Guzik assured the caller the problems were temporary.

On February 24, 1931, Al Capone was ordered to appear before Federal Judge James J. Wilkerson on a contempt charge, stemming from his failure to answer a federal grand jury subpoena after the Saint Valentine's Day Massacre. Wilkerson, a handsome man in his early fifties, was openly appalled by the corruption that had swept through Chicago and was determined to give Capone his day in court. Adding to the intrigue was the likelihood that Capone, if he were indicted for income tax evasion or Prohibition violations, would be tried in Wilkerson's courtroom.

After spies who tracked Capone's activities in Florida contradicted the defendant's claim that he had been too ill to appear, the judge found Capone guilty and sentenced him to a six-month term in the Cook County Jail. He was, however, allowed to remain free on bail, pending an appeal. George E. Q. Johnson was thrilled. He and the other prosecutors believed they had finally found a no-nonsense jurist who was willing to handle Capone without fear of retribution.

As aggressive as Ness and his Untouchables had grown in recent months, nothing could match the brazenness of their next act if, in fact, it actually took place. Historians have been troubled by the lack of documentation of the event and the absence of newspaper coverage, let alone eyewitnesses. According to the story detailed in *The Untouchables* and passed along by word of mouth, the idea was hatched when Ness learned that the trucks and other vehicles seized during the raids on Capone's breweries and warehouses were headed for the auction block. Ness gleefully made plans for one of the most bizarre public displays downtown Chicago had ever seen.

He summoned the Capone Squad to a federal government warehouse to help wash and wax each of the vehicles. Early the next morning, he telephoned the Lexington Hotel, talked his way through a desk clerk, and spoke directly to Capone.

"Whad'ya want?" Capone grumbled.

"Well, Mr. Capone, I just wanted to tell you that, if you look out your front windows down on Michigan Avenue at exactly eleven o'clock, you'll see something that will interest you."

Ness hung up before Capone could respond. One can only speculate as to Capone's concern about this telephone call or, for that matter, the Untouchables themselves. There is little documentation to support the long-held assumption that Capone was obsessed with the work of Ness and his men.

At the designated time, Ness and his team, joined by about three dozen recruits from the Prohibition Bureau, arrived at the garage and took their positions aboard the shiny trucks. They fell in behind a police escort and formed a line that covered three city blocks. With sirens wailing and lights flashing, the caravan lumbered forward on Michigan Avenue.

Forty-five vehicles seized during Prohibition Bureau raids paraded steadily toward the Lexington. Ness rode in the lead car, armed with a sawed-off shotgun, more for show than security.

Capone appeared at an upstairs window with his bodyguards and flew into a violent rage when he realized what was happening. He allegedly lifted two chairs and smashed them over a table, screaming, "I'll kill 'im! I'll kill 'im with my own bare hands." Ness, in his memoirs, called the parade "a brilliant psychological counterstroke."

"What we had done this day was enrage the bloodiest mob in criminal history," Ness explained. "We had hurled the defiance of the Untouchables into their teeth; they surely knew by now that we were prepared to fight to the finish."

According to Ness's account, two nights later, he and Edna were relaxing at their apartment, listening to an opera on their phonograph, a cat sleeping on Eliot's lap, when the phone rang. The raspy voice at the other end warned the federal agent that his days were numbered. "You won't know when, and you won't know where," said the caller. "The next time I see you will be at your funeral."

In *The Untouchables*, Ness claimed that he took several steps to tighten security. He spent most nights in hotels rather than drive home and expose Edna to any danger. He also changed the routes he used to report to the Transportation Building, and he arranged to have a car with two agents follow him whenever he was on the road.

In his memoirs Ness claimed that three attempts on his life followed in quick succession after the telephone warning. In the first he barely escaped a hail of bullets from a passing car:

> I hardly noticed the parked car facing in the opposite direction. But as I approached to within a few yards, there was a bright flash from the front window and I ducked instinctively as my windshield splintered in tune with the bark of the revolver. Without thinking, I jammed the accelerator to the floor. As my car leaped forward, there was another flash, and the window on my left rear door was smashed by another slug. Only the uncertain lighting

and my sudden acceleration had saved me. I drove back into the
city with my gun on my lap.

During the second attempt he was almost run down by a speeding automobile that veered toward him as he and Lahart crossed an
intersection outside his office. Just days later, according to the sensationalized Ness-Fraley account, the federal agent noticed something amiss with the hood of his car as he balanced his briefcase on
the fender.

"Very cautiously, I raised the hood," he recounted. "Attached to
the wiring system just under the thin panel separating the driver's
seat from the motor was a dynamite bomb. I carefully lowered the
hood and called the police. 'If you had touched that starter,' said the
Police Department explosives expert as he gingerly removed the
bomb from the car, 'you'd have been blown to kingdom come.' I was
severely shaken, and sat for a long time in my car, trembling."

Historians and other researchers are split on whether any of
these episodes actually occurred. There is, however, at least a grain
of truth in the reports. Mike Graham, a prominent Chicago journalist who studied the Roaring Twenties, found ample evidence
that Capone or his close operatives really did want to eliminate
Ness. The assassination would have been carried out, if not for the
better judgment of his associates.

"People with cooler heads—lieutenants in the organization—recognized that Capone was a marked man," Graham told a National
Public Radio interviewer. "He really represented the old order of
doing things. The garishness, the glamour and the violence were
things that were going to have to be eliminated if the others were
going to continue on when Capone went to jail."

Growing desperate, Capone moved to consolidate his criminal
enterprises and prepare for the expected repeal of the Volstead Act
and the legalization of alcoholic beverages. He positioned his syndicate to gain a monopoly on the bottling of soda water and ginger ale
as a source of post-Prohibition income.

As the summer of 1931 arrived, Ness turned his attention to
paperwork that have been accumulated by the Capone Squad. He
and Lyle Chapman had filled three file cabinets with documents and

were ordered by the prosecution team to reduce the material to the essentials for a grand jury. The two had moved some of the more significant evidence to safety-deposit boxes in a Chicago bank after a break-in at the Transportation Building a few months earlier.

Finally, after more than two years of investigation, the federal government was prepared to move forward in its prosecution of Al Capone on two fronts. In early June, Frank Wilson and his Treasury Department colleagues presented only a small portion of their evidence, and a grand jury quickly responded by indicting Capone on twenty-two counts of income tax evasion.

"Capone's Days Are Numbered," heralded a Chicago newspaper.

A week later, Ness carried two briefcases with summaries of his evidence into the Federal Building. He took a seat in the corner of the building's impressive lobby and leaned back to collect his thoughts. Ness stared up at the high ceiling, which echoed with the dull roar of the business below, and tried to envision his appearance on the witness stand. Beads of perspiration formed on his head as his heart began to pound in nervous anticipation. His mind was racing as he leafed through the documents in his briefcases and lit a cigarette. The minutes seemed to pass like hours. After only a few puffs, he snuffed out the cigarette, gathered his evidence, and proceeded upstairs to the courtroom.

For the first time in his life, Eliot Ness was center stage. The sheer volume of evidence presented during Ness's three-hour stint on the witness stand was staggering, supporting more than five thousand offenses by Capone and his allies. He read from lists of confiscated equipment and from transcripts, as well as testimony presented during the trials of Ralph Capone and Jack Guzik. Jurors also heard laboratory reports on the contents of beer and other illicit beverages seized during raids of Capone's facilities.

The government's case dated back some ten years, when Capone, as "Al Brown," took charge of beer production so Johnny Torrio could focus on vice operations. Evidence revealed that the World Motor Service trucking company incorporated by Capone and aides Joseph Fusco, Bert Delaney, and Nick Juffra in 1921 was a cover for bootlegging. Over the next decade, this organization made as much as $200 million by selling illicit beverages, the prosecution alleged.

Based primarily on the Untouchables' work, the grand jury brought indictments against Capone and sixty-eight members of his mob for conspiracy to violate the Volstead Act.

The *New York Times,* in a page-one headline, hailed Ness as a hero: "Faced Many Perils in Capone Roundup. Squad of Seven Young Dry Agents Credited with Successful Drive on Chicago Gangster. Leader Only 28 Years Old; Impervious to Threats of Death or Bribes. They Have Been Styled 'The Untouchables.'"

"What of the offers of bribes and the threats of death that came the way of Eliot Ness and his youthful assistants?" the accompanying story read. "Ness is reluctant to talk about them. He calls them side incidents in the larger task of doing a job and doing it well."

Ness's photo appeared in newspapers across the nation. "This indictment not only represents the first time the 'big shots' of a gang have been hit by liquor law charges, but virtually assures the undoing of Capone," said the *Chicago Tribune.* "His gang is said to be almost insolvent due to the wrecking of his huge breweries by raiders, the large amounts paid for protection, the high bonds required of his gangsters in the federal courts, and business depression."

George Johnson deflected the praise to Ness and his Untouchables, who were unnamed except for their leader. "They were the men on the firing line," Johnson said.

"One 28-year-old federal agent played a prominent part in gathering evidence on Capone," the *Boston Traveler* wrote. "Eliot Ness was threatened, attacked, offered bribes and persistently stalked, yet on he worked, content with his $2,800 a year and his conscience."

"Each of the men—Ness and Capone—is a product of this democracy of ours," said the *Birmingham (Alabama) News.* "Obviously it is the duty of sociologists to peer deeper into the social environment and the hereditary background of America to discover what active forces are at work that act so diversely. . . . One of the things that brought malignant power to Capone was a passion for owning things—material things. If one may judge the mind and spirit of young Ness by his first public service, its passion lies in making a better social state—a passion for clean and fine things, something quite apart from the acquisitive passion."

"This country owes to this young man and the other unnamed workers who assisted him a great debt of gratitude," said the *Hollywood Daily Citizen*. "There is an inspiration in that young fellow's work not only for other young men but for the older people who have grown discouraged in the battle for good government."

The federal government's "debt of gratitude" to Ness was paid in the form of a promotion, as well as a salary increase to thirty-eight hundred dollars. His new title was assistant special agent-in-charge for a sprawling region that included Illinois, Iowa, Wisconsin, Minnesota, North Dakota, and South Dakota. Despite the broad jurisdiction, Ness was ordered by the Justice Department to continue to focus his immediate attention on Chicago.

As the heat on Al Capone intensified, his lawyers again tried to strike a deal with George Johnson. He would plead guilty to a portion of the tax evasion and Prohibition charges if Johnson would recommend a sentence of no more than two and one-half years.

Privately, the U.S. attorney was thrilled with the offer. Not only would the plea represent a measure of success after many months of frustration, it would also immediately put the volatile Capone behind bars. Johnson recognized as well that the longer Capone's lawyers postponed their client's trial, the greater the chance that hired guns could remove some of the government's key witnesses. In addition, Johnson and others knew the U.S. Supreme Court was poised to revise its statute of limitations. If a new statute took effect, much of the government's tax evasion case against Capone would crumble.

As the prosecution team prepared to work out the details of the plea agreement, Ness and the Untouchables went back to work. With Capone about to fall, other criminal organizations were maneuvering to cash in on the multimillion-dollar bootlegging business. These rivals were naturally eager to share with Ness any information they had on the location of Capone's production and distribution facilities, and Ness was pleased to oblige.

An anonymous telephone call to Ness told of a large brewery in an abandoned garage at 1712 North Kilbourn Avenue on Chicago's North Side. Surveillance by two agents confirmed the report. Ness's team took the brewery without resistance, crashing through the front doors after posting agents at each exit. Less than a week later, based on information gathered by Leeson and Seager, the team blasted into another Capone brewery at 2024 South State Street. These two raids resulted in eleven arrests and the destruction or confiscation of equipment and supplies valued at close to three hundred thousand dollars.

Agent Marty Lahart orchestrated one of the most daring raids, which took place at a massive beer distribution center at 222 East Twenty-fifth Street. Ness and Lahart donned dirty work suits and drove a beat-up Ford to the East Side. They positioned the car partly in the road and opened the hood. When Lahart spotted one of Capone's delivery trucks approaching, he bravely stepped out in the road, forcing the driver to stop.

"Can you give us a hand?" he yelled through the driver's-side window.

"Go to hell!" the driver responded, stomping on the accelerator. As the truck started to pull away, Ness and Lahart grabbed the tailgate, and hoisted themselves up and in. They crouched under a tarp, concealed as they huddled between two rows of beer barrels.

A quick toot of the horn brought open the warehouse doors, and the truck eased inside. As the workers milled around a makeshift lunchroom, Ness and Lahart quietly slipped over the tailgate, raised their guns, and walked slowly toward the table. Not until the agents were about twenty feet away did anyone notice them.

"What the hell are you—," one of them declared, stopping in midsentence as he realized what was happening.

"Federal raid, boys," Ness shot back. "Just stay where you are. You guys ought to be used to this by now."

Lahart walked backward toward the double doors, his revolver still trained on the four mobsters, and released the latch. Robsky, Leeson, Cloonan, and Friel charged through, guns in hand.

"Relax, fellas," Lahart assured them. "These guys are sitting ducks."

Inside the warehouse was a Prohibition agent's dream—a virtual treasure of moonshine, including dozens of cases of premium Canadian whiskey ready for shipment; 300 barrels of beer; 56 cases of bottled beer; and a wide assortment of notebooks and ledgers documenting delivery routes and payments, as well as 96 speakeasies being serviced. A few minutes later, a second truck pulled into the brewery and its two occupants were also arrested. Ness recognized one of them, Albert Johnson, who went by the alias of Harry Alcock, as the same man who had tried to bribe him several months earlier.

Soon a half-dozen newspaper reporters and photographers were on the scene. Robsky lifted one of the whiskey bottles to pose for the photographers, the bright warehouse lights highlighting the deep-amber liquid.

An anonymous phone call in the wake of the raid gave Ness the final pieces of a puzzle he had been trying to solve for months. The Montmartre telephone conversations continually referred to liquor supplies coming from "Joyce." Ness assumed it was a code name for a Canadian whiskey runner, until the tipster directed agents to a six-story building on Chicago's Diversey Avenue. A legitimate business, the Joyce Company, occupied the first few floors. On the top two stories were the headquarters of a mysterious enterprise known as Sennett Paint Company.

Ness and Lahart visited the building one night, climbing a narrow, rusty fire escape that creaked and shook with every step. When they finally reached the fifth floor, they peered through the window to discover a still so massive that a wide hole had been cut into the ceiling to accommodate it.

Ness returned to the Joyce Company the next day, posing as a real estate speculator interested in buying the building. The owners said they did not want to sell, especially now that the Sennett Paint Company had moved in and begun making generous rent payments, always early and always in cash.

Large freight elevators serviced each floor, but Ness feared the arrival of the elevator car would alert Capone's men that something was amiss. That night, just before midnight, he and Lahart crept up the fire escape to the fifth floor and smashed through a window. They aimed their guns at two startled workers who sat at a table in the corner of the huge room. One of them was Nick Juffra, alias Frankie Rose, one of Capone's leading henchmen.

The still was capable of producing twenty thousand gallons of alcohol per day. Bottles and other supplies moved in and out under the cover of wooden crates marked with a Sennett Paint Company logo.

A new machine seized as part of the raid was being used to imprint a diamond-shaped outline bearing a number on each crate. Speakeasy owners who were "obligated" to buy their stock from Capone used the numbering system to verify the source of each shipment.

The days of Capone's men boldly driving their big beer trucks down the city streets in broad daylight were over, due in large part to the Untouchables' dogged efforts. Instead, the organization resorted to hauling its beer three or four barrels at a time in passenger cars that had been gutted of all seats except the driver's. Larger shipments were made under the guise of ice delivery trucks.

"This is a radical departure from the old Capone method of making deliveries in huge and expensive trucks," Ness told a reporter. "We have seized so many of their trucks that the syndicate is running short on finances. Also, they probably thought they could fool the agents with their small automobiles."

An increasing amount of moonshine was smuggled in from outside the city. Obsessed with drying up the Midwest, and anxious to demonstrate that he was equal to his new responsibilities, Ness sent his men out to intercept these shipments. They were also dispatched to the remote areas beyond Cook County to track down Capone's suppliers.

Covering all the bases, the Untouchables started watching rail stations and confiscating shipments of corn sugar. At times, they would allow the sugar to be loaded and then follow the trucks to their destinations—often isolated farmhouses where stills had been set up to produce corn whiskey.

On one occasion, the agents arrested all three members of a small-town police force for operating a still in a shed behind the police station. Perhaps it was a sign of the times that the community's outrage was directed not at the police chief, but at Ness and his Untouchables.

CHAPTER THIRTEEN

Federal Convict No. 40886

SKIES WERE SUNNY IN Chicago on June 16, 1931, as Al Capone, dressed in a bright yellow suit, appeared at the Federal Building. A fat cigar drooped from the corner of his mouth, dangling below the heavy makeup that covered his facial scar. Reporters shouted questions that he ignored as three bodyguards and a pair of uniformed officers cleared a path for him. The entourage headed toward an elevator just as a judge tried to enter it. "You can't use this, bud," the elevator operator told the jurist. "It's reserved for Mr. Capone."

In a brief court session that was little more than a formality, Capone entered his guilty plea and Johnson recommended the two-and-one-half-year sentence that had been agreed to. Judge Wilkerson adjourned the hearing to study the facts before pronouncing sentence.

"Smug" is the way one journalist described Capone during a discussion with reporters in his Lexington Hotel suite that afternoon. Dressed in white-bordered silk pajamas and pacing around his parlor, Capone decried the distortions that Hollywood was giving American movie fans.

"You know, these gang pictures, that's terrible kid stuff," Capone said. "Why, they ought to take them all and throw them into the lake. They're doing nothing but harm to the younger element in this country. You remember dime novels, maybe, when you were a kid? Well, you know how it made you want to get out and kill pirates and look for buried treasure? Well, these gang movies are making a lot of kids want to be tough guys and they don't serve any useful purpose."

Capone declared himself a scapegoat. "I've been made an issue, and I'm not complaining, but why don't they go after all these bankers who took the savings of thousands of poor people and lost them in bank failures? How about that? Isn't it lots worse to take the last few dollars some small family has saved, perhaps to live on while the head of a family is out of a job, than to sell a little beer, a little alky? Believe me, I can't see where the fellow who sells it is any worse than the fellow who buys and drinks it."

One reporter asked what would become of Capone's gang during his absence.

"It's really a shame to disabuse the public—to destroy one of their myths—but honestly there is not, nor has there ever been, what might be called a Capone gang," he replied. Capone said Johnny Torrio would assume responsibility for his "business enterprises" while he was serving his sentence. He speculated that good behavior would reduce the term to far less than the anticipated thirty months.

Adding insult to injury, while Capone awaited sentencing, two of Ness's agents raided another of his breweries. At 2636 Calumet Avenue they found twelve thousand dollars' worth of iced beer ready for delivery. James Calloway, one of the men nabbed with Bert Delaney in the South Wabash Street stakeout, dashed from the brewery and was pursued by policemen who happened upon the raid. One of the officers fired two shots into the air, prompting Calloway to surrender.

On July 30, Judge Wilkerson dropped a bombshell that echoed all across America. "The parties to a criminal case may not stipulate as to the judgment to be entered," he announced. "The court may not now say to the defendant that it will enter the judgment suggested by the prosecution. It is time for somebody to impress upon the defendant that it is utterly impossible to bargain with a federal court."

Capone's jaw, which had been busily working on a thick wad of chewing gum, dropped as he looked at his lawyers in confusion.

After huddling with their client, they announced that Capone would withdraw his guilty plea and proceed to trial.

"Very well," Wilkerson said. "The court calendar will be cleared for two weeks in October."

After the gavel sounded, Johnson turned to Ness, seated on the first bench behind the prosecution table, and motioned for him to join them. "This changes everything, Eliot," he said. "You'd better go back through your files and make sure you're ready to go to trial on the conspiracy case. It looks like we might have to hit him with both barrels." Ness nodded his approval, but in reality he did not have much to do. The evidence was ready; the witnesses were subpoenaed and prepared to testify; all he needed was a forum.

A handful of the sixty-eight defendants indicted along with Capone had disappeared and subsequently eluded authorities. One of them, twenty-four-year-old Frank Uva, was spotted driving a beer delivery truck on September 8. Ness recognized Uva as he approached Lake Shore Drive from Clark Street. Ness and a deputy attempted to block Uva's path, but a car that was trailing the beer truck forced Ness to swerve away. A high-speed chase through the heart of Chicago's Gold Coast ensued before Uva leaped from the truck and began running. Ness and his partner quickly cornered Uva, and he surrendered without a struggle.

This was Ness's first official act in his new capacity as chief investigator of the Chicago Prohibition Office, a promotion that was made with considerable fanfare by Amos W. Woodcock, director of the Justice Department's Prohibition Bureau.

"Mr. Ness's work with the special agents extends over a considerable territory in the Middle West, an area that is too large for him to cover effectively," the director said. "He will be more valuable if allowed to help in the more purely local investigations, and there is no question that much work remains to be done in the Chicago area. Mr. Ness has a proven track record in Chicago and his appointment should serve notice to the violators of the Volstead Act that their days are numbered."

Capone, seemingly unconcerned about his legal battles, opened another highly publicized soup kitchen on South State Street. He pooh-poohed his recent indictments. "Oh, they're only trying to scare me," Capone declared. "They know very well there'd be hell in this city if they put me away. Who else can keep the smalltime racketeers from annoying decent folks? This is going to be a terrible winter. Us fellas has gotta open our pocketbooks and keep them open if we want any of us to survive. We can't wait for Congress or Mr. Hoover or anyone else. We must keep tummies filled and bodies warm."

Behind the scenes, Capone's men were taking great pains to ensure a positive outcome from the trial. They obtained a list of potential jurors and set about winning their favor through threats of violence and offers of cash, jobs, and prizefight tickets. When Judge Wilkerson was informed of this serious breach in security, he appeared unconcerned.

On the morning of October 6, a motorcade of Chicago police squad cars brought Capone to the Federal Building for jury selection. He was a bloated figure, too big for his blue suit. A white handkerchief was neatly stuffed in his breast pocket. Crowding around the prosecution table with George Johnson were four assistant U.S. attorneys. Among the witnesses seated directly behind them was Ness, complete with a bulging leather briefcase.

The sixth-floor courtroom of Judge Wilkerson abounded in patriotic and legal imagery, from its massive walls finished with white marble to the gilded scrolls near the ceiling. Electric bulbs in chandeliers and sconces burned throughout the courtroom. Some walls, darkened by age, were devoted to large murals depicting the Founding Fathers. Behind the judge's bench, Benjamin Franklin addressed the Continental Congress, his right hand outstretched to George Washington.

About twenty newspaper reporters filled several rows in the front of the courtroom. Wilkerson emerged from his chambers, his deep-set eyes and oval face expressionless as he took his seat on the extreme edge of a swivel chair. He glanced at the tainted jurors, then summoned a court attendant.

"Judge Edwards has another trial commencing today," he announced. "Go to Judge Edwards's courtroom and bring me the entire panel of jurors. Take my entire panel to Judge Edwards."

Capone remained rigid in his chair, bleakly studying the decor and avoiding eye contact with everyone as his facial features clouded with fury. Moments later, a group of small-town tradesmen, mechanics, a real estate manager, and an insurance salesman filled the twelve seats in the jury box. The judge made it clear to them that Capone was being tried on charges of violating the income tax laws and nothing else.

Assistant prosecutor Dwight Green and George Johnson soon embarked on an evidence spree that left Capone and his lawyers speechless. Three witnesses gave testimony confirming Capone's involvement with the Hawthorne Smoke Shop. They were followed to the stand by a surprise witness, Capone's Hawthorne bookkeeper, Leslie "Lou" Shumway. A pole-thin, nervous man, Shumway had been tracked down in Florida by Frank Wilson, secretly interviewed, threatened with a long prison term, and protected until the trial.

Shumway told the court that profits from the shop during the two years he kept the records exceeded $550,000. He also detailed the entries he made in thirty-four loose-leaf notebooks documenting gambling activities. These ledgers, seized during the raid that followed Billy McSwiggin's murder, had been uncovered and cataloged by Wilson several months before the trial.

The prosecution also entered into evidence the letter from tax attorney Lawrence Mattingly that conceded Capone's taxable income. Parker Henderson, a Florida hotel manager, told the jurors how he befriended Capone and fronted him in the purchase of a Palm Island estate. Henderson testified that he also regularly signed Western Union transfers of one thousand to five thousand dollars and turned the money over to Capone. A series of witnesses recounted their selling goods and services to Al Capone—everything from real estate and jewelry to fancy clothes and prime cuts of meat.

One of the few interruptions in the fast-moving trial was the removal of Capone crony Philip D'Andrea from the courtroom. D'Andrea, whose menacing look may have intimidated some witnesses, was found to be carrying a .38-caliber revolver.

Wilson still had to buttress Shumway's testimony tying the Hawthorne Smoke Shop profits to Capone. For that he turned to Fred Ries, brought back from his South American hideout. Ries delivered the prosecution's knockout punch. He implicated Capone and his associates in financial dealings involving hundreds of thousands of dollars.

Capone's defense team was comprised of Michael Ahern, noticeably tall and elegant in his gray suit and tan shoes, and Albert Fink, a round-bellied tax law specialist who came out of retirement to take the case. They argued that Capone's income was more than offset by heavy losses in other business enterprises and at the horse racetrack. "The numbers just don't add up," insisted Fink, his gold-rimmed glasses riding the tip of his pointed nose. "There's no tax liability at all."

Johnson poked holes in the defense's argument with citations of previous cases specifying that gambling losses can only be deducted from gambling winnings for tax purposes, and Capone's attorneys had already insisted their client hardly ever won when he gambled.

Waving his arms high, defense counsel Fink urged jurors to consider Capone's intent. Clearly, he argued, his client had demonstrated a willingness to pay income taxes by signing the affidavit drawn up by Mattingly. Fink also told the jurors that, if they believed Capone was a man of considerable wealth, they must also question whether he would be foolish enough to risk a prison term by failing to pay taxes.

"Don't let yourselves be drawn away from the truth by the claim that Al Capone is a bad man," Fink cautioned. "He may be the worst man who ever lived, but there is not a scintilla of evidence that he willfully attempted to defraud the government out of income tax."

Fink continued, "In Rome during the Punic Wars, there lived a senator named Cato. Cato passed upon the morals of the people. He decided what they would wear, what they should drink, and what they should think. Carthage fell twice, but Carthage grew again and was once more powerful. Cato concluded every speech he made in the Senate by thundering, 'Carthage must be destroyed!' These censors of ours, these persecutors, the newspapers, all say, 'Capone must be destroyed!' Be careful of taking liberty from this defendant. You are the last barrier between the defendant and the encroachment and perversion of government and the law."

The prosecution team chose George Johnson to cement the issue of Capone's guilt in the jurors' minds. His winglike coiffure flapping with the vehemence of his emotions, Johnson stressed the importance of the tax laws to the welfare of the nation:

Gentlemen, the United States government has no more important laws to enforce than the revenue laws. Thousands upon thousands of persons go to work daily and all of them who earn more than $1,500 a year must pay income tax. If a time ever came when it has to go out and force the collection of taxes, the Army and the Navy will disband, courts will be swept aside, civilization will revert back to the jungle days when every man was for himself. Who is this man who has become such a glamorous figure? Is he the little boy from the Second Reader who has found the pot of gold at the end of the rainbow that he can spend money so lavishly? He has been called Robin Hood by his counsel. Robin Hood took from the strong to feed the weak. Did this Robin Hood buy $8,000 worth of belt buckles for the unemployed? Was his $6,000 meat bill in a few weeks for the hungry? No, it went to the Capone home on Palm Island to feed the guests at the nightly poker party.

Capone cast despairing eyes around him, as if appealing to the audience. His usual smile was missing as he squirmed from his slumped position while the jurors left for their deliberations.

The prosecution team, Ness included, retired to Johnson's office to wait. Capone paced in the corridor, forcing a smile now and then for the people who stared at him from behind a cordon of guards. After several hours, he returned to the Lexington, where he smoked cigars and continued walking the floors, staying close to the telephone.

Newspaper reporters entertained themselves by holding their own mock deliberations. They were split down the middle on whether Capone would be convicted or acquitted. Inside the jury room, the polling was not nearly as close. Only one juror expressed any doubt about Capone's guilt. For eight hours, the dissenter held his ground before bowing to the majority.

Court officials summoned all of the important players just before midnight. The reporters scurried for their seats in the front rows. Johnson, Ness, and the others hurried downstairs and pushed through the crowd to reach the courtroom. Ness took his customary seat in the first row behind the prosecution table. A soft murmur echoed around the courtroom.

At the Lexington, Capone never removed the cigar from his mouth as he answered the phone on the first ring. "Yeah?" he grunted, followed by a brief silence. "All right. How's it look?" More silence. "Let's get it over with."

Capone hung up the phone and snuffed out his cigar. Donning his overcoat and fedora, he led an entourage out to the limousine that would take him the three miles to the Federal Building. By the time Capone settled into his seat at the defense table, he was perspiring profusely. He cleared his throat and leaned forward, resting his elbows on the table, before Judge Wilkerson ordered him to stand. The clerk read the verdict:

- guilty on three counts of income tax evasion from 1925, 1926, and 1927
- guilty of failing to file a tax return for 1928 and 1929
- not guilty on assorted other charges

The crowd erupted in spontaneous applause, and reporters hurried for the nearest telephones. Capone looked at his lawyers, then at the floor, before he returned to his seat. His supporters sat motionless amid the revelry.

Defense attorney Fink sprang from his seat to announce that he would appeal. "You are certainly within your rights to do so," Judge Wilkerson responded. "In the meantime, I plan to spend the next five to seven days studying the record of these proceedings and reviewing case law before I render my sentence. Until that time, Mr. Capone, I will allow you to remain free on bond which has been posted, but I would also advise you not to leave the area." Capone nodded.

Outside the courtroom, Capone told friends he was not surprised by the verdict. He rationalized that it would be good to live in an environment where rival gangsters could not reach him, then emerge as a man who had "paid his debt to society."

Judge Wilkerson entered the courtroom for the October 24 sentencing hearing looking grimmer than usual. Capone, dressed in a dark purple suit, accented by a white handkerchief, approached the bench, locking his hands behind his back as he heard his fate.

"On Count One," Wilkerson announced, "the defendant shall go to the penitentiary for five years, pay a fine of ten thousand dollars and pay all costs of prosecution."

Capone looked calmly at his lawyers, his fingers twisting and turning behind his back. The defense had expected the five-year sentence for one tax evasion count and the other sentences to run concurrently.

Wilkerson followed a different script. To the horror of Capone and his attorneys, he imposed a separate five-year sentence for the 1926 and 1927 violations then tacked on another year for Capone's failure to file a tax return in 1929. The total sentence was eleven years in prison, plus a fine of eighty thousand dollars.

All eyes in the courtroom fell on Capone. His tongue moved in his cheeks, and his fingers, still locked behind his back, twitched and twisted. He looked helplessly at the defense table.

Fink stared incredulously at the judge. "Your Honor," he said, "we request that our client remain free until such time as a timely appeal can be filed."

"Motion denied!" Wilkerson snapped back. He ordered a U.S. marshal to remove Capone to the Cook County Jail, where he would be held during the appeal process.

On his way out of the courtroom, Capone was approached by an Internal Revenue Service agent, who nervously announced that a tax lien had been placed on all property of Alphonse and Mae Capone. "Please do not attempt to transfer your assets, Mr. Capone, until we settle this tax matter first," the agent said in a near monotone. Capone muttered an obscenity and drew back his foot to kick the IRS man before he regained his composure. He slung his coat across his left arm and clamped his fedora down on his head.

"Get enough, boys," Capone said angrily, as newspaper photographers elbowed for position while he was escorted to a waiting police car. "You won't see me again for a long time."

Johnson, Wilson, and Ness remained in the courtroom long after the crowd dispersed. They knew Capone had the money and political connections to fight the conviction and sentence on every imaginable front.

"You better hold on to everything you have—and keep it in a safe place," Johnson instructed Ness. "The more we have against this guy, the better. Who knows if this'll hold up? We're in uncharted waters, really."

"I'll guard it with my life," Ness assured him.

Reporters peppered Johnson with questions as the prosecutors filed out of the courtroom. He stopped long enough to express his faith in the criminal justice system and his appreciation to Judge Wilkerson and the jurors. Johnson added that the battle against Capone could never have been won without the combined efforts of public crimefighters and private financiers. "It was a victory of an aroused public that demanded justice. I believe this is the beginning of the end of gangs as Chicago has known them for the last ten years."

"Capone's conviction was the culmination of five years of hard work, brilliant work, by a team that my father headed," said George E. Q. Johnson Jr., the prosecutor's son, many years later. "No single man put Al Capone in jail—it was teamwork. And if there were any unsung heroes, I'd say it was the witnesses and the jurors. These people were brave and community-minded. They were in a very dangerous position and they still gave of themselves for the good of the community and got little or no credit."

Public reaction to the downfall of Capone was mixed. For every citizen who applauded the government for finally subduing him there was another who thought that limiting the charges to tax evasion was a miscarriage of justice. Ness may have shared that sentiment, since the outcome of the trial denied him the chance to be in the limelight, but he never said so publicly.

Of the verdict and the sentence, the *New York Times* editorialized: "Chicago has been terrorized by its gangsters or rather that part of the population of the city which came closest to them has been. They seemed invincible. It has probably made the career of the gangster somewhat less alluring. In that fact, and in the realization that gang rule cannot exist without the connivance or tolerance of great numbers of people who consider themselves law-abiding, may lie Chicago's hopes."

One person who took special pride in the fall of Al Capone was Peter Ness, an immigrant who believed that the keys to lasting success were hard work and playing by the rules. To have both a son and a son-in-law so involved meant a great deal to him, even as he lay in a bed at Chicago's Roseland Community Hospital, partially paralyzed by a stroke he suffered in mid-1931. Peter Ness had been forced to sell his bakeries a few years earlier as the infirmities of age overcame him.

On December 23, 1931, Peter Ness drifted off to sleep in the late afternoon and never awoke. Obituaries referred to him as "a prominent, community-minded, industrious Norwegian master baker" and "the father of the courageous Chicago crimefighter, Eliot Ness."

Even as a convicted felon, Capone exerted his influence at the Cook County Jail. He was placed in a private cell, from which he could place telephone calls and send telegrams to lawyers, bookies, organizational contacts, and well-placed city officials. One of his closest friends from outside the world of organized crime, Doc Kearns, paid him a call.

"What are you going to do?" Kearns asked, eyeing a photo of thirteen-year-old Sonny Capone on a bedside dresser.

"I got no idea," Capone said with a frown. "I guess it ain't too stiff of a rap. The organization should sort of hold together until I get back. 'Course, you never know what a difference a few years can make, and there's no tellin' how things might be, one way or another, when I finally get out. Hell, the booze racket's about shot to hell right now."

Eliot Ness and his colleagues made one final sweep of the bootlegging rackets. They rounded up more than a dozen other Chicago mobsters, at least some of whom were affiliated with Capone. Among them was George Howlett, known in gangland as Capone's "society lieutenant," who had been wanted by the government for failing to pay more than fifty thousand dollars in income taxes. Howlett had been at large since the indictments were handed down against Capone and the sixty-eight others. He made the mistake of attending the Northwestern-Indiana college football game at Dyche Field. Ness spotted Howlett in the crowd, chased him down at the corner of Sheridan Road and Irving Park Drive, and arrested him.

The U.S. District Court of Appeals denied Capone's bid for a new trial on February 27, 1932. Two months later, the Supreme Court refused to review the decision. Out of options, Capone was ordered to begin serving his sentence in the federal penitentiary at Atlanta.

Largely as a symbolic gesture to lessen the sting of prohibition violations never coming to trial, Johnson designated Ness and his Untouchables to escort Capone to Dearborn Station. There he was to be handed over to the federal marshals manning the Dixie Flyer for the long ride to Atlanta. Rumors that some of Capone's men might make a desperate attempt to spring him from federal custody prompted officials to ensure that security was extremely tight.

At the Cook County Jail, Capone bade farewell to Mae, Sonny, and other family members. He and another prisoner, a car thief named Vito Morici, were led out into the jail's courtyard, where photographers were waiting.

At the end of the sidewalk leading through the courtyard to the prison gates, Capone for the first time came face-to-face with the man who had worked so hard to reduce his once-lucrative boot-legging business to a shambles. He paused as he looked up at Ness, perhaps connecting a real, live face with the image he had seen in newspaper photographs. Capone fumbled to find something to say as Ness made eye contact with him.

"Geez," he muttered sarcastically, looking out into the early evening sunset. "You'd think Mussolini was passin' through, with all the fuss you guys are makin'."

Ness painted this picture in *The Untouchables:*

> I was determined to see there would be no rescue or that no
> assassin's bullet would cheat the law. We arranged a five-car cara-
> van to escort Snorky from the jail to Dearborn. Lahart, Seager
> and I were to ride in the first car. Behind it was to be another car
> with Capone, followed by Robsky, Cloonan and King in another,
> followed by two automobiles carrying Chicago policemen. All of
> us were heavily-armed; my crew was ready with sawed-off shot-
> guns, revolvers and automatics loose in shoulder holsters.

"It was every driver for himself," wrote a Chicago journalist covering the event. "Fenders and bumpers clashed and pedestrians were trampled in the stampede to avoid being hit by the fast-moving officials' motors. Police officials described the ride to Dearborn Station as the wildest and noisiest in their experience."

With their sirens wailing, the police cars moved along Ogden Avenue to Clark Street. Capone looked out at the old warehouse where the Saint Valentine's Day Massacre had occurred and at the Federal Building where his freedom had slipped away.

How did Al Capone feel about the man who had the courage to raid his breweries and who now escorted him to the prison train? Historians can only speculate, because there's no record of Capone's acknowledging Ness's existence, despite the many newspaper accounts of Ness's activities.

"At first he probably thought, 'What's this? A Prohibition agent who doesn't take bribes? This can't be true!'" suggested John Binder, a Chicago writer and founder of the Merry Gangsters Literary Society. "Once he accepted it, Capone probably had some admiration for Ness. I don't think he hated honest public officials. He probably admired them for doing their job—'you're on your side of the fence and I'm on mine.' Later on, he probably resented the fact that Ness took reporters and photographers along on his raids and figured Ness was just another politician or publicity hound trying to get ahead at Capone's expense. That was the way Capone thought."

Alphonse Capone—Snorky, Scarface, Big Al, the Boss—left the city with yet another name: Federal Convict No. 40886.

A blood test administered at the federal prison in Atlanta conclusively showed that Capone suffered from "central nervous system syphilis." After years of latency, the disease had erupted into the tertiary stage. His battles now would be private ones. Capone had given the rival gangs, the cops, and the politicians all they could handle. Now he was fighting for his sanity and for his very life.

PART TWO

Cleveland

CHAPTER FOURTEEN

Change of Scene

ORGANIZED CRIME CONTINUED TO flourish in Chicago as rival gangs flexed their muscles. Many of the rules had changed. Gangland murders, which numbered almost seven hundred between 1920 and 1931, were becoming rare.

The most notable slaying occurred on February 15, 1933, in Biscayne Bay, Florida. That afternoon, Chicago Mayor Anton "Tony" Cermak, a well-connected Democrat who had upset Big Bill Thompson in the 1931 election, was attending a reception for President-elect Franklin D. Roosevelt. Walking toward Roosevelt's car in a crowded amphitheater, Cermak was struck in the right armpit by a .32-caliber bullet. The gunman was Guiseppe Zangara, a former soldier in the Italian army.

Most assumed that Zangara had meant to assassinate Roosevelt, but some observers of the Chicago mob have long contended that he got his man. Cermak died nineteen days later. Following a guilty plea to homicide charges, Zangara, described by doctors as a psychopath, was silenced forever by the electric chair.

Back in Chicago, Eliot Ness packed away the evidence he never needed. Although he had not had his day on the witness stand in the public trial of Capone, publicity about his activities resulted in one lasting memorial. An innovative comic strip by Chester Gould, entitled "Dick Tracy," began to appear in the *Chicago Tribune* and other newspapers. Unlike many cartoonists of his day whose strips relied on fantasy heroes such as Buck Rogers or Tarzan, Gould drew his from the news of the day.

Writer Max Allen Collins quoted Gould as saying that the inspiration for his detective came from Ness, whom Gould envisioned as a latter-day Sherlock Holmes—fearless, technologically adept, and committed to direct action. Al Capone also appeared in the strip as a character labeled "Big Boy."

Chicago residents still had a thirst, and even if Capone wasn't available to quench it, there was no shortage of underworld outfits anxious to fill the void. Joe Fusco, still under indictment for Prohibition violations, opened a handful of breweries, many of which were promptly raided by Ness and his squad.

The next logical career step for Ness was the Federal Bureau of Investigation. His reputation as a Prohibition agent and special investigator for the Treasury and Justice Departments was unquestionably solid. Yet Ness's dream of becoming an agent in the Justice Department's Investigations Bureau, as it was called at the time, remained unfulfilled. In all likelihood, this was due to the paranoia, jealousy, and pettiness of director J. Edgar Hoover.

Hoover believed that George Johnson, Ness, and the others had made his agency look bad. He was particularly troubled by Ness's self-promotion and his "play by the rules" attitude, an approach that ran counter to Hoover's "the end justifies the means" philosophy of law enforcement. Therefore, a strong endorsement letter that Johnson sent to the director recommending Ness for an Investigations Bureau appointment had little impact.

The director went so far as to establish a confidential file on Ness, charting his activities with the same degree of thoroughness as the FBI employed with suspected criminals. This file, made public many years later under the Freedom of Information Act, contains numerous handwritten notes by Hoover ordering FBI personnel to have nothing to do with Ness. The records reveal that Hoover considered Ness a dangerous, reckless vigilante. He was largely the victim of his own success. Instead of joining the FBI, Ness remained on a Prohibition career track, and his promotion to chief investigator of Prohibition forces for the entire Chicago Division was soon rendered meaningless.

The vast majority of Americans saw Prohibition for what it was—a failed social experiment. It was costing the nation more than $1 billion in lost taxes and import duties. Clandestine drinking had become a very symbol of personal liberty. In February 1933 Congress voted to submit the Twenty-first Amendment, repealing Prohibition, to the states. By the end of the year, President Roosevelt proclaimed that the necessary thirty-six states had ratified the amendment, putting an end to the dry law.

As the Prohibition Bureau was dismantled, many of the Untouchables moved into other roles within the federal government. Joe Leeson and Paul Robsky remained in Chicago to help Ness with the "mop-up duty." Eventually, Leeson was transferred to Kansas City. Robsky went on to chase smugglers off the coast of Florida and Georgia, intercepting their shipments of whiskey from the Bahamas. He later entered private detective work and became a security guard in Florida, a virtual unknown despite his affiliation with the Untouchables. Lyle Chapman reenlisted in the army, became a major in World War II, and spent his later years as a football handicapper.

Some of the Prohibition Bureau's responsibilities were turned over to a new Alcohol Tax Unit within the Bureau of Internal Revenue (Treasury Department). The same U.S. government that had stalked the producers of alcohol as criminals now sought to share in their gains through taxation. The government also regulated the quality of alcoholic beverages. Of greatest concern was the sudden growth of moonshining by those who found the cost of liquor prohibitive because of federal taxes and new market dynamics. Often dangerous and potentially lethal concoctions were made available on the black market.

Nowhere in America was this problem worse than in the "Moonshine Mountains" of Ohio, Kentucky, and Tennessee. Chicago mobsters may not have been inclined to shoot federal agents, but the same rules did not apply to these mountain moonshiners. They saw any intrusion by the government into their affairs as an affront to their lifestyle.

The Bureau of Internal Revenue needed a leader with experience, integrity, and courage to enforce the federal liquor laws in that volatile region. Eliot Ness, now thirty, eagerly accepted the offer. He was dispatched to the Cincinnati district in early 1934 to become assistant investigator-in-charge for the southern Ohio, Kentucky, and Tennessee region. The new assignment posed all the danger and offered none of the glory of his Chicago work. Ness was given little direction and not nearly enough agents.

Ness received minimal support from local officials or, for that matter, the federal government itself as he tried to establish undercover and surveillance operations in and around the Cincinnati area. He had little confidence in any of his officers, with the exception of Barney Cloonan, who was also transferred to the Alcohol Tax Unit.

"Our unit has been passing through a rather unsettled period, due to the fact that many men have been dismissed," Ness wrote to one colleague. "Authority for the supervision of wiretaps has been slow in coming through from Washington, which I guess is due to the unsettled state of our unit."

Thousands of stills were in operation across a vast and hostile territory that had its own code of silence. During less than a year as a "revenooer," Ness narrowly missed being shot from ambush several times during raids on hillbilly stills. "Those mountain men and their squirrel rifles gave me almost as many chills as the Capone mob," Ness told one interviewer.

Ness's nephew and childhood friend, Wallace Jamie, who was assistant safety director in Saint Paul, Minnesota, offered him an administrative job with the police department in that city. Ness discussed the invitation in detail with Edna and others, but he opted to remain a federal employee, believing it would enhance his chances of becoming an FBI agent.

He finally did escape the Moonshine Mountains on August 16, 1934, when he accepted an appointment as investigator-in-charge of the Alcohol Tax Unit for northern Ohio. The federal government had labeled Cleveland as the worst spot in the nation for bootleg liquor, because vast quantities were sent to other eastern cities by way of Cleveland. Even with the repeal of Prohibition, the number of stills had remained steady or perhaps even increased as buyers sought to avoid stiff federal and state taxes.

Ness and his modest four-member staff settled into an office at the Standard Bank Building in Cleveland, a block from City Hall. He was provided with a large black Ford coupe to supplement his thirty-eight-hundred-dollar salary.

Edna, who had remained behind in Chicago during her husband's stint in Cincinnati, joined him at a modest gray cottage on the lakefront in Bay Village, an hour away from downtown Cleveland. There they put the pressures of Chicago and the dangers of the mountain moonshiners behind them and enjoyed a more traditional lifestyle.

The modest, one-story home came with a garden, a small reflecting pond, and plenty of room for their six cats to roam. In their cozy living room they could build a fire, sit back, and read or talk. Ness, however, soon found himself staying on the job until 10 P.M. He pleaded his case for additional agents from the outset and was pleased to see a steady stream of new officers join the unit. Ness relied on civil service ratings and personal interviews to fill the new positions, seeking to avoid political influences, corruption, and lethargy.

The agents were responsible for combating tax evasion by manufacturers and dispensers of illicit liquor, but they were also on the lookout for other crimes. They uncovered hundreds of moonshining operations throughout Ohio's Cuyahoga and Lake Counties. Smugglers brought tax-free Canadian liquor into the Cleveland area, cutting it with water and other substances, and selling it at high markups. They also took raw alcohol, added artificial colors and flavorings, and slapped counterfeit labels and tax stamps on the bottles. Empty bottles of legal liquor became a valuable commodity for these "repackagers."

Evaluations of Ness during his service with the Alcohol Tax Unit described him as a "tireless worker, liked and respected by his men, and a stern disciplinarian when laxity by subordinates handicaps his investigations."

He often joined his agents for their more complicated raids, one of which took place very close to home. As a result of an anonymous tip, Ness learned that Canadian rumrunners were storing their supplies near a boat harbor on the bay. One night, he and two agents apprehended a trio of smugglers as they approached their getaway car after unloading a small shipment. Ness not only arrested the men, he also seized their vehicle and arranged for it to be donated to Bay Village, which until that time did not have a police car.

The most bizarre raid took place after Ness uncovered a major bootlegging, liquor smuggling, and bribery racket being operated out of the sheriff's office and jail in Summit County, Ohio. An undercover federal officer purchased a case of corn whiskey from a sheriff's deputy, John Lavery. Under questioning, Lavery confessed and revealed details of the operation that county sheriff Ray Potts had directed for many years.

"It is incredible to me that a county sheriff and five members of his staff could so brazenly operate what amounts to a miniature liquor empire!" Ness told reporters. The plot actually ran much deeper than bootlegging, courtroom testimony would reveal. Sheriff Potts and his deputies regularly stopped rumrunners from Steubenville, Ohio, and demanded payoffs before allowing them to continue on their delivery routes.

Lavery's testimony was corroborated by bank records reflecting real estate investments far in excess of what Potts could afford on his sheriff's salary. Handwriting expert William Souders, a consultant in the government's case against Bruno Hauptmann for the murder of Charles Lindbergh Jr., testified that Potts manually recorded names of bootleggers and the amount of monthly tribute they paid. Most of the producers on the list were rounded up by Ness's group and encouraged to testify in return for leniency.

Ness was chagrined to learn that two members of the Alcohol Tax Unit were part of the scheme as well. They were quietly ushered out of government service. Charges were also filed against Leo Isaar, the former "Corn Sugar King" of northern Ohio, for providing supplies that fueled a major still operated by the sheriff and his staff at Oakwood Road.

All told, some thirty-three men were indicted by a grand jury convened to hear the evidence in July 1935. Ten of them avoided trial by pleading guilty and agreeing to testify in the trial of Potts and fifteen other defendants. Seven of the men who were indicted fled the area, including deputy sheriff Jack Potts, the sheriff's brother.

The largest of the Alcohol Tax Unit raids was at a massive distillery operating behind the cover of a paint company at 6300 Kinsman Road in Cleveland. Agents seized and demolished equipment capable of producing two thousand gallons of bootleg liquor a day, which cheated the government out of approximately sixty thousand dollars each week in taxes. Ness declared the elaborate distillery part of a major northern Ohio alcohol ring.

Three weeks later, agents arrested three men and destroyed seventy-five thousand dollars' worth of equipment at the former Orchid Sue Night Club on East Thirtieth Street. A warehouse, bar, and a storefront disguised as a picnic supply center were also part of the scheme.

At another time, Ness was tipped off that a suspicious substance with the odor of molasses was flowing into the Cuyahoga River from a warehouse beneath the Detroit-Superior High Level Bridge. One whiff of the discharge was all he needed to identify the source as a large distillery hidden behind the brick façade of an abandoned garage.

Ness plotted the attack with all the thoroughness of a Chicago-style brewery raid. At the sound of a handheld whistle, four Alcohol Tax Unit agents climbed through a skylight and descended a rope into the warehouse. Four others, Ness among them, barged through the front doors. In the basement they discovered a huge boiler unit being manned by a lone employee. He was arrested on the spot, as were six other workers caught by surprise as they reported for night shift duties.

Next a group of investigators under Ness's command took over the offices of a bootlegging business at 1345 East Ninetieth Street, where Fred Morello was in charge of huge stills servicing both speakeasies and legitimate taverns and nightclubs. For four hours they answered telephone calls complaining about late deliveries. Afterward the agents promptly visited dozens of establishments marketing the illegal brew and arrested the proprietors.

Successful investigations inspired Ness's men to follow their chief's lead by working extended hours, often going without sleep for long periods to uncover and destroy illicit stills. Moonshiners, meanwhile, devised elaborate schemes to avoid detection. One time, Ness and another investigator raided a distillery in the basement of a garage on Avon Avenue in Cleveland and found themselves trapped. The electric power operating the lights, exhaust fans, and trap door had been shut off, and the officers were surrounded by darkness and little oxygen. Fortunately for them, two other agents staked outside became concerned when Ness and the other officer failed to return. They battered a hole through the concrete floor of the garage and helped their colleagues to safety. A search of the adjacent house led the officers to apprehend the owner, Charles Rinaldo, hiding in a closet. The team confiscated two hundred gallons of whiskey, six thousand gallons of mash, and a pair of three-hundred-gallon stills.

A few days later, Cleveland newspapers carried a story about "Alky," a German shepherd puppy who led Ness's team to another still. Agents had been watching the house on 154th Street for some time but didn't have the evidence they needed until a puppy wandered over to greet them. The dog reeked of alcohol, and the officers took their cue. They followed the pup into the home and arrested its master, Joseph Urban, who was tending to a 250-gallon still roaring at full blast.

Later that same day, Ness's team moved in on a six-car garage along West Eighty-third Street. They watched through a knothole as a huge man tended to a five-hundred-gallon still. After reinforcements arrived at about 4 A.M., a half-dozen officers forced their way into the garage and arrested the operator, Hoseeb Farris, and two other men. They noticed that a car had been circling the block repeatedly. At Ness's direction, four of the officers tracked down the vehicle, which was operated by Louis Fadil, a prominent professional wrestler known far and wide as "Big Louie." Fadil was carrying a notebook showing a series of delivery stops. Ness determined that the West Eighty-third Street distillery serviced more than one hundred joints on Cleveland's West Side.

"I am pleased to say that Mr. Fadil offered no resistance," Ness quipped. "Had he done so, I seriously doubt that we would be having this conversation today."

Several other raids made the headlines in Cleveland's dailies, particularly if they had a twist that made them more interesting than a routine arrest report and seizure inventory. A house on Thornhill Drive that children believed was haunted by ghosts after a murder occurred there was actually occupied by other "spirits." After neighbors reported strange sounds and suspicious odors emanating from the abandoned house, Ness and his team staged a raid that produced three arrests and a two-hundred-gallon still. The owner claimed she had rented the house to "some Italian gentleman" and knew nothing of what occurred in the basement. "But the still," Ness told reporters, "extended all the way from the basement up through the kitchen and even into the upstairs bedroom, where her son lay sleeping as we searched the home."

The Alcohol Tax Unit was also drawn into a federal crackdown on a massive underworld narcotics and counterfeiting ring centered in Chicago and Cleveland. Almost two hundred people in the Cleveland area were arrested, two dozen of them by Ness and his agents. By that time, Ness had captured the attention of Cleveland's crime reporters, who largely admired the young lawman's work. They also enjoyed Ness's company as he often joined them for drinks and camaraderie after work before driving back out to Bay Village.

Among his closest friends in this group of reporters was Charles "Wes" Lawrence, a respected journalist with the *Cleveland Plain Dealer*. Once he became acquainted with Ness, Lawrence was anxious to paint a portrait of his friend as "the man who brought down Al Capone," but Ness was having none of it. In fact, he went out of his way to set the record straight.

"We did our part, of course," Ness told him. "But the real work of sending Capone to prison was done by the tax investigators. Our job was more spectacular, that's all."

Most citizens considered the flow of illegal liquor trivial when compared with Cleveland's problems with organized crime, corruption of officials, gambling, youth gang violence, and prostitution. The city had other woes as well. Its post-depression economy was sluggish, its traffic control chaotic, and its air so polluted that a dark cloud hung over the city, sometimes obscuring any view of the massive Terminal Tower that protruded from the landscape like a lone candle. On the sidewalks, panhandlers, pimps, and prostitutes prowled among the passing pedestrians.

Ness, raised in a city where the lakefront was sacred, now had to look down upon an oily, yellow Cuyahoga River that flowed out to

Lake Erie. *Cuyahoga,* an Indian word meaning "crooked," was also adopted as the name of the county surrounding Cleveland. The river snaked crazily through the industrial valley known to Cleveland residents as "the Flats." Steel mills, oil refineries, huge factories, and warehouses sprawled through this bottomland section where a railroad line passed decaying docks and scattered industrial debris. At night, the Flats was a world of darkness cut only by an occasional street lamp or the muted glow of a rundown waterfront bar.

Cleveland's political climate was similar to Chicago's. The public had long ago lost faith in its city institutions. Cleveland did not have a public enemy as identifiable as Al Capone, but its police department was an embarrassment. Corruption ran rampant, from the beat cop all the way to the judge's chambers. Due in large part to the police department's lethargy, the underworld had rapidly expanded its domain with little interference, and often with complicity, from the people who were supposed to be enforcing the law. Prohibition had helped many mobsters acquire enormous wealth and power. In addition, union racketeering had spread throughout blue-collar Cleveland.

Voters elected a reform ticket in November 1935, headed by Harold Hitz Burton, a Harvard-educated former war hero. Burton vowed to clean up corruption, wage war on crime, and make the city streets safe again. To do so, he knew he would need a clean and competent director of public safety. The public safety director had supreme authority over municipal law enforcement and ancillary services. The incumbent, Martin J. Lavelle, and his predecessors had made a mockery of the position and outraged many citizens in the process. Burton sought an individual of integrity and skill to command the entire system of crime prevention, firefighting, and traffic control. Among the names on his short list was Eliot Ness.

Burton had never heard of Ness, but local newspaper reporters, businessmen, and reliable city officials spoke highly of this recent arrival from Chicago. U.S. attorney Dwight W. Green, one of the federal prosecutors in the Capone case and a future governor of Illinois, gave Ness a ringing endorsement. Echoing Green's opinion was Wes Lawrence, who had Mayor Burton's ear. Ness was also enthusiastically supported by William Clegg, a politically connected Chicago stockbroker who was foreman of the federal grand jury that indicted Al Capone on Prohibition and conspiracy violations as a result of Ness's testimony.

The fact that Ness was an outsider appealed to Burton. When he learned that Ness had turned down bribes and made a point of exposing those who accepted payoffs, Burton knew he had his man.

Ness first heard that he was under consideration from a couple of Cleveland newspaper reporters. His excitement was tempered by Edna's lack of enthusiasm. Nevertheless, when Burton summoned Ness to City Hall for an interview on December 11, 1935, Ness eagerly accepted the invitation. Less than an hour later, he took the oath of office and became Cleveland's director of public safety at an annual salary of seventy-five hundred dollars.

When Ness returned to his Alcohol Tax Unit office to share the news, his colleagues had a dozen roses waiting for him. They had been tipped off by a reporter moments after Ness was sworn in. Photographers snapped away as Ness emptied his filing cabinet, hugged several members of his staff and shook hands with others, and prepared for the next chapter in his career.

Newspapers the next day trumpeted Ness's appointment. Burton was applauded for bringing in an outsider with a G-man's mentality and no local political ties, although one Republican was quoted as saying, "What did this Ness guy ever do to elect Burton?"

On his first day of work, the youngest public safety director in the city's history arrived at City Hall in a tan camelhair topcoat and snap-brim fedora. His first appointment was with the mayor.

"What I really wanted to know was how far I could go," Ness wrote of the meeting. "Were these men serious about cleaning house, or was I just hired for window dressing? I had no intention of remaining in Cleveland if the people around me weren't as serious about my mission as I intended to be."

Burton had enjoyed a successful legal career in Cleveland, but he yearned to leave a mark on the city. According to Ness's description of their first meeting, Burton began to pace the floor before stopping in front of the tall, wide window that allowed him to look out over the smoky landscape. He struck a match and lit a long Havana cigar. Blowing a cloud of smoke into the air, he turned to face Ness.

"We checked up on you. Did you know that?"

"I'm not surprised," Ness replied. "I'd do the same thing if I were you."

"You seem to get high marks all the way around. Maybe a little too aggressive from time to time. That's something you're going to have to watch around here."

"Agreed. I'm aware of it."

"I don't really know too much about you, other than the fact that you helped out on the Capone matter and kept your nose clean."

"I guess that about sums it up," Ness said, loosening his tie and reaching for the coffee Burton's secretary had just delivered.

The mayor went on to detail Ness's duties. He said the new director's inexperience might work in his favor, since he had no ties to Cleveland's political machinery. However, Burton cautioned Ness that he would have to step on some big toes to perform his duties effectively. While he was expected to attack the problems of corruption and inefficiency in the police department, Ness also had to avoid alienating members of the city council, who controlled the purse strings.

"I think I can handle it, under one condition," Ness said. "I don't want to be deskbound. I want to be out on the beat. That's where I function the best."

"I don't have a problem with that," the mayor responded. "If you're visible, you'll get attention, and the publicity could really do us some good at budget time, if it's the right kind of publicity."

The idea of commanding the police force and fire department at first seemed overwhelming to Ness.

"Here I was, one of the youngest men employed in city government, and suddenly I was put in charge of more than 2,500 men," he wrote. "Perhaps I had gotten more than I bargained for."

After his meeting with Burton, Ness drove his Ford to Central Police Station, a four-story sandstone fortress at Twenty-first and Payne on Cleveland's East Side. There he spent an hour with George J. Matowitz, Cleveland's chief of police. A thirty-one-year veteran of the department, Matowitz was immediately defensive, though Ness took great pains to put him at ease.

The chief, a stocky six-footer, struck Ness as uninspired, perhaps even lazy, a common perception around Cleveland. No one had accused Matowitz of tolerating police corruption, but there were suspicions that he was so uninvolved, he had no idea how far the cancer had spread. Ness left the meeting believing that as long as Matowitz knew people were watching, the chief would be an important ally.

Cleveland news reporters caught up with Ness as he left Central Station. Having heard of his activities in Chicago, those who had not yet met Ness expected to see a stern, nondescript lawman. Many were surprised to find that the new public safety director was a well-dressed, handsome young man with a pleasant smile and a soft voice.

"I'm not going to be a remote director," Ness promised them. "I plan to be right in the front lines combating crime, but only after I become a little more familiar with the police force and the local crime scene."

Dropping a heavy load of books, pamphlets, and file folders on the passenger's seat of his car, Ness walked around to the driver's side and opened the door. "This is my homework," he said, pointing to the city charter, a crime and law enforcement survey, and other material spread out on the car seat. "I'll know a lot more tomorrow and a lot more than that the next day. I'm going to do plenty of studying."

CHAPTER FIFTEEN

One Tough Town

ELIOT NESS DEMONSTRATED HIS commitment to the new job the very first night. He and Edna joined another couple for dinner at a downtown Cleveland restaurant. Interrupted by his driver, who heard a police radio transmission detailing the discovery of a burglary near the eatery, Ness dropped a wad of bills on the table, instructed Edna to take a cab home, then bolted for the door.

Shielding himself from a strong wind that blew in from Lake Erie, he spotted the flashing red light of a police car two blocks away and ran to the scene. Ness was greeted by a uniformed officer who was keeping the gathering crowd away from a two-story brick office building. Officers had chased two suspects caught in the act of burglarizing the City Savings and Loan Company onto the roof and discovered they had jumped to an adjacent building and escaped into the night.

As the policemen regrouped at their squad cars, Ness accepted an invitation to join the patrols in the crime-ridden third precinct, the so-called Roaring Third. Brothels and gambling houses operated unimpeded on virtually every street. Asked by Ness why they ignored the obvious criminal activity, the officers said they were ordered not to make arrests in vice cases without the approval of their precinct captain.

Later the patrolmen responded to a five-alarm warehouse fire at Neville Street and Wentworth Avenue. Ness was shocked by the inefficiency he observed, as well as the outdated, unreliable equipment the firemen were forced to use.

As the clock neared 2 A.M., the officers were summoned to assist with a raid at a small brothel on Orange Avenue. By the time police broke through the door, the prostitutes and their customers were gone. One of the officers conceded to Ness that the targets of the raid had, in all likelihood, been forewarned by a contact in the police department, business-as-usual in Cleveland.

"That was a quick getaway," Ness said with a grin to a newspaper reporter. "At least they're jittery."

The episode didn't sit well with Edna. Upon Ness's return home in the predawn hours, she told Eliot he had embarrassed her in the restaurant and ruined their evening together because of his restless craving for adventure. If relations were strained for Ness at home, they were growing cozier with the press. Not only did Ness seek to polish his own image, he also recognized the importance of building public support for his plans. He was page-one news the next day.

"Six feet and 172 pounds of fight and vigor, an expert criminologist who looks like a collegian but can battle crime with the best of them, Eliot Ness is beginning his job of upholding law and order in Cleveland," read one story. Mayor Burton was given high marks in the story for "hiring a Safety Director without political ties or aspirations who has a spotless record of battling corruption in a major American city."

Less than a week later, Ness sent an even louder message to all of Cleveland. He investigated a tip that two veteran patrolmen, Michael Corrigan and Joseph Dunne, were drinking while on duty. Not only did Ness verify the report, he also learned that Dunne was a habitual offender. When the men arrived for work the next morning, Ness demanded their badges.

"I will not stand for this," Ness vowed to a *Cleveland Plain Dealer* reporter who heard of the dismissals. (It is unclear whether Ness spread the news himself or merely acknowledged his actions when confronted by the reporter.) "It is this simple," he continued. "Either we have a decent, law-abiding community, or we don't. These men don't fit."

Some of the top brass in the police department, stunned by Ness's abrupt action, demanded that Dunne and Corrigan be reinstated. At least two newspaper editorialists joined the chorus, charging the safety director with overstepping his authority. One of them called on city officials to replace the gung-ho Ness with a director who was more in tune with Cleveland's way of life.

"Boy Scout" and "College Cop" were among the derisive terms used by police department veterans to describe him, based in large part on first impressions. Those who met Ness were surprised to see not an abrupt, hard-nosed man, but a smiling, blue-eyed young gentleman who couldn't keep a stray lock of light brown hair from falling over his brow and who reacted to information with such mild expressions as "gee" and "gosh." But Ness would not yield an inch, especially after Cleveland's newspapers called on their readers to support his efforts to mold the police force in his own image.

"In a decently-operated police department, semi-military disciplinary action wouldn't have been worth mentioning," wrote Philip Porter. "It would have been customary and expected. But a quarter century of police favoritism, phenagling and chiseling has left the honest cops disheartened. The ones who either stood in with the mob or simply did nothing got the promotions and the good jobs."

Next, Ness met with traffic commissioner Edward Donahue and urged him to insist that traffic police practice salesmanship and courtesy, instead of carrying "the big stick."

Just before Christmas, Ness announced a major shakeup of the police department. With concurrence from Chief Matowitz, he transferred the head of the detective bureau—a political affiliate of the former mayor—to a special traffic assignment, shifted captains and lieutenants to new precincts, and reassigned nearly one hundred officers to new beats. His aim was to sever the cozy alliances that many officers had developed with the city's criminals.

One by one, he summoned the precinct captains to his office and warned them that they would be held personally responsible for any misconduct by the men who were under their command. More serious offenses would be punishable by immediate suspension of both the officer involved and his precinct captain.

Ness closed out his first month on the job by designating John R. Flynn, a thirty-seven-year-old lawyer with a military background, to ferret out graft and corruption in the police department. The lingering political alliances of Flynn, a six-foot-four former Notre Dame football player, were a concern to Ness, but he recognized the need for a gradual transition.

Veteran police officers huddled to discuss ways to force the safety director out, but Ness took his case to the court of public opinion. At thirty-three, he was the youngest public safety director in the city's history. With his Scandinavian good looks, wearing the latest double-breasted suits, and living with an attractive wife in Bay Village, Ness was seen by many as the dynamic symbol depression-weary Clevelanders needed.

Ness spelled out his mission during a speech to the Cleveland Advertising Club in early January 1936, and he made sure the press was there to hear him. "In any city where corruption continues, it follows that some officials are playing ball with the underworld. . . . The dishonest public servant hiding behind a badge or political office is more detestable than any street criminal or mob boss. If town officials are committed to a program of protection of the lawmakers, police work becomes exceedingly difficult, and the officer on the beat, being discouraged from his duty, decides it is best to see as little crime as possible."

Ness said many Cleveland police officers were regularly accepting bribes, tipping off criminals about impending raids, and even serving as enforcers for the mob. Other policemen were apathetic and lazy, and many were drinking while on duty, he reported. "And the worst part is that we have officers who match all three descriptions—crooked, lazy, and drunk!"

He pointed out that political favoritism, rather than merit, was traditionally the basis for promotion, and he vowed to replace patronage with civil service testing. Playing to his audience, Ness pointed out that the police department's shortcomings were allowing the mob to flourish, exacerbating the city's economic woes. Skyrocketing profits from gambling and bootlegging had led to unabated growth of organizations such as the Cleveland Syndicate and the Mayfield Road Mob, a vicious gang of Jewish and Italian criminals working in profitable harmony. The most lucrative of their enterprises, even with the demise of Prohibition, was bootlegging. The mob produced its own whiskey and smuggled truckloads of Canadian liquor across Lake Erie.

Much of the alcohol produced by other smaller operators could also be traced to the large criminal organizations, which controlled the supply of corn sugar. The easiest substance to convert into alcohol, corn sugar had long been a lucrative business for Cleveland crime figures, dating back to the Prohibition days' "Corn Sugar Wars." Supplies had been controlled by the Lonardo brothers and, later, the Porello family, both from Cleveland's "Big Italy" section in the Woodland neighborhood. By the mid-1930s, the Mayfield Road Mob had won undisputed control of the corn sugar business.

This was, in large part, testimony to the effectiveness of Morris "Moe" Dalitz. A diminutive figure with a prominent nose and affable smile, Dalitz landed in the Mayfield Road Mob after cutting his teeth with Detroit's notorious "Purple Gang."

Other underworld figures were being attracted to Cleveland because of the vast opportunities that abounded. Ness estimated that organized crime was robbing Cleveland's economy of more than $1 million monthly from illegal gambling alone. He surprised many businessmen present when he questioned the wisdom of outlawing gambling—a position that ran counter to Mayor Burton's pronouncements. He said legalizing gambling would cut deeply into the mob's profits. Ness, however, also acknowledged that any attempt to make gambling legal would be politically suicidal.

"It's debatable whether gambling is morally wrong, but from the policing standpoint I have an entirely different picture," Ness said. "Illegal gambling brings into financial power men recognized as law violators. They collect large sums of money, which must be distributed among many people, some of them public officials. Gradually, with their money, they make inroads into the police departments and the courts."

"Policy" was one of the most popular forms of gambling in the city, having survived antigambling crusades for decades. A forerunner of today's state lotteries, policy involves the random selection of numbered balls, with prizes awarded according to gamblers' correct guesses. It was so entrenched in the city that Ness ordered one of his deputy inspectors to summon prominent policy operators for a meeting at a downtown police station to warn them of an impending crackdown. They were advised to "close up shop now, or be prepared to be arrested, because you will be."

"Horse rooms," similar to today's off-track betting parlors, were also operating throughout the city. They typically featured enormous racing-odds boards, loudspeakers, betting windows, and operators busily tracking the results of horseraces by telephone or telegraph. Clevelanders' affinity for gambling had even reached the city's school grounds. Money furnished to needy pupils by the National Youth Administration for books, lunches, and other necessities ended up instead in the pockets of neighborhood youth gangs.

The penchant for gambling fueled the widespread popularity of the Harvard Club, a notorious nightspot on the outskirts of Newburgh Heights, which was outside the jurisdiction of the city police. Ness was shocked to discover that this full-scale casino had, for more than five years, operated openly and unmolested by local law officers. The Harvard Club not only defied the law, it also cheated customers out of large sums of money with rigged equipment, loaded dice, and an assortment of other tricks. Its chief operator was James "Shimmy" Patton, one of three co-owners who directed the majority of gambling profits to the Cleveland Syndicate. The Mayfield Road Mob controlled the club's lucrative alcohol business.

Not far from there was the Thomas Club in Mayfield Heights, run by another of the Mayfield Road Mob, "Gameboy" Miller. Moe Dalitz also had his own place, the Mounds Club, in Lake County, just outside Cleveland.

Ness found a natural ally in Cuyahoga County prosecutor Frank T. Cullitan, who shared his disgust that these gambling houses operated with apparent immunity. Cullitan was a respected tactician whose strong courtroom oratory had helped him send seven murderers to the electric chair.

On January 10, 1936, Cullitan shocked the underworld by secretly deputizing almost two dozen private detectives and sending them out, warrants in hand, to shut down the gambling dens.

At the Thomas Club, the raiders were admitted after starting to batter down a heavy front door with a long wooden bench. They seized gambling equipment and more than fifty thousand dollars in cash, along with a schedule showing the stops of a seven-passenger sedan that ran a circuit into Cleveland and around to the Harvard Club and the Thomas Club.

Their stiffest resistance came at the Harvard Club, where Shimmy Patton's bouncers greeted Cullitan's chief assistant, Charles J. McNamee, with submachine guns. Eventually, Patton himself, a short, chubby man with black hair plastered back on his head, appeared at the door and threatened McNamee and his officers.

"You just step inside and let the fellows you've got with you try to come in and we'll mow them down," Patton shouted. Cullitan arrived a short time later, fresh from the Thomas Club raid, and received a similar threat. "Anybody that goes in there gets their f— head knocked off," Patton said.

After a long standoff, the prosecutor retreated to a gas station a half-block away and telephoned Cuyahoga County sheriff "Honest John" Sulzmann, with predictable results. Sulzmann declared that his department would not assist in the raid unless the Newburgh Heights mayor requested the sheriff's intervention. This "home rule" argument had shielded Sulzmann from any responsibility to enforce the law on repeated occasions.

Cullitan eventually tracked down Eliot Ness at a Cleveland city council meeting. "This is the most brazen defiance of the law I've ever seen," an excited Cullitan fumed. Ness, as expected, was eager to help, but Mayor Burton did not share his enthusiasm. The mayor finally agreed to let city police officers serve as special deputies of the Cuyahoga County prosecutor's office, with the understanding that they were acting independent of any affiliation with the city.

Ness rounded up twenty-seven willing volunteers. Among those accepting the invitation was Lt. Ernest Molnar. A veteran officer, Molnar had already made a name for himself by assembling a squad of courageous officers who became known as "Molnar's Raiders." Meanwhile, upward of two hundred spectators who had gathered along the fringes at the Harvard Club to watch the drama unfold suddenly found themselves in darkness when the operators turned off the parking lot lights.

Ness and Molnar led a caravan that rolled into Newburgh Heights at about 11 P.M. Only moments behind them were three cars carrying newspaper reporters and photographers, responding to vague reports that the public safety director was about to generate some interesting news.

This army of volunteers, armed with an assortment of revolvers, high-powered rifles, sawed-off shotguns, and tear-gas guns, caught Cullitan by surprise. He emphasized that under no circumstances were shots to be fired.

The Harvard Club was a barnlike building that had once served as a warehouse. A fancy New Orleans–style façade erected in the front could not obscure the building's actual purpose. Wooden cowls covered all of the windows.

Ness directed each driver to maneuver his vehicle into place in the parking area, leaving the headlights on to illuminate the club. Many of the customers who rushed out at the first sign of trouble returned to watch the raid from a safe distance. Ness and Cullitan did not know it at the time, but among those who had left in all the commotion was one of the FBI's most wanted criminals, Alvin "Creepy" Karpis, suspected in several murders and two kidnappings. About twenty gamblers remained on the premises, seemingly unconcerned.

A half-dozen officers hurried to the back of the building to cover that exit. Without a word, Ness, unarmed, broke from the pack. Easily distinguishable by his camelhair overcoat and badge, Ness boldly walked up the porch steps to the heavy steel door at the front, took a deep breath, and knocked loudly. The tiny speakeasy slot flew open and slammed shut just as quickly.

Ness returned to the parking lot, where he and Cullitan stood quietly, their heavy breathing sending clouds of steam into the cold night air. The Harvard Club standoff continued for another five minutes before the front door slowly opened and a husky character in a tuxedo invited the group to enter. The men followed Ness, moving quickly into the nearly empty room. Most of the gambling apparatus had been dismantled and carried out. Shimmy Patton was nowhere to be found. Another of the operators, Arthur Hebebrand, climbed out a small window, dropped ten feet to the ground, and disappeared into the night. A brief scuffle broke out when a newspaper photographer was knocked to the floor while he began snapping pictures.

Despite some of the more sensationalized accounts that would be published, the raid was fairly uneventful, except for its symbolic value. Ness drew quiet satisfaction from shuttering a notable gambling den and letting the Cleveland Syndicate and the Mayfield Road Mob know that he meant business. He was especially pleased to see city police officers taking an interest in the raid on a voluntary basis.

Cleveland's three daily newspapers had a field day with the raid. "At 10:20, with sirens screaming, the safety director and his men hove into sight," reported the *Cleveland News*. "Four-score armed men, led by the unarmed Ness, came marching forward in a solid phalanx toward the club."

From the *Cleveland Press:* "Behind that door thugs held machine guns. They strutted and preened themselves, promising to 'mow down' anyone who tried to enter and alternately cursing and threatening."

The *Cleveland Plain Dealer* reported: "With Ness marching in front of them, the 42 policemen and 20 constables, armed with sawed-off shotguns, tear gas pistols and revolvers stormed the club. . . . Ness shoved open the front door and told Cullitan's constables to finish the job."

Cullitan bristled when a reporter called the raid a failure. His ire had been rising for two years, and he had received little support from local authorities. "Our objective was to close the place and we did it," Cullitan snapped at a reporter. Ness declared the closing of the two clubs "the beginning of the end of gangdom rule in Cleveland."

Ness also used the raid as a rallying cry. During a speech before a Cleveland civic organization a few days later, he said, "I'll tell you, gentlemen, I never saw such a situation, even when in the government service. I repeatedly raided the Capone outfit's places, but this situation was different. They were not bluffing—they meant business. . . . I don't think there is any doubt but that if Cullitan had gone into the Harvard Club earlier in the evening, he would have been murdered."

"So what did you do when you were faced with similar circumstances in Chicago?" one of the reporters asked.

Ness paused then said quietly, "We went in."

Sheriff Sulzmann came under fire. Clevelanders' sentiment was perhaps best summarized by columnist Jack Kennon: "He cooked his political goose blacker than a chunk of coal when he failed to aid his Democratic brother, Cullitan, threatened with his life by a coterie of yeggs who should have been hanged and quartered long ago." As forecasted, Sulzmann was defeated in the next election.

By the end of January, Ness had transferred 28 lieutenants, half of the force's 126 sergeants, and almost 400 of the 1,150 patrolmen. A handful of the police officers resigned, since the safety director let it be known that he would not be inclined to pursue charges against many of those who were no longer on the city payroll.

News reporters, unaccustomed to such access to a city law enforcement official, applauded Ness for his get-tough approach. Less supportive were many members of the police department. Some officers, including those who were clean, clammed up when Ness summoned them individually and grilled them about their knowledge of corruption among the ranks. Newspaper reports telling of the safety director's ire over this lack of cooperation only strengthened the conspiracy of silence within the department.

If the police wouldn't talk, Ness reasoned, maybe the criminals would. A series of meetings with prosecutor Cullitan resulted in a new policy that encouraged offenders to tell what they knew about police corruption. Among the inducements were reduced sentences, immunity from prosecution, protection against retaliation, and money. Police captains were also notified that if bookie joints and other vice operations reopened after being raided or warned, they would be held personally responsible.

Nobody could fault Ness's thoroughness or his commitment to this purge of the police department. Considering the poor credibility of many informants, he knew it was imperative to verify every accusation and to give each officer a fair hearing. Ness did much of the fieldwork himself. At night, despite his wife's protestations, he could be found talking to prostitutes, pimps, and other criminals in bars and back alleys. Ness also made a habit of visiting precinct stations in the middle of the night to check up on the late-shifters and see if they were enforcing the vice laws.

Gradually, veterans of the police force grew less inclined to scoff at Ness or mock his Ivy League appearance and quiet manner. Officers who had nothing to hide began to respect him for his tenacity. All the while, Ness was recruiting young officers. He found one of them on the handball court at Fenn College (now Cleveland State University), where Gus Zukie dropped by to play one Saturday afternoon. Zukie and his partner were disturbed to find the court they had reserved occupied by Ness and his crony, and they made no effort to hide their disgust.

"We decided to throw them off the court," said Zukie, chuckling. "I just about kicked Ness's ass."

Born in a multiethnic Cleveland neighborhood in 1913, Zukie was in his second year at Fenn College and working as a barroom bouncer when he had his first encounter with Ness. Zukie, who was a solid 230-pounder, recalled the conversation: "Ness walked up to me afterward and said, 'I think you'd make a pretty good police officer. You know how to stand up for your rights.' I said, 'I don't know who in the hell you are, but where I come from, nobody likes cops.' Ness persisted and I ended up taking the job."

A small news item buried behind the headlines of the January 27 newspapers drew little attention from Clevelanders. It told of a dismembered female body discovered in an alley near East Twentieth Street and Central Avenue. The body parts were wrapped in newspapers and packed in two half-bushel baskets, covered with burlap bags, and left in the snow behind the Hart Manufacturing Plant. Through fingerprints, police identified the victim as Flo Polillo, a forty-one-year-old prostitute and part-time waitress who lived a few blocks from the spot where her remains were found. She had been killed by the precise surgical amputation of her head.

CHAPTER SIXTEEN

Crooked Cops
Pay the Price

E LIOT NESS WAS RIDING high, and his popularity exceeded that of
Mayor Harold Burton. He was a featured speaker at business
luncheons and was hired to deliver law enforcement lectures at
Cleveland College. As long as Ness expressed no political ambitions, the mayor welcomed all the positive publicity his administration could garner.

Ness fit the mold of an all-American hero, with his glimmering
eyes and modest voice. Among those enamored by Ness was Clayton
Fritchey, a prominent reporter and nationally syndicated columnist
with the *Cleveland Press*. Fritchey, recognizable to most Clevelanders
by his round glasses and polka-dot bow tie, was respected for his
courage and thoroughness in covering the city government beat. He
had been anxious to ally himself with Ness and capitalize on the
safety director's fast-growing popularity, so when he stumbled onto
evidence linking a prominent police official with the Cleveland mob,
Fritchey knew just where to turn.

It began with a series of investigative news stories on the sale of
cemetery plots, some of which didn't even exist, to the immigrant
population of Cleveland. Frank T. Cullitan used much of Fritchey's
information to bring charges against a handful of police officers with
known underworld connections.

Fritchey continued to be bothered by the repeated appearance of one name, John S. Dacek, on ledgers, memos, and canceled checks seized during Cullitan's probe. There was no mention of Dacek in any official records. Eventually, it dawned on Fritchey that, by switching a couple of letters, the name resembled that of sixteenth precinct police Capt. Louis J. Cadek.

Long suspected of having mob connections, Cadek, a thirty-year veteran of the department, had hidden behind a wall of protection and political power he had built over the years. "Nobody went to the bathroom without Cadek's permission," recalled one of his colleagues. "He called the shots. There wasn't a cop on the force who carried more clout."

Convinced that he had solved the riddle, Fritchey met with Ness to share his evidence. Thus began a relationship that would be mutually beneficial for the remainder of Ness's days in Cleveland. Fritchey, in effect, became an extra investigator for the city. In return, he obtained exclusive material that improved the *Cleveland Press*'s stature in the highly competitive newspaper business.

Ness and Fritchey determined that Cadek's involvement with bribery and conspiracy dated back at least fifteen years. Bank records subpoenaed by Ness revealed that under the aliases of Louis J. Cadeb, John L. Dombrowski, and John S. Dacek, Cadek had been making large, unexplained investments since 1921. Cadek's savings account showed a balance of $150,000, despite an annual salary that had only recently been increased to $3,500. He had also received two fancy Cadillacs as gifts from men with known underworld connections.

The investigation spread out into the sixteenth precinct, where Ness and Fritchey found the incriminating evidence they needed. In return for immunity from prosecution, operators of speakeasies and gambling houses agreed to testify that Cadek had extorted tens of thousands of dollars from them during Prohibition, promising police protection in return. The prosecutors verified more than $109,000 in bribes and protection payments.

Cadek's conviction sent shock waves through the police department, particularly after the captain bargained for a reduced sentence by pointing the finger at some of his colleagues. Clevelanders now realized how widespread the corruption in their police force had become, and there were more prosecutions pending.

Ness's actions also caught the city's vice lords off guard. They had anticipated a banner year in 1936, with Cleveland hosting hundreds of thousands of visitors for the Great Lakes Exposition, the National American Legion Convention, and the Republican National Convention.

While Ness continued to focus on police corruption, investigators were called to the Kingsbury Run area on Cleveland's Lower East Side on June 5, 1936. Many Clevelanders and drifters dispossessed by the Great Depression had gravitated to Kingsbury Run, a prehistoric riverbed attached to the section known as the Flats. Bordered on the north by Woodland Avenue and on the south by Broadway, Kingsbury Run in the 1930s was filled with trash and other debris as well as makeshift shanties occupied by hoboes and vagrants. Today, the run itself is less distinguishable, obscured by railroad and rapid-transit tracks.

Two boys, ages eleven and thirteen, had set out for a day of fishing near the Kinsman Road bridge when they discovered the head of a white male wrapped in a pair of trousers close to the East Fifty-fifth Street Bridge. The next day, a couple of railroad workers found the body about one-quarter mile away, dumped in front of the Nickel Plate Railroad Building. Clean and nearly drained of blood, the corpse was intact except for the head. The cause of death was decapitation. Despite the presence of six distinctive tattoos on the body, this victim was never identified. Although found in hobo country, he was probably not one of them. He appeared to be clean, well nourished, and well dressed. Judging by the volume of blood at the scene, investigators concluded that the victim was probably killed at the same place the body was discovered.

Although police were not telling the public as much, they now believed they had discovered the work of a serial killer. Back in September 1934, a young Frank Lagassie was strolling along the shores of Lake Erie, east of Bratenahl, when he discovered the lower half of a woman's torso, thighs still attached but legs amputated at the knees. Cuyahoga County coroner Arthur J. Pearse was intrigued by the presence of a chemical preservative on the skin. A subsequent search yielded other scattered body parts. The woman, apparently in her early thirties, was not identified. She had been dead for about six months and came to be known later by investigators and researchers as "the Lady of the Lake."

Almost a year to the day of that morbid discovery, sixteen-year-old Jimmy Wagner and twelve-year-old Peter Kostura discovered the decapitated, emasculated corpse of a white male near the dead ends of East Forty-ninth and East Fiftieth Streets in the Kingsbury Run area, at the base of a section known as Jackass Hill. This body was nude, except for a pair of socks, and drained of blood. He was eventually identified as twenty-nine-year-old Edward Andrassy, no stranger to the police. Andrassy had been arrested on several occasions for excessive drinking, fighting, and weapons charges.

Even more shocking, while searching for evidence connected with Andrassy's murder, police came across the body of another man, also decapitated and emasculated. Both heads were found buried in a shallow pit nearby. This second victim, believed to be about forty-five years old, had been dead for several weeks. His body was covered with the same chemical preservative. There were enough common threads between these killings and the others to convince police that they were the work of at least one man who likely prowled the dark, dreary Kingsbury Run section in search of victims.

There has been considerable debate over the years on the extent of Eliot Ness's involvement in the search for the Kingsbury Run serial killer. In the initial stages, Ness tried to distance himself and focus most of his attention on police corruption and organized crime. He was also preoccupied by other assignments. Mayor Burton insisted that Ness oversee security and other arrangements for the 1936 Republican National Convention in Cleveland. Burton saw the event as an opportunity for the city to improve its poor public image and tell the world that Cleveland was on the rise, with the population increasing and the economy improving.

Cleveland police debuted fifteen "Voice of Safety" Oldsmobiles during the event, moving slowly around the congested streets with public address systems to direct and handle the increased vehicular and pedestrian traffic. The convention went off without a hitch, the delegates choosing Gov. Alf Landon of Kansas to "win back the presidency" from Franklin D. Roosevelt.

Public outcry over the Kingsbury Run serial killer was renewed in July 1936 when newspaper stories trumpeted the discovery of another murder victim. A seventeen-year-old girl came upon the decapitated body of a white male in a wooded area near Clinton Road and Big Creek on the West Side. The head, as well as a pile of blood-soaked clothing, was found nearby. The victim, about forty years old, had been dead for approximately eight weeks. He was never identified.

City officials tried to downplay the murders and assure the public they had many promising leads. In reality, there was little evidence to go on. Ness believed that one of the best hopes of finding the killer was in establishing the identity of his victims. He secretly commissioned a plaster artist to work with the coroner's office in creating casts of the unidentified victims' faces. These life-size "death masks" would be as realistic as possible, based on the victims' hair color, bone structure, and other clues.

Ness needed another diversion, and he got one when Anton Vehovec of Collinwood, an outspoken, politically connected Cleveland city council member, made serious allegations against a high-ranking police officer, Capt. Michael J. Harwood of the fourteenth precinct in southwest Cleveland. He alleged that Harwood had been accepting bribes for many years to protect racketeers. Pressed for specifics, the self-styled crusader pointed to the popularity and apparent legal immunity of the Blackhawk Inn, a gambling house at 1775 Ivanhoe Road.

So began the bitterest of any police corruption investigation Ness would pursue. Harwood, a twenty-five-year veteran of the force, was a heavyweight in Cleveland. He and his son, Edward Harwood, had invested heavily in nightclubs, resorts, and other popular social venues. Captain Harwood, described by the *Cleveland Press* as a "flamboyant, two-fisted outspoken fighter," had survived numerous political battles and allegations.

Ness listened intently as councilman Vehovec detailed an elaborate system of bribery dating as far back as 1928. Harwood was also accused of allowing the Blackhawk Inn, owned by his son, to operate without police interference. At Vehovec's invitation, Ness went to have a look for himself.

The Blackhawk was ostensibly a restaurant and licensed tavern, but many patrons entered through a back door protected by a security guard. Together with detective Walter Walker and councilman Vehovec, Ness attempted to enter the back room and was denied. The sudden departure of about thirty men and women through another door told Ness all he needed to know. He and Walker forced open the door and discovered about a dozen men surrounded by horseracing charts, betting slips, a bank of telephones—some of which were ringing—blackjack tables, and other gambling apparatus.

Moments later, Edward Harwood arrived. He denied any knowledge of gambling activities, claiming he rented the back room to a man named "Joe"; he was unable to recall his tenant's last name. Harwood was permitted to make a telephone call. A short time later, a short, pudgy man with a cigar dangling from his lower lip appeared in the room.

"I'm Joe McCarthy—you lookin' for me?" he asked, looking alternately at Ness, Walker, and Vehovec. "What's the problem here?"

"Didn't Harwood just telephone you to come down here?" Ness replied.

"No, I'm the owner. I've had the place for about two weeks."

"You're quite sure you want to take the rap on this?"

"Well, it's my joint, if that's what you mean."

"So, how much rent do you pay, Mr. McCarthy?" Ness inquired.

"I don't know. Mr. Harwood and I haven't worked that out yet."

"Your story sounds a little thin to me, Joe. Is there anything else you'd like to tell us that might save you a whole lot of trouble? That's what you're heading for, and I mean a *lot* of trouble."

"Not really."

McCarthy was then arrested on gambling charges. In the meantime, Ness discovered an alarm system that could be triggered by the bartender to warn gamblers of an impending raid. He also determined that none of the keys on McCarthy's key ring matched the lock to the gambling room, whereas Harwood had a key that fit. A search of the premises revealed a box of horserace betting slips just outside the door of an upstairs apartment where Edward Harwood resided. Ness also found several cases of bootleg whiskey being dispensed at the restaurant and tavern.

Evidence from the Blackhawk raid and testimony from more than a dozen speakeasy operators who paid bribes during Prohibition resulted in indictments against Michael Harwood and seven other police officers. Recognizing the writing on the wall, Harwood immediately resigned—he had already been suspended—and applied for his $140-per-month pension. Some members of the police establishment believed Harwood should be permitted to collect the pension and escape criminal prosecution, but Ness held firm.

The issue soon became a political controversy, as reporters revealed serious differences of opinion between Ness and deputy police inspector Andrew J. Hagan. When Hagan sought to circumvent Ness by pushing through pension requests, Ness intervened. Pointing out that pensions, once granted, were irrevocable, he sabotaged the plan by refusing to accept the resignation of any officer suspected or accused of a crime.

"This is just another reminder that some powerful influences would have crooked policemen rewarded and that the community and its legal institutions are impotent to deal with the situation," Vehovec said of Hagan's plot.

Ness continued to bear down on Harwood's corruption-ridden precinct. Further investigation confirmed the severity of the problem. Gambling and liquor raids were nearly nonexistent in the fourteenth and fifteenth precincts, where Harwood had authority, except in those cases where operators refused demands to pay graft.

"The matter has gone far beyond the operation of a single bootlegging and gambling operation," he pointed out. "It is a question of police efficiency, discipline, and honesty throughout the fourteenth precinct." With that, Ness transferred twenty-eight officers to other precincts.

While Cleveland police officers recognized that Ness meant business, they also knew that severing their ties with the underworld was not without its own risks. Many opted for early retirement, which allowed Ness to continue filling the ranks with a new breed of officer. At the same time, honest policemen who had resisted the bribes welcomed the support that had been denied them for so long and began coming forward with incriminating evidence against their corrupt colleagues. There was also an increase in tips from citizens and a greater willingness—in some cases, eagerness—by witnesses to testify.

While the tide was turning in favor of honest, effective law enforcement, Ness was putting together plans for an Untouchables-style raid on a West Side gambling house. For more than a decade, the casino on West Twenty-fifth Street in the aptly named Rowdy Run area had operated under the cover of an establishment known as McGinty's.

A handpicked team of proven officers infiltrated McGinty's, posing as gamblers, and gathered descriptions of the organizational structure, games in operation, a layout of the building, and gambling by city police officers. To test police response, Ness had an undercover officer plant a tip with deputy inspector Timothy Costello and waited to see if any action would be taken. The fact that Costello's three sons worked for owner Tommy McGinty suggested police complicity. Two weeks later, with no action having been taken, Ness made his move.

Seventy-seven gamblers were issued summonses on the spot and nine employees were taken into custody. The raiders seized stacks of financial records, including evidence tying McGinty's to Arthur Hebebrand, a co-owner of the Harvard Club. Another veteran police captain, Adolph Lenahan, whose eighth precinct officers were so tolerant of McGinty's, was suspended for drinking on the job and neglecting his duty.

Ten more gambling raids followed in downtown Cleveland during July, all under Ness's orders and a few with the public safety director's personal involvement. In some cases, records were shared with the U.S. Treasury Department for tax evasion investigations.

"Ness is an enigma to police, to politicians, to underworld contact men, and even to his closest associates," wrote Jack Kennon of the *Cleveland News*. "He takes no one into his confidence and this is especially true in respect to ranking police officials. No one knows his mind, what he will do next, where he will strike. Yet his actions of the last nine months clearly define his objective as Safety Director. He is out to clean up the police department and to crush the underworld as best he can and finally place younger men on the force. . . . He personally has led raids. Why? He doesn't relish being labeled a 'bookie raider,' but he firmly believes a direct connection exists between gambling and more serious forms of crime. He tells you this over and over again."

Kennon went on to report that although Ness had been issued a Smith and Wesson service revolver, he rarely if ever carried it. Others confirmed that conclusion. There is no record of Ness ever discharging a firearm in the line of duty, with the exception of the brewery raid in Chicago, when his pistol made short work of the padlock.

Other press reports praised Ness for his aggressive attitude. The July 26, 1936, *Plain Dealer* reported:

> Eliot Ness, with his boyish face and enigmatic manner, is well aware of what is going on in the department, and attending to one matter at a time. The cops were at first inclined to scoff at him, but by now are aware he knows his business. It is fairly obvious that he considers his business the rebuilding of a police force which has gone badly to seed. His greatest handicap is that he must investigate by himself, and can trust so few others.

That situation was about to change with the appointment of Robert Chamberlin to the new position of administrative assistant in the public safety director's office, succeeding John R. Flynn. The differences between Ness and Flynn, while never bitter, had grown as the director's crackdown on police corruption intensified. Flynn was closely aligned with Cleveland's Republican establishment and was rumored to be considering a challenge to Harold Burton in the 1937 Republican primary. As supervisor of patronage in the safety director's office before Ness arrived, Flynn had promoted and hired police officers with strong political connections, even though they ranked low on civil service lists.

Chamberlin, a young attorney and Ohio National Guard officer, was well known throughout the Cleveland area as a high school football star. He was tall, rangy, and dark-haired, with dark eyes and sharp features, a natural complement to the dynamic young safety director. The son of E. P. Chamberlin, assistant attorney general in the Taft administration, he went on to attend Michigan University and John

Marshall College of Law. He was a captain of the National Guard and a compensation referee for the State Industrial Commission before accepting the administrative assistant job.

He and his wife had befriended Eliot and Edna Ness soon after they rented their Bay Village cottage from the Chamberlins, who owned a large home next door.

"We used to visit back and forth and we became friends," Chamberlin said. "I grew to think of Eliot much as I would my own brother. I'd kid him about his work as a federal agent. I told him once that I'd hardly call it 'work,' so we went out on a raid together, and I'll never forget the way he pushed open the door. He didn't know what was behind it and he didn't seem to care. He just didn't know what fear was."

"Ness was always on the go, never keeping regular hours," said Jook Chamberlin, Robert's brother. "If something was happening, he'd say, 'We'd better take a look,' and the next thing you know he'd be across town and whoever happened to be with him went sailing along, too."

One of those passengers was Viktor Schreckengost, a Cleveland Heights resident who befriended Ness in the 1930s. He shared his memories during a 1997 interview with reporter Brian Albrecht of the *Cleveland Plain Dealer*. Schreckengost recalled attending a party in Cleveland Heights where Ness, after receiving an urgent phone call, invited him along for a ride into the city. The next thing Schreckengost knew, he was part of a convoy of cars roaring down congested Euclid Avenue at speeds of eighty miles per hour, sirens screaming, hearts pounding.

Once they arrived at the scene, Ness instructed his passenger to stay in the car. "He came out after ten or fifteen minutes and said, 'No problem. We got it solved.' I never did find out what the call was all about."

Schreckengost said this was one of many surprising things he learned about Ness. "The first time we met, I was looking for a big fellow, and here's this quiet guy who never liked to brag. He would just sit back, look you in the eye and listen, and then ask his questions. He always seemed to want to know more, almost daring you to tell him more because he seemed sincerely interested in what you were saying, kind of like a fascinated kid. He'd say, 'Come on, come on!' Not the kind of fellow you expected to be a gangbuster at all. In fact, he was the last person you'd think would have anything to do with Al Capone."

Schreckengost recalled that Ness did not carry his gun on most assignments. "I asked him why and he said, 'I don't need it, the holster's enough.' What he meant by that, I don't know."

In the midst of the police reorganization and crackdown on crime, Ness and his team had their attention diverted to the Great Lakes Exposition of August 1936, which brought an estimated four million visitors to Cleveland. Ness spent a great deal of time organizing security for the event and preparing an award-winning booth designed to boost Cleveland's image and rally public support for law enforcement. He also used the event to display the first "death mask," portraying the tattooed man, in the faint hope that somebody might recognize the victim.

Despite all the attention that was showered upon him during the expo, Ness welcomed the opportunity to return to the business at hand.

In September 1936, a transient sitting on an embankment along East Thirty-seventh Street in Kingsbury Run spotted the upper half of a man's torso rolling in the slow-moving waters. A white male, approximately twenty-five years old, the unidentified victim had been dead for about forty-eight hours. For the first time, the newspapers were reporting that police considered as many as six Cleveland-area murders to be the work of the same man, now called the "Mad Butcher" or "Torso Killer."

Pressured by politicians to calm public fears, Mayor Burton announced that Ness would be working with coroner Arthur J. Pearse to solve the crimes. Reluctantly, Ness visited the city morgue to view the remains and confer with the investigators. He then traveled to the area where the victim was found. Conferring with police, Ness summoned a search-and-rescue crew to dredge a nearby pool of stagnant water. As hundreds of people looked on in shock, the divers emerged with the lower half of the torso and parts of both legs. The following day's newspapers were crammed with sensationalized reports, biting editorials, reckless speculation, and revealing photographs. All of Cleveland now knew a monster was on the loose.

Ness immediately assigned twenty-five detectives to fan out over all of Cleveland and track down every lead, no matter how remote. He also organized a brutal roundup of all the vagrants and hoboes inhabiting Kingsbury Run. Officers paraded their hapless captives into police headquarters, where detectives grilled them extensively. Only a handful reported seeing anything that might be connected with the murders, and those clues were either inconsequential or discredited by further investigation.

Exhausted and frustrated by the five hours of interrogations, Ness had no sooner stepped out the door of Central Station than he was surrounded by newspaper reporters and photographers.

"You're the big G-man who's supposed to be solving this," one of the reporters shouted. "What are you doing?"

"Like everyone else, I want to see this psychopath caught," Ness responded angrily. "I'm going to do all I can to assist in the investigation, but I'm not going to be much help to you folks." Ness pushed his way through the crowd toward his car, ignoring further questions. This was the first time he had been anything but accommodating to the press, and his brusqueness was duly noted in the next day's editions.

Seeing that Ness needed some positive publicity, Clayton Fritchey provided it. "Thousand Young Dick Tracys Thrill & Cheer As Ness Tells How G-Men Got Capone Gang," read a banner headline in the *Cleveland Press* over Fritchey's story on Eliot's appearance before a group of Boy Scouts.

An editorial in the same edition cited a recent crime statistics summary. "There is one interesting—very interesting—paragraph in the report of Cleveland's Safety Director: 'Cases of vandalism totaled 89 this year, as against 300 for the same period last year.' For that single sentence, Mr. Ness, you are entitled to take a bow."

Ness designated Det. Sgt. James T. Hogan, his chief of homicide, to take charge of the Mad Butcher probe. James Badal, English professor at Cuyahoga County Community College and perhaps the foremost authority on the serial killings, said, "It has always been my feeling that Ness didn't particularly want any part of it. This was a man used to dealing with men like Al Capone who committed crimes for understandable reasons—greed, jealousy, power—and

Ness was smart enough to realize this was something new in the annals of crime, so he didn't want to get involved."

Hogan, working in conjunction with David Cowles, head of the police crime laboratory, summoned thirty-five Cleveland area law enforcement officials for a brainstorming session at the Central Station. They concluded that the killer probably lived in or near the third precinct, close to Kingsbury Run. His lifestyle or profession brought him into contact with vagrants and alcoholics on a regular basis. Considering the precision of the dismemberments, officials concluded that the murderer had probably received some type of medical and/or surgical training.

Based on the condition of the bodies, the absence of blood where most of the victims were found, and the likelihood that they had been carried or dragged a long distance, Ness told the group the killer was undoubtedly "a big man with the strength of an ox." He suggested investigators look for some type of "bloody laboratory" where the Mad Butcher performed his operations, even if that meant a house-to-house search of the region. Ness agreed to establish a special telephone exchange at City Hall, where the public could report evidence that might help police.

As a result of the lengthy meeting, two of the detective bureau's top men, Peter Merylo and Martin Zalewski, were assigned primary responsibility for the investigation. So began the most massive police investigation in Cleveland history. By the time the case—still "open" even today—would run its course, at least three thousand people would be interviewed, fifteen hundred of them by Merylo and Zalewski.

A study of homicide records within a three-hundred-mile radius of Cleveland produced two reports of dismemberments. One victim was a white male whose headless, decomposed body was found along some railroad tracks in Haverstraw, New York, about twenty miles from New York City. Investigators could find no other similarities between that slaying and the Mad Butcher's work.

The other killing, equally gruesome, was more intriguing. The nude, headless corpse of a male was discovered in the rail yards just outside the western Pennsylvania community of New Castle. Based on the way the victim had been decapitated and the rail link between

New Castle and Cleveland, Merylo and Zalewski concluded that the
Mad Butcher had struck again.

Ness sought to deflect the public's attention from the serial
killings by releasing results of his exhaustive investigation of police
corruption. His eighty-six-page report identified twenty high- or
midlevel officers alleged to be on the take; nine were immediately
suspended. Ness was able to document more than $1 million in
graft, calling it a "mere fraction" of the actual payments over the
past several years. The report told a shocking tale of bribery, intimidation, frame-ups, conspiracy, and case fixing. Clayton Fritchey put
his own spin on the report:

> For three months Mr. Ness has been working day and night run-
> ning down clues and amassing evidence. I have worked with him.
> For three months we turned the city inside out for elusive wit-
> nesses. The corruption uncovered stems from higher circles than
> the police department; the rank and file who have taken money
> were in many cases the victims of an evil system. In short, the
> department has been so controlled for the last twenty years that it
> could not breed or attract men of high character. The director
> discovered that young men coming into the department got off to
> a bad start by having to pay several hundred dollars for their job;
> anywhere from $500 to $750 for a sergeantcy, more for a lieu-
> tenancy and as much as $5,000 for a captaincy. The rank and file
> got their baptism of corruption at gambling and drinking parties
> given for superior officers and attended by one hundred or two
> hundred patrolmen.

Police padded their salaries by strong-arming businessmen and
others to purchase tickets or donate prizes to "police benefits," some of
which had already been held or never would be held. Ness and Fritchey
also revealed evidence of bootleg whiskey being sold out of the fourteenth precinct police station. Officers there were so brazen that they
would occasionally raid the homes of their buyers so they could confiscate the whiskey and sell it again. The names of dozens of witnesses
willing to testify against the offenders were turned over to county prosecutor Frank Cullitan. "Any action now is up to the prosecutor," Ness
told reporters at a press conference. "I'm going on vacation."

Cullitan, facing a tough challenge in the upcoming election, glee-fully prepared arrest warrants while Eliot and Edna Ness spent the next two weeks enjoying each other's company. They took cruises on Lake Erie, dined in the finest restaurants, and slept late into the morning hours. This was a trip that was long overdue. Eliot's time away from home, either attending to business or unwinding with his reporter friends, left Edna with only her cats for company. She longed for the good times—when they would sit back and talk, look through travel books making plans, attend a movie, or go small-boat sailing. Eliot apologized and said the long hours would end after he rid the police department of its bad apples, but there was no sign that would happen anytime soon.

Cullitan was reelected by a huge margin, but county coroner Arthur J. Pearse was not so fortunate. He was upset by a Democratic challenger, Samuel R. Gerber, who had seized on the Mad Butcher case to suggest Pearse was inept. Gerber, small and charismatic with a thin mustache and wavy, graying hair, was intelligent and industrious. He let it be known from the outset that he was unimpressed by the safety director's handling of the investigation.

Ness would not engage in verbal sparring. To reporters who asked him to comment on Gerber's declarations, he replied, "As I've said before, we are investigating these homicides and doing every-thing within our power to bring the killer or killers to justice. Just because a homicide investigation is under way doesn't mean we should drop all of our other work."

Michael Harwood went down fighting. With his trial on bribery and solicitation charges drawing near, his operatives learned the iden-tity of witnesses poised to testify against the captain. Some of them were lured to an apartment and plied with liquor by women decoys. In their intoxicated state, they were urged to repudiate their grand jury testimony and fabricate a scenario under which Ness was to have paid them to lie about Harwood.

Harwood, smiling and confident at the outset of his trial, soon bore a look of concern when he realized his witness-tampering plot had failed. Ness also attended the trial, but he was not a participant. Dressed in a natty brown suit and red tie, he glanced occasionally at Harwood and the jurors while trying to keep a low profile. Harwood was convicted of six of the seven felony counts against him and sentenced to a prison term of two to twenty years.

In a scene straight from Hollywood, the captain's daughter shuffled past Ness on her way out of the courtroom and spat on his shoulder, muttering a sarcastic, "Thank you, Mr. Ness." Ness, reaching for his handkerchief, did not respond. Later, he told a reporter, "I want to say one thing: There is nothing personal about this case. I am fighting for principle, that's all."

This was typical of Ness's approach to his job. "His style was to stop and think about a situation, then decide a response," said Dan Moore, one of Ness's closest friends during his years in Cleveland. "He wouldn't think of responding angrily to a woman who insulted him. Eliot tried to get along with as little conflict as possible, to be as nice to people as he could. In situations where normal people might get mad or resort to violence, Eliot would accomplish more with diplomacy. It was quite a character attribute."

Two lieutenants and four other officers implicated in the Harwood case either pleaded guilty or were convicted. Ness used evidence presented during the trial to suspend five more officers. Dozens of others faced less drastic disciplinary measures for misconduct or negligence. In some instances, to avoid a messy trial, Ness merely confronted the offender and asked for his resignation.

Cleveland's crackdown on police corruption was trumpeted in newspapers across the country. The *Cleveland Press* earned an award for civic achievement, while Ness received a citation from the Ohio Supreme Court for "outstanding completeness and care with which he assembled evidence against police officers." The Veterans of Foreign Wars honored Ness as the Outstanding Citizen of Cuyahoga County.

CHAPTER SEVENTEEN

A Better Cleveland

THE ONLY WAY TO give the city a respectable law enforcement agency, Eliot Ness believed, was to set that tone early in each officer's career. Using that argument, he persuaded the city council to provide money for a new three-month training program that would create an untainted, more professional police force. Lt. Patrick Lenahan was dispatched to the FBI National Academy to help develop the curriculum. Ness also contributed to the plan, based on information he obtained from the School of Police Science at the University of Chicago. A military philosophy of continuous training was incorporated into the system, with veteran officers required to attend training courses and pass written tests and physical examinations.

But the major focus was on the rookie officers, beginning even before they arrived for training. "The lack of character investigation of men appointed to the Cleveland Police Department is almost incomprehensible," Ness observed. "We need to attract a new class of men to police service." He insisted on full background checks and criminal history investigations of all recruits.

Officer candidates had to meet rigid eligibility standards. Once inside, they were required to demonstrate their proficiency in crime detection, marksmanship, self-defense, approach psychology, arrest procedure, and other aspects of modern law enforcement. Then they had to pass a civil service qualifying examination, which more than half of them failed. The training school Ness established eventually became the highly respected Cleveland Police Academy.

Ness swore in one class of rookie officers with this advice:

> If people have been accustomed to giving you things for nothing prior to your becoming a policeman, I suppose it's all right for you to continue to accept those things. However, if people who never gave you anything for free before now want to give you something without charge, you can conclude they are buying your badge and your uniform. . . . Avoid these entangling alliances. The first problem of the police department is to recognize the public we want to serve. Ninety-nine percent of the public wants the racketeers and the gangsters chased out of town and the law enforced. One percent of the public apparently doesn't. In the past the Police Department apparently has not always understood what public it is serving. From my investigations I know there has been a powerful, centrally organized underworld with a lot of influence. I think everyone knows I want a Police Department free from the influences of the underworld.

That same week, Ness appeared before the local League of Women Voters chapter, not only to promote his reforms, but also to garner support for his efforts to increase the number of officers on the force. He produced statistics confirming that Cleveland's police department was seriously understaffed when compared to other major U.S. cities. He urged the public not to expect miracles, reminding his audience that to be effective, an officer has to be "a diplomat, a marksman, a memory expert, a boxer, a wrestler, a sprinter, and an authority on a wide variety of subjects."

A handful of the more outstanding graduates were enrolled in follow-up training supervised by Ness. Under a cloak of secrecy, they learned the fine points of undercover work—from wiretapping and infiltration of known criminal outposts, to cultivating informants and tailing suspects. Among the early students was James M. Timber, who would become one of Cleveland's most famous law enforcement figures. Also in the original group was Richard Wagner, who later served as Cleveland's chief of police.

"Ness laid down the law," Wagner recalled. "He said, 'Here's my private phone number. If anyone asks you to take any money at any time, call me immediately. If you do get asked and don't call me, don't plan on being a police officer for very long.' He meant it, and it worked."

To nudge his recruits up in the ranks, Ness revamped the promotion system so marksmanship and other skills helped compensate for advancement historically awarded for mere seniority or, worse, payoffs to higher-ups. Many of Cleveland's more intelligent and capable young people were attracted to careers in law enforcement, recognizing that they had an opportunity to learn some of the best methods of police administration.

In a scenario similar to the Secret Six arrangement in Chicago, Ness secured donations from the chamber of commerce and the American Legion to launch an undercover fund. Many of the donors were Cleveland-area businessmen suffering from the mob's widening infiltration of commercial enterprises, both legal and illegal.

Ness looked for officers who distinguished themselves during training. He wanted men who were smart, brave, discreet, and above all, honest. From among the more promising recruits, Ness formed two units to combat corruption and inefficiency. The Minute Men, so named by reporters who followed the public safety director's activities, were a visible presence on the street. They reminded gamblers, bootleggers, prostitutes, extortionists, and even some police officers that times had changed. The presence of the Minute Men was also a cover for a second group, the Unknowns, consisting of "untouchable" police officers and detectives who collected information on patrolmen or commanders suspected of being corrupt.

The identity of the Unknowns was a closely guarded secret. Among the group were Arnold Sagalyn, a recent police academy graduate; Tom Clothey, who came in fresh from an investigation of police corruption in Saint Paul, Minnesota; and Keith Wilson, a former Alcohol Tax Unit agent who had worked for Ness earlier in his career and would eventually become a judge in Chicago.

Assistant safety director Robert Chamberlin was one of the few people who could persuade Ness to take time off. They took long walks together and sometimes attended football games or other sports events. Even during these off-hours, Chamberlin recalled, Ness had a hard time keeping his mind off his work.

Because of his strong local ties, Chamberlin assumed a major role in the investigation of union racketeering in the city. Through their strong-arm tactics, union thugs were scaring away out-of-town developers at a time when Cleveland could least afford to lose them. Ness and Chamberlin, working with the Unknowns, set up a sting operation at the massive Northern Ohio Food Terminal, where extortionists from local labor unions and the underworld had long been preying on farmers who sold their goods there. Through their wholesale acts of terrorism, they enforced their shakedown racket. The farmers either passed these added expenses on to their customers, or they avoided the market altogether, if they dared to. Truckers were also victims of the extortionists. If the demands weren't met, terminal employees refused to help, and produce was either confiscated or left to rot.

Officers posing as farmers' representatives gathered evidence that resulted in criminal charges against two of the city's most powerful union bosses: Harry Barrington, business agent of the Carpenters Union, and Harry Wayne, an officer of the Kosher Butchers Union. Grand jury indictments did not come easily; Ness's men investigated more than one hundred reports of witnesses being assaulted or threatened. The case would "blow the lid off racketeering practices in Cleveland," Ness said. As soon as Barrington was released on bail, he fled.

At the same time, another high-ranking police official was convicted on bribery charges. Deputy inspector Edwin C. Burns, a twenty-five-year veteran of the force and commanding officer of the corruption-filled Collinwood district, accepted bribes to protect dozens of criminal enterprises in his district.

Lt. John H. Nebe, another officer in this third decade with the department, was the next to fall. Head of the plainclothes police squad in Collinwood, Nebe was convicted of soliciting and accepting bribes. Witnesses testified that not only did Nebe demand twenty-five dollars or more per month to protect their bootlegging activities, he also allowed them to store their corn whiskey in the lieutenant's basement after being tipped off to an impending federal raid. "You have observed the depths to which a policeman can sink," chief assistant prosecutor Charles J. McNamee told jurors. "It is a despicable thing, falling just a little short of treason."

Among the more satisfying honors bestowed on Ness was the National Safety Council Award, recognizing his work in Cleveland during 1936. "The next time anybody tells you that individual opportunity is as dead as a dodo in this corporate age and the chance for adventure along with it, please introduce him to Eliot Ness," wrote one Chicago columnist, reporting on the honor. He continued:

> The former Chicago South Ender is director of public safety for Cleveland. The remarkable young man who found a dramatic challenge in an ordinary job represents a brand new school of crime smashers. . . . When the customary political favors were asked of him during his first days on the job, he would maintain a deadpan and draw doodlegrams on a pad until his callers got discouraged and left. He was handed a politics-ridden police force which was honeycombed with corruption, handed a shrinking budget and told in all seriousness to go ahead and enforce the law. What Ness proceeded to do for that city might well be examined by any city in America. In fact, other cities have begun to adopt some of Ness's ideas.

The Chicago column and much of the other publicity Ness received did not escape the notice of J. Edgar Hoover. Privately, Hoover was furious at the entire law enforcement establishment of Cleveland for an episode dating back to 1934. According to the director, FBI agents were on the brink of capturing Public Enemy Number One, Alvin Karpis, and another wanted criminal when local politicians and police officials in Cleveland tipped off the wanted men. Hoover also believed Cleveland policemen had helped Karpis and others pay huge sums to a skilled surgeon to alter their facial features to hide their identity.

Additionally, Hoover had an inherent distrust of Ness, which is reflected in the contents of a file found in Hoover's official papers. Hoover collected news clippings of Ness's appointment as director of public safety, along with a January 1, 1936, memo to the field, in which the FBI director described Ness as "not very cordially disposed to the

Bureau." Hoover took a strong personal interest in the Harvard Club raid, highlighting news clippings that lauded Ness for his role. One internal FBI memo went so far as to suggest "the raid was so planned to give Eliot Ness, recently appointed Safety Director, a political buildup."

Hoover was not inclined to share the spotlight with anyone. He wanted his agents to be efficient and anonymous, so a maverick who drew attention to himself did not fit. "An egomaniac" is the way an embittered George E. Q. Johnson Jr. described Hoover. "As far as Hoover was concerned, nobody else had anything to do with crime or deserved any credit. He was jealous of the publicity Eliot Ness got, and there was also friction between Hoover and my father because of the fame my father got at the time."

Ironically, Ness told anyone who would listen how much he admired J. Edgar Hoover, or at least his public persona. He often distributed to police officers a copy of a speech Hoover had delivered to support his premise that law enforcement must shift its focus "from crime detection to crime prevention."

These conflicting sentiments were the backdrop as Ness and U.S. district attorney Emerick B. Freed arranged for a meeting in Washington with the FBI director. Ostensibly, the session was called to iron out jurisdictional issues with the enforcement of federal laws covering police graft, bootlegging, tax evasion, prostitution, and high-stakes gambling. Ness also hoped to persuade Hoover to provide instructors for Cleveland's police academy. And Ness was anxious to impress the director in the hope of fulfilling his dream of joining the bureau.

He was disappointed to discover, however, that Hoover could spare only a few minutes for him and Freed, and then the director appeared to show little interest in the Cleveland situation. "The director's position appears to be that local criminal activities are best handled locally, unless they rise to a certain level," Ness wrote in a memo to Mayor Harold Burton. "As to what that level might be, one can only speculate, because it was not made clear."

In the wake of the Burns and Nebe corruption trials, the Mad Butcher struck again. On February 23, 1937, the partial remains of a seventh victim washed ashore along Lake Erie, east of Bratenahl. The upper portion of a woman's torso was discovered by Robert

Smith while he was combing the beach for driftwood. This was the same area where the mutilated torso of another woman had come ashore in 1934. Unlike any of the other victims, this woman had not died of decapitation. Her head had been removed after her death. The lower portion of the torso would float ashore some three months later. She was never identified.

There were similarities to the Kingsbury Run murders. The torso was severed at the waist. "Neatly done, with surgical skill," county coroner Samuel R. Gerber reported. Like the others, the head had been removed with a clean, bold stroke.

Ness called upon his friends in the press to downplay the discovery, to no avail, particularly after Gerber released detailed information. Ness then pulled both the Minute Men and the Unknowns off their assignments so they could search the streets, mental hospitals, taverns, and slums for evidence. He also drew the Nickel Plate Railroad police into the case, pressuring them to interrogate the hoboes and vagabonds who hopped the trains at Kingsbury Run.

Taking their cue from the victims themselves, several policemen—Lt. J. Peter Merylo among them—dressed as derelicts and set themselves up as potential targets in the shantytowns and taverns. Merylo and a couple of others even posed as hoboes in boxcars and lived in the shack enclaves, hoping to lure the Mad Butcher to approach them. They referred to themselves as "butcher bait."

Police asked citizens who noticed bloodstains in unusual places to notify authorities. Rewards of up to five thousand dollars were posted, prompting one nineteen-year-old man to accidentally shoot himself in the leg while stalking the killer.

Desperate for leads, police targeted entire groups for scrutiny, from medical professionals and slaughterhouse workers to game hunters and mental patients. With each killing, more theories abounded. One investigator suggested the killer was a victim of trypanosomiasis—a disease that destroys red blood corpuscles—and was seeking blood replenishment.

It's unclear whether the Mad Butcher was aware of these measures or not, but what is clear is that his killing spree continued. In June 1937 fourteen-year-old Russell Lauer discovered a human skull in a field under the Lorain-Carnegie Bridge. Next to it was a burlap bag containing the decaying remains of a petite black woman eventually identified as forty-year-old Rose Wallace, a resident of Scovill Avenue. Police interrogated everyone they could find who may have had contact with the victim, but none of the leads moved them any closer to the killer.

Public unrest was growing, and much of the criticism was being directed at Mayor Burton and Ness. Many wondered why Cleveland's chief law enforcement officers devoted so much attention to wrongdoing by police officers and union operatives while the Mad Butcher's killing spree continued.

At about this time the national news media focused on the aggressive actions of the G-man who fearlessly attacked Al Capone's breweries a few years earlier. From the *Christian Science Monitor:*

> A year of Eliot Ness as Cleveland's Safety Director has been marked by the transition from conspicuous crime to conspicuous crime prevention. Hunted underworld characters no longer feel safe here, where they formerly sought and found refuge. Gamblers and promoters of vice, whose activities honeycombed certain sections of the city, have run to cover. Mild-mannered, soft-spoken and quick to smile, Mr. Ness looks like anything but a giant-killer, but he's proved all of that when he's come to grips with the giants of crime.

Two of Cleveland's crime lords found themselves with a dose of double trouble in the summer of 1937, the result of a raid that Ness and Chamberlin orchestrated during the recess of a highly publicized tax evasion trial. Defendants Maxie Diamond and Philip Goldberg, charged with defrauding the government out of more than $150,000 in taxes, made the mistake of visiting Diamond's gambling joint at 1446 East Ninth Street, near Superior Avenue, for a lunch break. Moments after their arrival, Chamberlin and six city police officers were on the scene and Ness was not far behind.

Diamond's joint had been raided three or four other times, but investigators found little evidence of gambling activities. On this occasion, however, to lessen the chance of a tip-off, Ness and Chamberlin obtained warrants through a reputable municipal court judge, rather than the politically infiltrated tax clerk's office at Central Police Station. Diamond and his cohorts had constructed a secret room in the back of this restaurant, with a trap door and hidden panel to permit gamblers to escape or hide when signaled by the bell-and-light alarm system. Secret recesses were built into the walls as hiding places for racing sheets, telephones, betting slips, playing cards, and other gambling paraphernalia.

Ten men, including Diamond and Goldberg, were arrested on the scene. Police also confiscated two loaded revolvers, race betting slips, blackjack equipment, and dice cups. Diamond was livid, telling reporters that Ness and Chamberlin had timed the raid in an effort to sway the jury in the tax evasion case.

"This was probably downtown Cleveland's busiest and biggest bookie and gambling joint," Ness replied. "Mr. Diamond should, quite frankly, be gratified that it was able to operate unimpeded for so long. This situation suggests we still have a lot of work to do in terms of cleaning up the Police Department."

Chief Matowitz, reacting to those strong comments, took a page from the book of Theodore Roosevelt, who had crusaded against gambling as New York City police commissioner almost forty years earlier. He ordered officers to patrol sections where there were gambling activities in progress and take down the names of each patron that entered. Many protested this as an invasion of privacy and pointed the finger of blame at Ness, accusing him of being too zealous.

Trouble was brewing for the administration from organized labor, as well. Union leaders labeled Burton and Ness as too sympathetic to wealthy industrialists bent on destroying the city's labor organizations. The situation came to a head after the Congress of Industrial Organizers ordered thousands of workers to walk off their jobs at the Republic Steel Mill in the Flats, prompting companies to bring in scab laborers. Brawls and vandalism ensued, and the industrial leaders turned to the mayor's office for help. Ness sent out the police, armed with clubs and tear gas, and ordered them to disperse the picketers. Barricades were erected outside the factories, and police were directed to arrest anyone who trespassed on these designated "dangerous strike zones."

After sympathetic union members arrived to swell the picketers' ranks, the mob crashed through the barricades and blocked the replacement workers from entering the factories. Mayor Burton pan-icked and called in the National Guard. Hundreds of guardsmen descended on the Flats, equipped with riot gear, rifles, and bayonets. Troopers were positioned at each entrance to allow employees, both union-busters and scabs, to report to work if they wished. Union members finally backed off and the plant reopened.

The peace, however, was short-lived. Weeks later, sixty people were injured and more than one hundred cars damaged in fighting between strikers and nonstrikers. The violence broke out at night and escalated rapidly. Tear-gas bombs flew, shots rang out, many strikers were hit by cars, and fistfights broke out. Away from Republic Steel, a union meeting hall was vandalized. The following morning, Ness sent dozens more police officers to join the National Guard members in keeping the strikers from positioning them-selves within five hundred yards of the steel mill. This quelled the disturbances while the steelworkers union and Republic moved closer to a settlement, and the violence finally subsided.

During ongoing patrols, Albert Mahaffey, one of the National Guardsmen, was peering into the waters of the Cuyahoga River off the Third Street Bridge as a tugboat passed. In the boat's wake what he at first thought to be a dressmaker's dummy was actually the lower half of a man's body. Over the next few days, searchers found many other body parts, including much of the upper torso wrapped in newspapers and crammed in a burlap bag. Investigators determined that the victim was a white male, approximately thirty years old. His abdomen and his heart had been ripped out, repre-senting a new element of violence in the killer's approach. The Mad Butcher's body count, as best as investigators could determine, now stood at nine.

Criticism of the city's police department had never been harsher. Ness took steps to deflect the negative publicity by calling a press conference to announce the latest crime statistics. They showed that serious crime had plummeted 25 percent during his first eighteen months as public safety director. Arrests and convictions were 20 percent higher than the previous year.

"Most important," Ness told the reporters, "organized crime is moving out of Cleveland and our police officers are more honest, more professional. We have made an excellent start and, with the public's support, we can make a lot more progress."

On the heels of the Republic Steel dispute, Ness and police chief Matowitz came under fire by the International Ladies' Garment Workers Union for breaking up picketers at the Federal Knitting Mills. Violence erupted when unionized workers at the Industrial Rayon Corporation tried to block laborers from entering the factory during a strike. The fact that Ness and Matowitz had the women arrested on assault charges prompted harsh criticism. Mayor Burton assigned a bodyguard, David Kerr, to accompany the safety director for about two weeks while the labor unrest was at its peak.

"Ness was a likable guy," Kerr recalled. "He attracted the newspaper men, that's for sure. He always had them around him when he had lunch, just about every day, but I can see why—he was making news, plus he would pick up the check."

Carpenters Union head Harry Barrington could run, but he could not hide. Federal agents found him in California and held him behind bars while extradition papers were prepared. Once Barrington was back in Cleveland, Ness and Chamberlin visited him in his prison cell, hoping to strike a deal. The feisty union boss initially wouldn't hear of it, but when faced with the possibility of a fifteen-year sentence on extortion charges, he had a change of heart. Barrington's information was a bonanza for investigators who had been trying for years to get the goods on two particularly powerful labor leaders: Donald A. Campbell, president of the Painters District Council and Glaziers Union, and John M. McGee, who headed the Laborers District Council and Window Washers Union.

The duo had built a brutal and efficient army of hitmen and professional bombers who terrorized hundreds of Cleveland-area business owners. Any builder or merchant who bought glass from suppliers other than those under Campbell's control paid a stiff price. Businesses had great difficulty purchasing insurance coverage. Even the window-washers were involved in the scheme.

The Painters Council was so powerful that homeowners needed "permission" to paint their own houses. If they didn't buy their paint from approved suppliers or hire the right painters, the consequences could be frightening, let alone expensive. Unions also exacted a "hiring fee" from business owners for any new worker added to the payroll. Construction projects were halted when union officials demanded additional payoffs. The stubborn few who resisted found their windows smashed or worse. Dynamite and acid bombs were also used by the union tacticians to get their point across.

Politicians intent on unseating Harold Burton made Eliot Ness's union-busting a major campaign issue. The Democratic forces said that what Cleveland needed was "not a G-man from Chicago," but rather a local safety director who understood and could effectively deal with the city's problems. Burton's response was straight and to the point: "Eliot Ness works hard and he serves the public, no one else."

As effective as his opponents' tactics were, Burton survived the 1937 election by a narrow margin and promptly reaffirmed his support for Ness, as did the *Plain Dealer:*

> Voters agree Harold Burton needs two more years to carry on the war against racketeers and other law violators started by Eliot Ness. The community hopes for prompt steps in this direction. Ness has been a great asset to the administration. With the free hand given him by Burton, his achievements in bringing big criminals to justice should be multiplied in the months now ahead.

To the Democrats, the *Plain Dealer* said, "The party needs to prove to the public that in its ranks there are men to whom government represents an opportunity for public service and not a call to the trough."

On November 7 Ness and Chamberlin drove to Ann Arbor, Michigan, to watch the Ohio State–Michigan college football game. Upon his return late that night, Ness received a telephone call from his brother, Charles, a successful businessman in Indianapolis, informing him that their mother had died of a heart attack in her sleep the previous night. Seventy-three-year-old Emma Ness had been living with Eliot's older sister, Effie, a public school teacher, since the death of her husband five years earlier. She was unknown in Cleveland, but the local newspapers still memorialized her.

"Mrs. Ness, a kindly, quiet-speaking woman, concealed her pride in the son who had been doing big things in law enforcement for a dozen years," the *Cleveland News* editorialized. "She acted as if it was to be expected of the boy who had made his own decisions as a youth."

The *Cleveland Press* added: "Mrs. Emma Ness was a mother. To her came the happiness of seeing her hopes and sacrifices rewarded by the fine careers of her children. The city and the nation owe a debt to her and mothers like her who mold character into their sons and daughters and thus determine the fate of the world."

Eliot and Edna drove to Illinois for a small funeral service attended by family members and a few close friends. This was the final time the five Ness siblings would be together; Eliot would never again set foot in Chicago.

Upon his return to Cleveland, Ness went after the labor racketeers with a vengeance. He rounded up dozens of witnesses, many of them from New York and Chicago, having been forced from the city by strong-arm tactics. "Capital has been driven out of Cleveland," Ness declared, "because those who wish to spend it here have come to believe that racketeering spokesmen for the unions must either be bought off or fought openly with little chance of victory."

One by one, almost forty business operators took the witness stand during a series of trials in February 1938 to tell how Campbell, McGee, and their accomplices bashed, bombed, and bullied them. This in itself was a coup for Ness, since businessmen had previously complained of the terrorism but steadfastly refused to testify for fear of retribution. Union members also risked the wrath of their colleagues to testify how Campbell and McGee had protected their leadership positions by fixing elections.

One of the prime witnesses was Ness's friend Vernon Stouffer, president of the restaurant chain that would evolve into a frozen-food empire. He testified about vandals smashing the windows of his downtown restaurant, Stouffer Playhouse Square Restaurant and Tavern, with ball bearings when he refused to bow to the extortionists' demands.

Campbell and McGee were convicted and sentenced to one to five years. Cleveland newspapers, though often sympathetic to union interests, heaped praise on Ness, as did the national news media. *Newsweek* lauded him for successfully combating police corruption, vice, and union racketeering. The magazine compared him with another Republican reformist, Thomas Dewey of New York.

Ness still had his enemies. The American Federation of Labor dispatched investigators to Washington to pore through Prohibition Bureau records in search of blemishes in the safety director's past. Except for an affinity for alcohol and suggestions of brutality early in his career, they found no ammunition.

He also came under fire from Samuel R. Gerber, the Cuyahoga County coroner. The two locked horns in April 1938 after the lower half of a woman's leg was discovered lodged against a tree limb over-hanging the flood-swollen waters of the Cuyahoga River. Gerber, who had both medical certification and a law degree, concluded that the Mad Butcher had struck again, but Ness considered the declaration premature and chided the coroner for what he perceived as an effort to discredit the police department. Following a heated exchange, Ness called in a respected pathologist from Western Reserve University to review the evidence. Gerber was so outraged that he blocked the entrance of the medical examiner's office and refused to allow the pathologist to see the limb.

Unfortunately for Ness, further evidence surfaced four weeks after the initial discovery and confirmed Gerber's suspicions. Two burlap bags were pulled from a section of the Cuyahoga near the West Third Street Bridge. They contained more severed body parts matching the leg of a woman now referred to as Victim No. 10. The same element of savagery evident with Victim No. 9 was present. Police tried to trace the course of the victim's head by dropping a ten-pound ham wrapped in a burlap bag into the river to check the flow of the current. A plaster death mask was also added to the police department's collection.

Desperate to silence his critics, Ness called in Chamberlin and detectives Merylo and Zalewski to sweep through the Kingsbury Run area in search of evidence. Police rummaged through tents, home-made shelters, junk piles, campfires, and abandoned railroad cars, looking for bones, bloodstains, saws, or any other evidence of the Mad Butcher's presence, but they came up empty.

"This killer has great cunning," Ness told the *Cleveland Plain Dealer.* "He certainly doesn't leave many, if any, clues. About all we have to go on is that one of the victims we've been able to identify was a pervert and another was a prostitute. This man seems to specialize in the sort of people nobody is likely to miss."

In contrast to Ness's low-key approach, Gerber used great anatomical detail in sharing with the public all of the evidence he had collected. Reporters hung on the coroner's every word, and Gerber's popularity continued to grow.

Ness was thankful that another public official was attracting the news media's attention. It gave him an opportunity to focus on a serious problem ignored by his predecessors: traffic control. Cleveland had more traffic-related deaths and injuries than almost any other American city. When police officials wanted to ease a veteran officer toward retirement, it was common practice to assign him to "Siberia," a derisive term for the poorly administered traffic division.

Ness took the opposite approach, appointing some of his most energetic and innovative officers to a new accident prevention bureau. He also sent word throughout "Siberia" that officers who were caught drinking on the job, taking bribes to ignore violations, or failing to take their work seriously could lose their jobs and their retirement benefits.

He tightened motor vehicle inspection standards, cracked down on speeders and drunken drivers, and worked with community leaders and city officials to restrict traffic to areas with high accident rates. One of the most obvious and most effective solutions was the establishment of one-way streets in narrow or congested sections. Posters and flyers appeared everywhere, thanks to the support Ness received from business groups, schools, churches, and civic organizations. Taxicab spare-tire covers carried the "Drive Safely, Walk Sensibly" slogan, as did huge posters at professional sports venues. Ness even persuaded the Cleveland Musicians Union to close each concert with a reminder to the audience to "Drive Safely, Walk Sensibly."

Mayor Burton appointed a Cleveland Traffic Committee composed of public-spirited citizens to consider improvements—engineering studies, increased lighting, police and court reforms, public education, and legislation. An incentive plan rewarded police officers in precincts that had the fewest traffic accidents and the most arrests. For the first time, drivers who failed to pay their fines or appear for hearings lost their privileges, and motorists who committed multiple violations were tracked down and jailed.

Police were required to attend specialized accident investigation training. "Whoopee Squads" assembled to keep watch over imbibing drivers on New Year's Eve became regular weekend fixtures on the more heavily traveled thoroughfares. Money flowing into the city's coffers from stiffer fines and increased arrests was used to finance new police cars and communications equipment. Cleveland police unveiled a fleet of thirty-two new red-white-and-light-cream Ford squad cars.

The Cleveland Police Emergency Mobile Patrol was established, consisting of twelve trucks operated by teams of police officers trained in first aid. These vehicles, forerunners of today's ambulances, were stocked with modern lifesaving equipment. Police cars and other emergency vehicles carried two-way radios patched into a communications center at Central Station. Anyone who needed to contact the police or the emergency mobile patrol could do so with a single telephone call. A teletype system helped criminal investigators exchange information with other cities.

The eyes of the nation's public safety officials were on Cleveland to see the impact and feasibility of implementing wide-scale scientific traffic control and accident-reduction safeguards in a major city.

To promote these reforms, precinct captains held neighborhood meetings, while Ness worked the luncheon circuit. Often, he brought along a two-way radio. As a test, he would summon police and measure how long it took for an officer to respond. Sometimes Ness arranged to have a policeman hide under the speakers' table. As soon as he placed the call, the officer would pop up and announce, "At your service, sir!" much to the audience's delight.

Ness's study of the fire department's deficiencies also began to bear fruit. After taking an inventory of leaky hoses, poor-fitting hydrant connectors, and dilapidated trucks, he persuaded the city council to approve a reorganization plan that called for stricter fire safety codes, new equipment, and advanced training for firefighters. All in all, it was an unprecedented effort for a major American city. Within a year's time, traffic fatalities dropped from 247 to 68 and nonfatal car accidents from 2,607 to 1,589.

Ness next turned his attention to a problem that had been festering in the city for generations.

CHAPTER EIGHTEEN

Troubled Times

SOME OF ELIOT NESS'S most impressive, least publicized, and longest-lasting accomplishments took place on the streets of Cleveland where violent youth gangs had staked out their territorial claims. Vandalism, fights, and burglaries had risen to alarming numbers, particularly in the "Roaring Third" precinct. Ness, dressed in a sweatshirt and casual slacks, met with the gang leaders on their own turf. With his quiet sincerity, he coaxed the restless youths to air their concerns and discuss their interests.

A language wall had developed between foreign-born parents who spoke little English and their American-born children, to whom English was first language. Many of the youths had rarely held a meaningful conversation with an adult. Once they got over their suspicions, they opened up to Ness. He won them over by focusing on the gang leaders, who saw it as a mark of prestige to be invited to meet with the safety director. Ness promised the youths that the city would provide recreational opportunities, including basketball courts, baseball fields, gymnasiums, swimming pools, tennis courts, and playgrounds. In return, they pledged to police their own ranks in curbing illegal activities.

Ness then went to work to keep his side of the bargain with a two-pronged approach, one designed to meet the needs of the juveniles and the other to help young men between the ages of eighteen and twenty-seven. He established Boy Scout troops and recruited young police officers and firemen to serve as leaders. Encouraged by police officers, many Cleveland merchants signed up as sponsors. Ness himself was named to the executive council of the Boy Scouts of America.

He also worked out partnerships with schools and churches for youths to use their recreational facilities. Ness spent many nights and weekend hours building rapport with the troubled youths, and he persuaded many of them to enter the Civilian Conservation Corps. For younger children, he organized a fun-based Dick Tracy Detective Squad, complete with membership cards, crime prevention materials, and safety tips. At its peak, the squad numbered more than one thousand members.

The police department reorganization of early 1938 resulted in five of the seventeen precinct stations being closed. These were turned over to the youth groups as headquarters for their activities. Within six months, more than five thousand young people had joined these "Boys' Clubs," which became centers of juvenile life and social activities. Activities ranged from athletic competition to movies, music education, and hobby clubs, many organized by police officers or other community volunteers.

"Keep them off the streets and keep them busy," was the public safety director's advice to civic leaders and city officials. "It's much better to spend time and money starting and keeping them straight than it is to spend even more time and money catching them in the wrong, then trying to set them straight. The value of this work is evident when you realize that more than 75 percent of all criminals of whatever age had experience as juvenile delinquents."

With the support of Mayor Harold Burton, Ness assembled a committee of one hundred citizens to study the causes and treatment of juvenile delinquency and devise the means of reducing crime with the idea of "reclaiming" young delinquents before they matured into serious offenders. Ness established a separate juvenile unit in the police department, designating some of his younger officers for a new beat that focused exclusively on youth problems, often in conjunction with family service agencies. One of the social workers who worked with this juvenile unit, Katharine Dorfeld, marveled at the young safety director's accomplishments.

"I knew some of the families of these salvaged kids," Dorfeld said. "They were very appreciative of Eliot Ness and his common-sense approach. He was certainly persistent, the kind of man who was able to command respect. Eliot never got the credit he deserved for helping the inner-city kids, but it was something he was proud of and something people should remember him for."

The needs of young men could best be met by getting them jobs that would make them self-supporting and give them a sense of responsibility. Numerous civic-minded employers were encouraged to make openings. With the help of the Works Progress Administration, night classes were instituted. Youths who lately had used blackjacks and guns were taught how to use slide rules, micrometers, and lathes. Ness took great pride in the fact that only a handful of these young people failed to make the grade with their new employers. After coming under fire by some opponents for "coddling punks," Ness silenced his critics by showing early statistics confirming a dramatic decrease in juvenile crime. After three years, more than five hundred young men had been placed in permanent positions.

At the same time, the summer of 1938 was passing with no new developments in the Mad Butcher case and fewer media reports criticizing the public safety director for failing to apprehend the killer. On August 16, however, three men foraging for scrap metal in a dump site at East Ninth and Lakeside, near what is now Burke Lakefront Airport, found the torso of a woman wrapped in a man's double-breasted blue blazer and then wrapped again in an old quilt. The victim's head, legs, and arms were discovered nearby, wrapped in brown butcher paper. As detective sergeant Hogan searched for something in which to carry the remains, he picked up a large can. Out rolled the skull of another man. Police combed the site, eventually coming across the skeletal remains of the other victim. Neither of these victims, each around thirty-five years old, was identified. The same pattern had been used to dismember them.

Coroner Samuel R. Gerber noted that the discovery "reminded police once more that somewhere in Cleveland lurks a headhunter, undoubtedly crazed, probably motivated by either true insanity of the schizophrenic type or else a borderline type of insanity such as a constitutional psychopathic state accompanied by aberrant sexual desires."

Lt. J. Peter Merylo was not as eloquent in his description: "He's as regular, as coldly efficient, and as relentless as an executioner when the mood to kill comes over him."

The next morning, Ness had to push himself through the mass of reporters who jammed City Hall, demanding answers. Mayor Burton and Ness conferred for more than an hour. Ness then left City Hall, ignoring the reporters, and traveled to Central Station to join police chief Matowitz, assistant safety director Chamberlin, and detectives Merylo and Zalewski. That session, which lasted for three hours, produced one of the most controversial acts in the history of Cleveland law enforcement.

Police officers from all over the city converged at Central Station on the night of August 18, 1938. At around midnight, the group emerged to form a caravan of eleven squad cars, four police vans, and three fire trucks. With news reporters and photographers falling in behind, the vehicles progressed to the Flats. They stopped at Canal Street, near the Eagle Street ramp, and huddled for a brief strategy session. In the distance, down a weed-covered knoll, several small campfires were burning, silhouetting a series of flimsy shacks and shelters where the Cuyahoga River twists behind Public Square.

About ten officers spread out around the perimeter of this makeshift village. Ness and twenty-five others, armed with guns, axes, and torches, then moved out in the direction of the vagrants' quarters. Reporters who tried to follow were ordered away. Ness, who walked several steps ahead of the others, carried a bright flashlight in one hand and an ax in the other. Once everyone was in position, he turned around and flashed a signal up the hill.

The area suddenly became illuminated by bright floodlights as the fire trucks rumbled forward. Ahead of them, Ness and the others charged through the heavy brush and rubbish, reaching the shanties in less than a minute. An assortment of hoboes and derelicts began to emerge, shielding their eyes from the bright lights in bewilderment. A few of them panicked and tried to flee, only to be chased down and handcuffed by officers. Within a matter of minutes, forty people were loaded into the police vehicles and taken to Central Station, where they were jammed into holding cells for later questioning.

The convoy progressed farther into the Flats and launched a similar raid on another enclave under the Lorain-Carnegie Bridge, then progressed to Kingsbury Run to clear out a third shantytown beneath the East Thirty-seventh Street Bridge. These two raids netted another twenty-five homeless people.

At daybreak, while police were still grilling the detainees, Ness and some of the other officers combed through the debris, hoping to find evidence of the Mad Butcher's presence. Then, as reporters looked on in disbelief, Ness ordered firemen to set the shacks ablaze. Within minutes, thick black clouds of smoke curled into the air and a heavy stench enveloped the Flats.

Nine of the men and two of the women were wanted on criminal charges. Another twenty-five people convinced police they were employed or had family members who would care for them. The rest were temporarily jailed on vagrancy charges and eventually directed to social service agencies.

As well intentioned as the act may have been, it produced no evidence that helped in the investigation. Ness declared that if nothing else, officials had cleaned up part of Cleveland and perhaps removed some of the Mad Butcher's potential victims. Furthermore, he pointed out almost ghoulishly, fingerprints taken from some of those who were detained might later help in the identification of murder victims.

Ness expected public praise for his aggressive action. Instead, he received mixed reviews. Some Clevelanders applauded him for eliminating an all-too-visible sign of the city's economic and social problems. At the same time, he was criticized for insensitivity to the city's less fortunate.

"To most of us, the arrest of the Mad Butcher would seem more important than the completing of arrangements for the identification of a possible corpse," scolded the *Cleveland Press* in a prominently placed editorial entitled "Misguided Zeal." "That such Shantytowns exist is a sorrowful reflection upon the state of society. The throwing into jail of men broken by experience and the burning of their wretched places of habitation will not solve the economic problem. Nor is it likely to lead to the solution of the most macabre mystery in Cleveland's history."

Ness weathered the storm of public criticism without complaint. Only a few close friends, Bob Chamberlin among them, realized that the public safety director was preoccupied. His private life was rapidly deteriorating, draining him of the enthusiasm and energy he had brought to the job.

Ness was not inclined to attend social functions at night, perhaps because he was enjoying them so frequently during the day. He and some of his cronies regularly joined the noontime gaiety at downtown Cleveland spots such as the Golden Pheasant and Lotus Gardens, where big-name bands entertained with midday sets. This was not an unusual phenomenon in the 1930s; executives, government leaders, and others who could afford it saw the lunch break as an opportunity to mix business with pleasure.

Earlier in their relationship, Edna had enjoyed dressing up, meeting important people, and appearing at her husband's side. As time passed, she felt imprisoned. Eliot wasn't home enough, and when he was, she felt a certain distance. When she was younger and more impressionable, Edna was blind to Eliot's shortcomings. Now, she believed, his career meant more to him than their relationship, and she was less tolerant.

The Nesses concluded that their relationship was irrevocably broken. Eliot agreed to move to a small apartment in the Hampton House complex, at the corner of West Boulevard and Clifton Street in Cleveland. Originally, Ness had secured this apartment at the request of Mayor Burton, who faced flak because his safety director was not a bona fide resident of Cleveland. Ness stayed there on occasion when he worked late into the night, but the Bay Village cottage had been his primary residence until the separation. He expressed concern that the divorce would damage his reputation in Cleveland and even entertained thoughts of resigning, but Edna talked him out of it. She assured him that, despite their problems, she would attend social functions with him to preserve his public image. Any chance of reconciliation, however, ended when Edna returned to Chicago to live with relatives. She and Eliot never spoke again.

Ness's immediate reaction was to bury himself even deeper in his work, spending sixteen or more hours on the job each day. He unveiled thirty new Harley-Davidson motorcycles, equipped with two-way radios controlled from Central Station. Citizens no longer had to call an individual police station, but could call one number for either the police or the emergency patrol.

When local industries thumbed their noses at the city's new anti-smoke code, designed to curb air pollution, Ness chartered an airplane to carry him and two assistants over the city, looking for violators. Some of those ignoring the ordinance were federal government defense contractors who used political connections to avoid prosecution.

Ness became a regular guest on a popular radio show, *Masterminds: Attention,* which aired on Cleveland's WGAR. Ness was among the celebrity panelists grilling witnesses who could answer yes or no to questions about a mystery. Ness was often so quick to solve the case that the show's producers had to scramble to fill the remaining airtime.

While coroner Gerber attracted most of the public attention, Ness quietly consulted with respected criminologists from across the country for advice on the Mad Butcher case. Still believing that the best way to identify the killer was to locate the building where he dismembered his victims, he formed six search teams, each consisting of three police officers and a fireman. They inspected every home, hotel, boarding house, and commercial establishment in the third precinct under the guise of fire safety code enforcement. The raiders discovered poverty and squalor beyond their worst expectations, but not a shred of evidence.

Editorial writers were chiding Ness, not only for his inability to find the Mad Butcher, but also for his visits to some of Cleveland's trendy nightspots with frequent and varied female companions. The city's conservative, Catholic population was critical of Ness when he calmly confirmed reports of his divorce. "It was a mutual decision," he told reporters. "We both realized a mistake was made, and we set out to correct it."

Tiring of his all-work-and-no-play lifestyle, Ness soon became such a regular visitor at the Bronze Room in the Hotel Cleveland and the Vogue Room of the Hollenden Hotel that the owners reserved a table for his exclusive use. He liked to dance into the early morning hours and not limit himself to just one or two dancing partners.

Occasionally, when he wanted to slip out of the public spotlight, he would board the C&D boat line. These long evening cruises featured gin rummy games and quiet relaxation as the boat traveled to Detroit then returned to Cleveland in the predawn hours. Observers said Ness enjoyed the card games, but often would slip out onto the deck to look out over the water or walk the boat's perimeter by himself.

Ness also liked to get together with his friend and eventual successor, Al Sutton, to shoot .22 rifles at cans and other targets along the Lake Erie shoreline. "Good, clean fun," Sutton said of the hobby. "Just a way to pass some time and relax. You couldn't do that today, though, without getting arrested."

The mischievous side of Ness also started to emerge. Once, he invited Gov. Martin L. Davey of Ohio and state securities commissioner Dan T. Moore Jr. to join him for a drink at a small nightclub. Ness and Moore had hit it off in their mutual pursuit of Cleveland crime figures. While the three men chatted, a man at the bar created commotion by threatening a waitress. A brief scuffle ensued, voices were raised, and suddenly a shot rang out. The governor, concerned about the publicity that would result from his presence at the scene, bolted for the fire escape. It turned out that Ness had hired two actors to play out a practical joke.

"I was in on it," recalled Moore during a 1995 interview. "Eliot had pulled that stunt on a couple of other people, but doing it to the governor was really something. That's just the way Eliot was at that stage of his life—a fun-loving guy who wasn't beyond some fun. He'd do things like invite a seven-foot-tall woman to a party and pair her up on a blind date with the shortest man in the room, just for laughs."

At times Ness seemed to be poking fun at some of the elite members of Cleveland's social scene. He told Moore he never felt comfortable in the high-society circles. Once, he planted recording devices at a party in his home and, late that night, blasted portions of the tapes for all to hear. Some of the victims of this prank were not amused and left in anger.

Despite his outward composure and a seemingly constant need to draw attention to himself, Ness could also be shy and nervous. He developed a habit of biting his fingernails to the quick and picking at his thumb with an index finger until the skin was shaved away. He smoked cigarettes, but usually extinguished them after taking only a few puffs. Sometimes he would unwrap a cigar and chew on the end until it was a mushy mess, never lighting it. He carried a silver dollar in his pocket, describing is as "my lucky coin," and often flipped it to reduce stress.

Ness had plenty of reasons to be nervous—the demise of his marriage, the negative publicity, the frustrations of the Mad Butcher case, the FBI's apparent lack of interest in him, and the pressures he felt as he faced off against some of Cleveland's most powerful underworld figures.

His Minute Men and Molnar's Raiders charged into a large home on East Thirty-sixth Street, where a dozen men working for crime boss "Big Angelo" Lonardo were arrested for running a multimillion dollar numbers racket. Among those taken into custody was Moe Dalitz, chief of the powerful Mayfield Road Mob.

Ness arranged for a secret grand jury to be convened on April 26, 1939, resulting in indictments against almost twenty-five gangland figures. Among the notables were "Big Angelo" Lonardo, "Little Angelo" Scirrca, Charles Pollizi, "Johnny King" Angersola, and Angersola's brother George. Several Mayfield Road Mob members were tipped off and fled Cleveland before the arrest warrants could be served, further evidence that the organization's stranglehold had been loosened.

Word leaked out that Moe Dalitz had offered substantial rewards in return for the identities of the jurors and the witnesses in the pending trials. Ness responded by placing jury members, witnesses, and some members of the prosecution team—himself included—under round-the-clock protection.

"We will not be bullied around by those forces who believe that they are above the law," he declared during a press conference. "We're a society of laws, not of men. Anyone who attempts to tamper with jurors or witnesses will be prosecuted to the full extent of the law."

While some of Cleveland's most notorious criminals were being brought to justice, Ness was also back in the news in Chicago, as reporters reviewed the work of the Untouchables following Johnny Torrio's guilty plea to tax evasion charges. Torrio was sentenced to a prison term of two and one-half years. During that same week, Al

Capone was transferred from Alcatraz to the new Federal Correctional Institute at Terminal Island near Los Angeles, where he was being treated for advanced syphilis.

Chicago reporters asked Jack Guzik if his old friend might someday return and pick up the pieces of his criminal organization.

"Naw," said Guzik. "Al's as nutty as a fruitcake."

Yours for a
Safer, Cleaner,
Better Cleveland,
Eliot Ness

VOTE FOR
[X] ELIOT NESS
FOR MAYOR OF CLEVELAND

Ness-for-Mayor Committee . . . Robert W. Chamberlin, Chairman

After the war Ness was enlisted as a partner in an import-export company, but when that failed he surprised his closest friends by announcing his candidacy for the mayor's office in Cleveland's election of 1947.

Eliot and Elisabeth (Betty, Ness's third wife) meet merchants at the West Side Market on West Twenty-fifth Street (*above*). The Nesses campaigned long and hard in the 1947 Cleveland mayoral campaign.

Cleveland Republicans had long tried to persuade Ness to run as their mayoral candidate. Donations from the business community and generous publicity from the newspapers boosted his campaign. The support from prominent and privileged Republicans, however, prompted the incumbent Democrat to brand Ness as a candidate of the moneyed establishment. Ness had made powerful enemies among organized labor, and he had been away from Cleveland for almost five years, which allowed his earlier accomplishments to dim in the public's memory.

Although the race was at times divisive, incumbent mayor Tom Burke (*left*) and Ness managed a handshake after a spirited debate.

Ness had been somewhat charismatic in his early Cleveland days, but now he was showing the effects of stress and an unhealthy lifestyle, with deep lines cutting through his face, slouching shoulders, and a noticeable paunch. During his speeches, he appeared nervous, stiff, and uninspiring. He paid little attention to current political issues, relying instead on broad principles and his faded fame as a crimefighter.

Ness cast his ballot in the 1947 election as newspaper photographers recorded the moment. He lost by a margin close to two to one: 168,412 to 85,990. Ness called Burke to congratulate him and was invited to a victory party at the mayor's home. He accepted, graciously joining in on the festivities. Ness stunned many of those present by toasting Burke with a snide remark, "Who'd want an honest politician anyway?"

Ness's good friend and one-time business partner Dan Moore, photographed in 1995, recalled the 1947 election. "[Eliot] thought he could win by standing on the street corner with Betty and shaking hands," he remembered. "One time I took out my pen and showed him the math, how he could shake hundreds of hands every day and still not ever see 90 percent of Cleveland's voters. Eliot didn't realize that he had to get himself some fresh publicity, and get the right people to work for him. Let's face it, politics wasn't his game."

Elisabeth Andersen Seaver (*left*) was an accomplished sculptor when Dan Moore introduced her to Ness in 1945. Moore noted, "Betty was sweet and outgoing, a real pleasure to talk to, and seemed to like the same things Eliot did." They were married in Baltimore on January 31, 1946.

In late January 1948, Eliot and Betty adopted a three-year-old boy, whom they named Robert Warren Ness (*below*). He brought a great deal of joy to the lives of his parents, especially since his father spent so much time away from home.

"Parenthood was a new experience for Eliot and he enjoyed it immensely, when he could find the time," said a friend of the Nesses. "He was spread too thin. He wanted to spend more time with Betty and Bobby, and they missed him, too. Betty tried to be understanding, but she felt abandoned at times."

Corinne Lawson, the former housekeeper of the Nesses, saw the hard times of the late 1940s in the Ness home. "It reached the point where some men did not like him and talked about him [behind his back]," she recalled, "but he was liked by the ladies because he was witty. As far as I'm concerned, he was a gentleman. Eliot and Betty were both very nice people."

G. Frank Shampanore (*left*) approached Ness to join in a business enterprise based on watermarked checks as a protection against counterfeiting. The company was founded in Cleveland as North Ridge Industrial Corporation and moved to Coudersport, Pennsylvania, to conserve expenses.

William Ayers (*below, front row, far left*) was a close friend and business partner of Ness during the trying times at North Ridge. The other men are (*front row, left to right*) Ayers, investor Pete Farmelo, a local grocer; Carl Reidy, legal counsel; (*back row, left to right*) an unidentified investor; George McKinney, treasurer; Joe Phelps, vice president; Ness, president; Verne Haight, executive vice president; investor Bruno Timpano, Pennsylvania State Police commanding officer; and founder Shampanore.

Pinch-hitting for her husband, Judge Walter P. Wells, Anne Wells engaged the switch to launch North Ridge Industrial Corporation operations in Coudersport. Company founder Shampanore and his wife, Del, are in the foreground. In the back are (*above, left to right*) employee Paul English, North Ridge vice president Verne Haight, and an unidentified onlooker.

These officers of North Ridge Industrial Corporation posed for a front page photograph in the Coudersport newspaper: (*below, from left*) Verne Haight, George McKinney, Joe Phelps, Ness, Shampanore, and Carl Reidy.

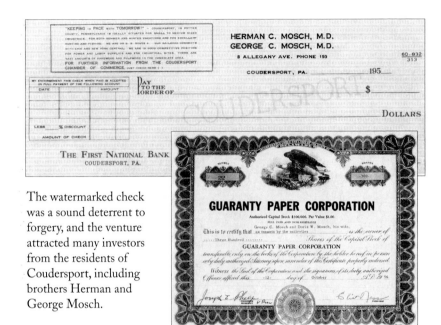

The watermarked check was a sound deterrent to forgery, and the venture attracted many investors from the residents of Coudersport, including brothers Herman and George Mosch.

Ness (*below right*) and company founder Shampanore pose for a newspaper photographer as they launched North Ridge Industrial Corporation. When the company failed to generate sufficient capital, Shampanore abandoned the project.

One office of North Ridge Industrial Corporation's two branches was on the second floor of this Coudersport building.

Marketing director Rube Pollan (*below left*) and Ness attended trade shows to advertise the products of the North Ridge Industrial Corporation's subsidiaries, Fidelity Check and Guaranty Paper Company.

In its heyday, the stately Old Hickory was a popular gathering place in Coudersport. Ness often visited the tavern in the basement after work.

Lewis Wilkinson (*left*) and his wife, Dorothy, frequently hosted Ness at their Coudersport home. Dorothy helped to type the original manuscript for *The Untouchables* as Eliot struggled to recall his adventures in Chicago.

Former school principal Fred Anderson recalled that the Nesses were very concerned about their son's education when he attended Coudersport Elementary School.

Former acquaintances of Ness gathered in 2000 to share their memories of him with a television production company from Great Britain and the author. They are (*from left to right*) Virginia Kallenborn, John Rigas, and William Ayers.

United Press Associations

INCORPORATED IN NEW YORK

GENERAL OFFICES

NEWS BUILDING NEW YORK CITY

May 6, 1956

Dear Eliot:

Finally finished the first two chapters and have given them to my agent to market. If anything is wrong, we can correct later.

You'll notice, I did a helluva lot of research to check facts and figures on Capone, etc., including dates & whatnot.

Don't get scared if we stray from the facts once in a while. We've got to make a real gang-buster out of this thing and after all, we have literary license.

I hope you have started your notebook deal, to jot down little things that come to mind now and then.

If and when we sell the book, we can really get down to cases. But meanwhile such a notebook will pile up a lot of valuable data.

PLEASE DON'T LOSE THE ENCLOSED CARBON COPY BUT MAIL IT BACK TO ME AFTER YOU'VE READ IT, TO MY HOME ADDRESS BELOW.

Quite often publishers mislay manuscripts and, without this carbon copy, I'd be in a helluva mess.

Let me know what you think of it and I hope you get to new york soon so we can talk some more. Give Joe my best.

Regards,

Oscar

Oscar Fraley
54 N. Woodhull
Huntington, L.I., N.Y.

Any doubt that certain passages in *The Untouchables,* Ness's autobiographical account of his career in Chicago, were exaggerated is removed by this letter from writer Oscar Fraley to Ness. The manuscript was picked up by Julian Messner, a New York publisher.

The years show in this 1952 photograph of Ness. A 1956 examination by his doctor, George C. Mosch, revealed an inactive rheumatic valvular disease. Ness was admonished to avoid exertion and continue taking a sedative. The stress of the struggle to keep North Ridge Corporation going proved to be too much, however. Ness died on May 16, 1957, of a heart attack, six months before *The Untouchables* was published. His death was noted in the Cleveland newspapers; the Chicago papers did not carry the story.

In April 1959 the *Desilu Playhouse* on CBS presented a two-part adaptation of *The Untouchables*. Its success inspired a weekly show, developed by ABC, and Robert Stack was cast to play Ness. The series generated 114 gritty black-and-white episodes, and Stack reprised the role for two television movies in 1987 and 1991.

The first edition of this work alerted the Cleveland Police Historical Society to the existence of the cremains of Eliot, Elisabeth, and Robert Ness at the suburban Cleveland home of Robert's widow. They were brought to Lake View Cemetery on September 10, 1997, for dispersment and a service attended by dignitaries from Cleveland, Chicago, and several federal agencies. Shown at the beginning of the ceremony (*from left to right*) are Lt. Debra Washington, local historian and research librarian Rebecca McFarland, Lt. Michael Doyle, and commander Robert Cermak.

Among those attending the dedication of the granite marker in the cemetery were (*from left to right*) James L. Brown, special agent in charge, U.S. Treasury Department, Bureau of Alcohol, Tobacco and Firearms; Al Sutton, former Federal Bureau of Investigation agent and Cleveland public safety director; William Denihan, Cleveland public safety director; two representatives of the pipes and drums corps and honor guard from Chicago and Cleveland; and Patrick Berarducci, senior special agent, U.S. Treasury Department, Bureau of Alcohol, Tobacco and Firearms.

CHAPTER NINETEEN

Social Protection

NESS DREW ATTENTION WHEREVER he went. Women were attracted by his good looks, his considerate manner, and his celebrity status. At Cleveland's nightspots, he was often accompanied by Evaline McAndrews, an attractive former model with dark brown hair and a ready smile. Evaline, at twenty-seven, was nine years younger than Eliot. A Chicago native, she had been acquainted with the Ness family during her childhood but hadn't seen Eliot in several years. She had studied at the Art Institute of Chicago and the University of Michigan before becoming a fashion designer. The two had renewed acquaintances on a train bound from Cleveland to Minneapolis, each on the rebound from a difficult divorce.

Eliot also socialized with Vernon Stouffer, who allowed him to move into the Stouffer family's four-story boathouse at the mouth of Rocky River on Clifton Lagoon. With Evaline at his side, Ness was often the life of the party. Newspaper reporters and politicians joined him for midnight swims and predawn motorboat rides, causing tongues to wag. They would party long into the night, yet Ness would maintain his early morning exercise regimen and arrive fresh at the office the next day.

Reporter Philip W. Porter, who watched the evolution of Ness from a workaholic lawman to a Cleveland socialite, recalled the Ness of mid-1939:

> Eliot was a gay, convivial soul who liked nothing better than to sit around 'til all hours, drinking with friends or dancing. It seemed to unwind him to visit nightclubs and hotel dance spots. He was not a heavy drinker, but he could keep at it for long periods without giving the appearance of being swacked. During his latter days as director, after he had pretty much finished his clean-up of the crooked police and racketeering unionists, he was seen more and more at public drinkeries, usually with newsmen. This made him vulnerable to backbiting by enemies. They spread the word that Ness was a lush; so how could a man who was on the sauce all the time be so all-fired virtuous?

Evaline set up an art studio on the top floor of the boathouse, taking advantage of the natural light provided by large windows on all four sides. It was an inspirational and scenic setting, with a splendid view of the deepest mooring place on Lake Erie and several impressive yachts anchored there.

In what some considered a spur-of-the-moment decision, Ness and Evaline drove to Chicago on October 13, 1939, and exchanged wedding vows before a justice of the peace. Only the couple's closest friends were informed of the plan. They decided to postpone their honeymoon until after the November election.

Two days later, Ness was back at his desk, where he found a file folder marked, "Eliot: Urgent!" Inside was a stack of newspaper clippings and notes from detective Merylo containing the latest news of the Mad Butcher. A group of boys looking for walnuts discovered the nude, headless corpse of a male in a weed patch about 150 yards from a railroad track near New Castle, Pennsylvania. That soggy wasteland had been labeled "Murder Swamp" because of the discovery of other victims there thirteen years earlier. The killer had apparently taken the body to the woods and attempted to burn it by igniting a pile of newspapers, one of which was a three-week-old edition of the *Youngstown (Ohio) Vindicator*. The victim's head was found almost a week later in a railroad car.

Merylo and Zalewski traveled to New Castle to inspect the remains. Based on the way the victim had been decapitated and other factors, Merylo speculated the killer was probably "a train-riding pervert who possibly holds forth in boxcars or hobo jungles, where he finds his victims and then uses a boxcar for an operating room." The victim was never identified. Investigators concluded he was likely a Cleveland-area vagabond who rode into Pennsylvania as a stowaway on the same train that carried his killer.

In Cleveland, Evaline Ness's career was blossoming. She designed advertising for Higbee's Department Store, supplied artwork for another retailer, and illustrated children's books. Her first few months as Mrs. Eliot Ness exceeded all her expectations. The two mixed business and pleasure in the proper doses, attending to their professional responsibilities by day and socializing with some of Cleveland's wealthiest and most influential couples at night. "I'm lucky in my profession because it's the sort of work that doesn't interfere with being a housewife, too," she told one reporter.

"That may have been the best part of Eliot's life," Evaline recalled. "He was a happy man who enjoyed what he was doing. He never really talked about his work much. We'd go out at night and have a good time, but there wouldn't be talk about his job. He always kept his emotions controlled. In fact, Eliot was probably the most controlled man I ever knew."

Among their closest friends were Ralph and Marian Kelly, a couple who worked for rival city newspapers. "The Nesses liked parties and they were good at having their own," Marian noted. "But Eliot always preferred to go to other people's houses. He had a curiosity about how others lived."

Ness avoided some of the popular nightclubs because of his suspicions about their mob connections. When he did visit nightspots, "he would always sit with his back to the wall, facing the door," Marian observed. "It wasn't that he was afraid. I suppose it was just the prudent thing to do, all things considered. We'd kid him about it and accuse him of seeing too many movies, but he'd just smile."

Kelly said she was very fond of Ness. "He was a pleasant person to associate with. Eliot had a tremendous line. He was one of the most attractive men I have ever seen or known. He wasn't handsome or flashy, but women were drawn to him. Sometimes I think it was because they wanted to mother him. Women threw themselves at Eliot. That was his trouble."

Ness resumed playing tennis whenever his schedule allowed and prided himself on remaining trim. He frequented a health club for jujitsu and handball. His fitness was remarkable, considering his drinking and eating habits. Ness rarely ate salads, vegetables, or spiced food; even the smell of a strong spice could make him ill. His diet was usually meat and potatoes. And he rarely had time for those who complained of minor illness or injury. Ness hardly ever missed a day of work himself and was not very sympathetic to those who did.

He sometimes walked the street beat with police officers, trying to keep in touch with the common citizens, particularly teenagers. Ted Kuhn, the former Chicago Prohibition agent who became an Alcohol Tax Unit officer in Cleveland, told of the time he and Ness stopped at an East Side tavern. Suddenly, a patron excitedly approached the bar and demanded a payoff for hitting the jackpot on the "Paces Races" pinball machine. Ness stopped the transaction, walked over to a pay phone, and summoned police to confiscate the machine.

"Who are you?" the bartender asked.

"I'm Eliot Ness, public safety director."

"No, you're not," said a wag at the end of the bar. "I know Ness personally, and you sure as hell aren't him."

Ness rose to button his overcoat and motioned for Kuhn to join him as he stepped away from the bar to leave. "If you don't believe me," he shouted back to the bartender, "just ask the cop who's been hiding in the corner since we came in. His drink is still on the bar."

The advent of World War II shifted law enforcement strategies, especially in major cities that might be vulnerable to attack. Ness's first action was to form a secret Industrial Safety Committee. More than three hundred industrial plants in the Cleveland area joined in a plan to establish a force to investigate suspicious employees or others who might be engaged in sabotage or espionage activities. Annual dues of one dollar per employee would be paid by the industries to finance the program, which involved the selection of two or more employees per plant to serve as undercover agents. Tom Clothey, one of the Unknowns, became chief investigator for the Industrial Safety Committee. The matter had a certain urgency in Ness's mind because several of the plants had contracted with the U.S. Navy to manufacture national defense materiel, aircraft parts in particular.

J. Edgar Hoover, ever protective of his turf, referred to Ness's plan as "repugnant to the bureau." In a memo to U.S. attorney general Frank Murphy, Hoover voiced strong opposition to the Industrial Safety Committee and pointed out that espionage or sabotage activities should be investigated by the FBI only.

"I cannot express too vigorously my complete disapproval of organizations of this kind which are designed to place the functions of law enforcement in the hands of untrained civilians functioning through vigilante groups," Hoover wrote. He accused Ness of "trying to capitalize upon the present emergency situation to his own advantage by attempting to usurp the functions of accredited law enforcement agencies."

Informed of Hoover's position, Ness took offense. He said the committee's investigators intended all along to refer evidence of sabotage or espionage to the FBI. "I'm in charge of the city and I'm worried about blowing up the downtown section or blowing up some Standard Oil tanks, which are all along the river, and the protection of the city," he declared. "If anything happens, I'll collect the blame." Taking a stand against Hoover certainly eliminated any chance Ness had of joining the FBI.

In early 1940, Ness restructured the fire department, using WPA funds to replace many firehouses and other sources to replace decrepit equipment. A new fire training school opened to provide rookie firemen with education on the most advanced techniques. World War II brought a sense of urgency to the effort, since the nation's civil defense plans called for police and fire departments in every major city to assume full authority in the event of an emergency.

Despite the war, the Mad Butcher case moved back to the front page on May 3—if only in retrospect—after the rotting remains of another victim were found stuffed into a burlap bag discovered on a boxcar after it arrived in McKees Rocks, Pennsylvania, from Ohio.

Inside another car, police found a second body sprawled on the floor, stripped naked and decapitated. A third butchered victim was discovered in another car. Evidence compiled over the next few days traced the murders to Struthers, Ohio, near the Pennsylvania border, sometime around Christmas 1939.

"I think it's safe to say that the Mad Butcher's victims now number twenty-three," J. Peter Merylo told a stunned Cleveland.

A conclusive body count was impossible to make; Merylo's figure was probably high. No other murders would be attributed to the Mad Butcher, which somewhat vindicated Ness for his decision to destroy the vagrants' quarters. Cleveland residents and the investigators were left to wonder if the murderer had died, gone elsewhere, been arrested for another crime, or otherwise been removed from society.

Some thought he was still on the loose, particularly after the decapitated, dismembered body of a man surfaced in the Monongahela River near Pittsburgh in May 1941. The amputations were surgically precise, and the victim was never identified.

One by one, Ness saw his colleagues move away. With World War II escalating, Bob Chamberlin left to join the Ohio National Guard. Tom Clothey, who had worked for Ness as one of the Unknowns, became assistant safety director before leaving to join U.S. Naval Intelligence. Ness lost another important ally when Mayor Harold Burton was elected to the U.S. Senate. He was succeeded by his assistant law director, Edward Blythin.

Ness's final attack on crime took place in mid-1940. Armed with incriminating evidence against one of Cleveland's remaining union power brokers, Albert Ruddy of the Carpenters District Council, Ness paid a call on Harry Barrington at the state prison farm in Mount Vernon. In return for his freedom, Barrington promised to detail for the court how he had carried out direct orders from Ruddy to pry shakedown money from dozens of Cleveland-area business owners. He was also able to point the finger at Ruddy for the 1936 murder of Albert Whitelock, a brutal union leader who rivaled Ruddy, and the 1933 bombing of a downtown Cleveland laundry.

Despite elaborate security precautions, Cleveland's union leaders learned of the meeting and sent word to Mount Vernon that Barrington would be executed if he talked. Ness knew he had to move quickly, so he rented an apartment in the Cleveland suburbs and held Barrington there under armed guard.

A grand jury indicted Ruddy and his enforcer, Vincent Dylinski, in June. Defense lawyers focused their attention on the credibility of Ness and his star witness. They argued that Ness was a self-promoting union-buster who would stop at nothing, including the fabrication of evidence, to advance his personal career. The attorneys also contended that Barrington, whose record included blackmail and extortion convictions, was merely trying to reduce his own jail time by presenting false testimony.

During a ten-day trial in October, some twenty witnesses, most of them building contractors and union carpenters, told jurors how they were strong-armed into paying tribute to Ruddy or Barrington. One quoted Ruddy as telling him, "For two thousand dollars we'll see to it that there are no strikes or trouble of any kind" at his new six-story office building.

"The racketeers and other criminals are doing their best to ruin legitimate labor in Cuyahoga County," prosecutor Frank T. Cullitan declared in his closing remarks.

Jurors lacked sufficient evidence to support a murder conviction, but they did find Ruddy guilty of racketeering. He was sentenced to a four-year prison term. The Cleveland newspapers praised Ness for his unwavering fight against the city's most elusive criminals. "Ness was never content to put Al Capone behind bars," the *Cleveland News* editorialized. "Apparently, he will not rest until every enemy of the people has been brought to justice."

By then Capone was a free man, obese, partly bald, and disoriented as he roamed the grounds of his Palm Island estate. Capone regularly expressed regret for his misdeeds and told visitors that he had accepted Jesus Christ as his savior.

Back in Cleveland, there was much speculation that the low-key interim mayor, Edward Blythin, would step down in 1941 to pave the way for Ness to run for the position. Some Republican friends tried to persuade Ness to throw his hat into the ring, but he declined, disavowing any political interest.

He probably could have been elected mayor, even though he had incensed the Republican loyalists by enthusiastically endorsing

Democrat Frank Cullitan for reelection as Cuyahoga County prosecutor. "I am primarily a law enforcement officer," he explained, "and I can honestly say that law enforcement has been magnificently served by Mr. Cullitan, which is much more important than what particular political party he represents."

Ness told friends that he was looking for new career opportunities outside of Cleveland, either in business or police administration. As the war effort escalated, the government sought a high-profile spokesman with experience in public safety education to warn military recruits about the dangers of venereal disease. Ness volunteered to fill the part-time position as a consultant to the new Federal Social Protection Program, even as he remained in office as public safety director. Critics chided Ness for his long absences as he traveled to government offices in New York and Washington and to military bases across the United States and Canada, promoting abstinence and safe sex. In response to his detractors, Ness cited the public service example set by New York mayor Fiorello La Guardia, who also served as the nation's civil defense chief.

When he was on the road, Ness spent a lot of his time in social clubs, failing to check in with Evaline for days at a time. The frequent separations took a toll on his marriage. Like Edna, Evaline understood his dedication to duty and the importance of his work, but she was lonely and restless, much too vibrant a woman to stay at home every night.

"Evaline liked being Eliot's wife, as long as he was home," said one of their friends. "She liked his prominence and power and fame. And he loved her, no question about that. He always called her 'Doll.' But Eliot started drifting back to his carefree lifestyle. She had her own ideas and wanted a more exciting life. Something had to give."

Ness's connections with Cleveland's political establishment were also loosening. Frank Lausche, the Democrat who was an easy winner in the November mayoral election, owed much of his success to Democratic county chairman Ray T. Miller, who was no fan of Ness. Miller had lined up solid union support for Lausche by promising, among other things, that Ness would be fired if Lausche were elected. Miller had even contacted another Ness opponent, J. Edgar Hoover, to line up a "qualified" replacement.

But Lausche admired and respected the safety director, dating back to the 1936 raid at the Harvard Club when, as a judge, Lausche had issued the warrant to county prosecutor Cullitan. Upon taking office in January 1942, he steadfastly refused to fire Ness.

"It's a safe guess that he will never confront a decision more difficult politically or one in which he will be subjected to greater pressure from opposing sides," the *Cleveland Press* editorialized. "Director Ness was obviously the most valuable asset of the Burton administration in its first two years. His work in helping to convict eight crooked union officials and a like number of corrupt police officers deserves the highest praise."

This show of independence would come to characterize Lausche's later career as governor of Ohio and a U.S. senator.

Other problems, however, were brewing for Ness. He was tipped off that Lt. Ernest Molnar of Molnar's Raiders was the mastermind of a massive policy racket being operated right under his nose, but he refused to believe it. He was unable to track down the kingpins of the dreaded National Death Incorporated insurance racket actively operating in Cleveland. Investors took out multiple life insurance policies on chronic alcoholics, then kept the insured parties supplied with copious quantities of alcohol until they either died from overconsumption or were hit by a car, sometimes intentionally.

His reputation slipping, Ness trotted out statistics showing that traffic fatalities in Cleveland had been reduced by 40 percent, resulting in a corresponding drop in auto insurance rates. Newspaper reports heralded the findings and gave much of the credit to Ness, but the public was more interested in the safety director's shortcomings.

He was being pressured to disband his undercover unit, the Unknowns, who had been hidden on the city's payroll as laborers. The Cleveland business community was not nearly as generous with donations to the special investigative fund, now that organized crime had lost much of its clout—a classic case of Ness being the victim of his own success.

CHAPTER TWENTY

Who Did It?

S PECULATION ABOUT THE IDENTITY of the Mad Butcher of Kingsbury Run dates back more than sixty years. Barring some dramatic development, however, no one will ever know who the killer was. Over the years, two names have continued to surface: Frank Dolezal and Francis Edward Sweeney.

On July 7, 1939, with great fanfare, Cuyahoga County sheriff Martin L. O'Donnell announced a break in the case. O'Donnell, who had succeeded "Honest John" Sulzmann, decided to take his turn solving the case after the killing spree had apparently stopped. He hired a detective, Patrick Lyons, who had already been working on the probe in a private capacity. Lyons's work led to the arrest of Frank Dolezal, a despondent Cleveland drifter who had worked as a bricklayer and a slaughterhouse laborer. One witness told police that Dolezal, fifty-two, liked to display an assortment of knives he carried wherever he went. Interestingly, not only had Dolezal lived for a while with Victim No. 3, Flo Polillo, he also had been at least casually acquainted with both Edward Andrassy (No. 1) and Rose Wallace (No. 8).

It was not much to go on, but Cleveland's law enforcement agencies were desperate, so they took Dolezal into custody and started peppering him with questions. Eventually, Dolezal signed a confession that, in all likelihood, was beaten out of him by police. The statement was an inconsistent blend of nearly incoherent ramblings coupled with clear, precise declarations, suggesting that it was coerced.

Ness was skeptical from the start. Publicly, he expressed his hope that police had found their man. Privately, he didn't believe Dolezal had murdered anyone. And the more Dolezal talked, the more the case against him crumbled. He had a variety of stories to tell, many of them inconsistent or contradictory. A week after his arrest, Dolezal was provided with an attorney. He withdrew his confession and told of being blindfolded and beaten by sheriff's deputies until he told them what they wanted to hear.

On August 24 the lifeless body of Dolezal was found leaning against the bars of his cell door at the Cuyahoga County Jail. Officials reported that he had hanged himself with a rope made of cleaning rags. Curiously, the five-foot, eight-inch Dolezal had allegedly attached his makeshift rope to a hook that was only five feet, seven inches off the ground. That prompted relatives to demand an autopsy by coroner Samuel R. Gerber. His examination revealed that six of Dolezal's ribs had been broken, strong corroboration of his claim that he had been beaten.

"Today, no one thinks Frank Dolezal was the Torso Killer," wrote James Badal, an English professor who has studied the case for many years, in an essay prepared for the Cleveland Police Historical Society. "He was merely the unfortunate victim of a very frightened city desperately in need of a scapegoat."

The situation with Francis Edward Sweeney, a medical doctor, is much more intriguing. In fact, Ness himself may have believed that Sweeney was the Mad Butcher, but he was never able to prove it.

Marilyn Bardsley, a former Cleveland resident now living in Great Falls, Virginia, has studied the Sweeney connection off and on since the early 1970s. Through the years, she has produced a profile of the doctor while, at the same time, compiling "evidence" that stops short of specifically connecting him with the crimes.

Born in Cleveland in 1894, the son of a laborer and grandson of Irish immigrants, Sweeney grew up on the East Side. After graduation from Central High School, he enlisted in the army during World War I and served in France. He later attended the Western Reserve School of Pharmacy and the Saint Louis School of Medicine. In 1928 Sweeney became a surgeon at Saint Alexis Hospital in Cleveland.

According to Bardsley, Sweeney married a nurse and the couple had two sons. Sometime in the mid- to late-1930s things started falling apart. Sweeney's affiliation with Saint Alexis ended and his wife divorced him in 1936; the paperwork included allegations by Sweeney's wife that he was habitually intoxicated and prone to violence. During this period of turmoil in Sweeney's life, the butchered bodies started showing up around Cleveland.

Ness and others involved in the investigation concluded that the killer had an intimate knowledge of human anatomy. Gerber went so far as to speculate that the Mad Butcher was probably a doctor or medical student "who performs the crime in the fury of a long drinking bout or derangement following the use of drugs." Police had focused on a wide variety of medical students, physicians, and male nurses, while paying particular attention to doctors who had a history of eccentricity or a weakness for illicit sex, drugs, or alcohol. Sweeney fit that bill. His military discharge papers cited a 25 percent disability, which was unspecified; some have speculated it was a head injury or mental disorder. In addition, he was large and strong, with a reputation for losing his temper.

Both Bardsley and Badal have documentation to support the conclusion that Sweeney was a suspect. In 1937 he was being watched merely because he was a physician with a drinking problem whose office was near Kingsbury Run. He was ruled out as a suspect, however, as soon as investigators determined that he was on record as a patient at Sandusky Soldiers and Sailors Home, a veterans' hospital in Sandusky, Ohio, when the murders occurred.

That changed after Lt. David L. Cowles, a forensics expert working for the Cleveland Police Department, was summoned to the Sandusky area, about two hours west of the city, in March 1938 to investigate an unrelated case. Recalling Sweeney's alibi, on a hunch Cowles visited the soldiers and sailors home. He determined that Sweeney had voluntarily admitted himself on several occasions for alcoholism treatment. Some of those times overlapped with periods when the Mad Butcher was believed to have been at work.

Digging deeper, Cowles learned that Sweeney was rarely monitored during his stays—not that the home had much of a security system anyhow. Cowles arranged to have Sweeney placed under surveillance, but the doctor soon discovered that he was under scrutiny and confronted the officers.

Whether voluntarily or by force, Sweeney was grilled by the investigators during a meeting at the Cleveland Hotel on Public Square in May 1938. Among those attending the meeting were Ness; Royal Grossman, a court psychiatrist; Cowles; Leonard Keeler, a polygraph expert from Chicago; and an assistant of Keeler's.

None of the participants discussed the meeting for many years. In 1974, however, Grossman did share some of the details with Marilyn Bardsley. He revealed that Sweeney had failed repeated polygraph tests when questioned about the murders and that Sweeney was taunting Ness.

Following the meeting, Sweeney entered the Sandusky Soldiers and Sailors Home once again. The circumstances behind the doctor's admission have never been clear. He spent the remainder of his life in institutions until his death in 1965, at the age of seventy, at the Veterans Administration Center in Dayton, Ohio.

Researchers and others have speculated that Sweeney escaped prosecution for the crimes due to not only a lack of evidence, but also political factors. The doctor's cousin was U.S. congressman Martin L. Sweeney who, together with Sheriff O'Donnell, controlled a powerful Democratic political machine in Cuyahoga County and Cleveland itself. In March 1937, Congressman Sweeney chided Mayor Harold Burton and "his alter ego, Eliot Ness," for "spending all their efforts persecuting cops that took $25 years ago," while major crimes such as the Kingsbury Run murders remained unsolved. A few months later, Sweeney called on voters in the Cleveland mayoral election to defeat Burton and "send back to Washington the prohibition agent who is now Safety Director."

Whether it was because of Sweeney's confinement, Ness's shantytown raid, or other factors, the Mad Butcher's killing spree ended and his identity remains a mystery. At least three people have quoted Ness as saying he believed Sweeney was the killer but lacked the evidence to bring criminal charges. Ness may not have used the doctor's name when discussing his suspicions, but the allusion is clear. If Sweeney was the murderer, he couldn't have been responsible for the four bodies found in southwest Pennsylvania in 1939–40.

In the early 1950s, long after Ness had left the public safety director's office, he received a series of five post cards from Dayton. Sweeney's name appears on three of them. Messages scribbled on the cards are difficult to comprehend and open to any number of interpretations. One is addressed to "Eliot (Head Man) Ness," perhaps a grisly pun or possibly a reference to Ness's previous position with the city. Others are addressed to "Eliot Ambig-u-ous Ness" and "Eliot Direct-Um Ness." Among the messages: "The better half of legal exaction will up on you one day," and, "The chimes peal for bell ringing effect or not is the MacBeathean questions." The post cards are now in the archives of the Western Reserve Historical Society.

Other evidence has surfaced over the years to confirm that Sweeney was a prime suspect. David Kerr, a former Cleveland policeman, had been on the force for just over a year when he joined the investigation. Kerr recalls the search narrowing to a single suspect—a doctor who was related to a well-known Cleveland political family and had fallen into disrepute because of alcohol abuse and sadistic tendencies.

Yet Sweeney is not everyone's primary suspect. Gus Zukie, a Cleveland policeman from 1936 to 1977, told *Cleveland Plain Dealer* reporter Brian Albrecht that a male nurse at Cleveland Hospital (now Metro General Hospital) had been linked by police to several of the victims, but investigators never had sufficient proof to make an arrest. Zukie said Lt. J. Peter Merylo told him the nurse was a suspect, but that phase of the investigation ended when the man died in the service during World War II.

Curiously, Zukie said the nurse, whose name was not made public, was—like Sweeney—related to a prominent Cleveland family. Zukie worked for a time with Merylo on the Mad Butcher case. He said the investigator told him he expected to be pulled from the assignment because of the suspect's political connections.

Zukie declared that he was skeptical of theories that Sweeney was the killer. "Listen, Mac," he told reporter Fred McGunagle in 1989. "I don't fool with theories. I've been too long in the business. You gotta have evidence."

Merylo continued to investigate, even after Cleveland police dismantled their "Torso Squad" in 1941. He left the force two years later and opened a private detective agency in Cleveland. Merylo died of a heart attack in 1958. His six-year mission resulted in hundreds of arrests for sex offenses, an unrelated murder, abortion, immigration law violations, drug trafficking, burglary, and white slavery operations.

"They couldn't have had a better man on the case," Zukie said of Merylo. "He was like a bulldog. He never gave up. He worked night and day. He was very meticulous about whatever he did."

The case became the subject of several books, some factual—albeit incomplete—and others clearly labeled fiction or part-fiction. Merylo himself had assisted in a manuscript written by Frank Otwell, a reporter for the *Cleveland News* who actually worked with the police in looking for the Mad Butcher in the mid-1930s. Otwell, who died in 1971, could not find a publisher willing to handle the work.

"Peter used to come out to the house a lot to talk to Frank about it," said Betty Otwell, widow of the reporter. "He'd tell the most grue-some stories I ever heard in my life. Peter was determined to get this fellow. One night he came over, gave Frank a revolver, and they went out to walk through the area where some of the bodies had been found. I stayed home, worrying. Everybody was a little panicky about it back then. I know I was frightened."

Books, magazine articles, television shows, and even a comic book series have focused on the Mad Butcher case. The most serious work is James Badal's forthcoming *In the Wake of the Butcher.*

One aspect that has frustrated researchers is the absence of offi-cial police records that have been lost, destroyed, or removed. In 1999, however, the daughter of J. Peter Merylo came forward with a collection of her father's notes and other records, including a journal in which he documented his investigation. These papers were instru-mental to Badal in the preparation of his manuscript.

Ness was apparently considering writing a book about his Cleve-land experiences, collaborating with Oscar Fraley, a United Press International sportswriter, but the work never materialized. Fraley is among the individuals who quoted Ness as speculating that Sweeney was the killer, even as he insisted that a pseudonym be used.

Every time a murder of similar nature took place, the public wondered if perhaps the Mad Butcher was still at work. This senti-ment was expressed as late as July 1950, when the nude, decapitated, and dismembered torso of forty-five-year-old Robert Robertson, a Cleveland drifter, was found under a pile of steel girders at East Twenty-first Street and Lakeside Avenue. The victim had been cut into five pieces with a heavy, sharp knife by someone familiar with human anatomy.

There was also conjecture that the Mad Butcher's victims were not all necessarily that. A doctor who ran an embalming college was no stranger to practical jokes and was rumored to have planted body parts to confuse investigators.

Perhaps crime writer John Bartlow Martin, in his 1950 book, *Butcher's Dozen and Other Murders,* said it best: "He was that almost unknown creature, a master criminal. . . . It can be argued powerfully that he was the greatest murderer of all time."

PART THREE

A Downward Spiral

CHAPTER TWENTY-ONE

"I'm Sure Having Fun"

WHILE THE CONTROVERSY OVER his future in Cleveland swirled, on March 5, 1942, Eliot Ness provided his political opponents with all the ammunition they needed. On a cold, rainy night, Evaline and he joined friends for several hours of dining, drinking, and dancing at the Vogue Room of the Hollenden Hotel. This fourteen-story red-brick Victorian structure near Public Square was considered the hub of Cleveland's downtown social life, and it drew the elite among its patrons. The Nesses and another couple stayed to close the lounge, then retired to a private room to continue their socializing. Finally, at about 4:30 A.M., they made their way to the parking lot and Eliot started to drive home.

During the night a frigid north wind had transformed an earlier rain into a frozen glare on the highways. Ness had just eased the couple's Cadillac onto Bulkley Boulevard, now the West Memorial Shoreway, when he spotted two tiny headlights approaching in the opposite lane. As the lights grew brighter, they flashed annoying reflections on the icy roadway. Suddenly, as Ness turned the steering wheel to negotiate a slight curve, his car started to slide sideways. The lights of the oncoming car filled most of Ness's field of vision and the vehicles collided.

Evaline was hurled, shoulder first, against the dashboard. Squinting her eyes and rubbing her head, she tried to get her bearings. Eliot hurried over to check on the other driver. He was Robert Sims, a twenty-one-year-old East Cleveland machinist who was still seated behind the wheel, his driver's-side door open and his feet resting on the car's running board. Sims had struck his head on the steering wheel and jammed his knee against the dashboard. After determining that Sims could still drive his car, Ness suggested he follow them to a nearby hospital.

Ness returned to his car, where he found Evaline sitting up, still groggy, and having trouble catching her breath. He felt his wife's head and discovered a bruise above her right ear. Although the metal of their car's left front panel had collapsed, there was still about an inch of clearance between the fender and the front tire.

What happened after that was never fully established. A motorist told police he had come along after the mishap, found the victim still sitting in his car, and persuaded Sims to accompany him to a hospital for observation. Hospital staffers reported that an anonymous man had called to inquire about Sims's condition.

Sims himself was able to solve the mystery. From his hospital bed, he told police that the other driver had failed to identify himself, but that the license plate of the 1941 sedan was EN-3. Visited at his home by two investigators just before noon, Ness admitted his involvement in the crash and suggested that the two officers downplay the episode. Uncomfortable with the safety director's request, they shared the information with their captain, who was among the police officials under investigation for improper conduct. The captain gleefully telephoned the Cleveland newspapers to share the details of Ness's crash.

Journalists found plenty of headline value in the revelation that the city's heralded public safety director, an aggressive enforcer of Prohibition laws, had crashed into an innocent motorist following a night of drinking. Three days after the crash, Ness broke his silence by calling a news conference. He admitted he had "had a few drinks" several hours before the crash, but he denied that his drinking was a cause of the collision or that it had influenced him in his cover-up attempt. Ness said several hours had passed between his drinking and the accident. He blamed the icy road surface and said he had every reason to believe Sims would follow him to the hospital. When he failed to see headlights behind him, Ness said, he circled back to the scene of the crash, but Sims was gone. By that time, Ness claimed, Evaline insisted that she would be all right and they drove home. Ness admitted that he phoned the hospital to inquire about Sims's condition. He further conceded that he declined to identify himself on the phone and subsequently pressured the investigating officers, because he wanted to avoid unflattering publicity. "I said that I would have my insurance adjuster on the job in the morning."

"It was very slippery and the thing just happened like that," Ness told reporters, snapping his fingers to reinforce the point. "My first thought was for my wife because I thought she was the most seriously injured. Then I got out of my car and went over to check on the other driver and told him who I was. . . . I have never regretted anything more in my life. It was a very unfortunate thing all the way through."

"I remember the accident," Evaline would later tell a reporter. "It was icy. I think I was telling Eliot something about a reporter I had told off, and we were laughing. It was an ordinary thing. We just slid into the car."

Evaline said the crash took a toll on her husband. "I don't think he could stand the criticism, especially when it came to his job. That's why he tried to avoid the publicity. It certainly did not reflect well on him."

No charges were filed, but the damage to Ness's image was irreversible. Mayor Frank Lausche wasn't satisfied with his explanation; neither were the people of Cleveland. The crash, coupled with the perception that Ness had lost enthusiasm for a job he had once performed in such spectacular style, caused many Clevelanders to question his judgment.

Lausche summoned Ness for a private meeting. There is no record of what transpired, but the following morning, April 30, 1942, Ness tendered his resignation as public safety director. He claimed his departure was the result of his promotion to the position of national director of the Federal Social Protection Program, which was under the Federal Office of Defense.

"Cleveland is a different place than it was when Eliot Ness became Safety Director," wrote columnist Clayton Fritchey in saying good-bye to his friend. "Ness restored a sense of hope and pride to a beleaguered community. Cleveland was in desperate need for a lawman with the talent and integrity of Eliot Ness. Today, policemen no longer have to tip their hats when they pass a gangster on the streets. Labor racketeers no longer parade down Euclid Avenue in limousines bearing placards deriding the public and law enforcement in general. Motorists have been taught and tamed into killing only about half as many people as they used to slaughter."

Philip Porter of the *Plain Dealer* was even more effusive in his praise:

> One way in which the Ness administration differed sharply from the others was that he rooted out and minimized departmental politics and when it popped up he got tough with it. He was always several jumps ahead of the chair-warmers and connivers in city government, and even to this day they can't figure him out, but have spent a good deal of their time criticizing him. As Ness enters full-time federal service, an era has ended here. The heights of law enforcement and competence which have been built up during Ness's six-year administration are so outstanding among American city experiences as to be a little amazing when you get away from town and begin to analyze and compare them. When he took office, the town was ridden with crooked police and crooked labor bosses. A dozen such were sent to prison, and scores of others scared into resignation or inactivity. There were gambling halls on every block and lush casinos in the suburbs. The little joints mostly folded and finally the big joints quit when a couple of Ness's honest cops were put in the sheriff's office. The town reached such a condition of comparative purity that about all the continual critics had to complain about was occasional bingo, strip-teasers and some policy games. We'll probably never have perfection in any municipal police administration, but we have gradually achieved something as near it as any big city is ever likely to, and we ought to be grateful to Ness for it.

Ness left an indelible mark on those who met him or followed his exploits in Cleveland. "Quite a guy, that Ness," recalled Alvin Sutton, a former FBI agent who took Ness's place as public safety director. "He commanded respect and drew a lot of attention to himself because he was handsome and plenty smart and decisive. He knew how to work the press and the reporters liked the way Ness cleaned house with the police department. He sent at least twelve cops to prison, so that has to tell you something."

The Nesses moved to Washington, D.C., where they settled into a luxurious home provided to them rent-free. Ness, now thirty-nine, tackled his new role with the same vigor he had once demonstrated in both Chicago and Cleveland. Most of his time was spent far from home at military bases. In one sense, Ness and Capone were fighting the same enemy—venereal disease. Ness attacked it as a lecturer at military installations. Capone's battle was more personal, as he drifted in and out of reality at his Miami compound.

One of Ness's assignments, an effort to stamp out prostitution, was to establish alliances with law enforcement authorities in communities that hosted or surrounded the military bases. This put him in a familiar situation—at odds with organized crime. In one bizarre episode, prostitutes and their supporters rallied around the site of an anticrime speech by Ness in Peoria, Illinois, harassing the audience and displaying signs decrying his actions as an affront to their personal liberties.

Labeling VD "military saboteur number one," an undaunted Ness dusted off the federal government's May Act, which imposed stiff penalties for prostitution near military bases or recruiting stations and gave the Justice Department control of local policing for repression of prostitution. He threatened to revoke the licenses of bars, hotels, cab services, and other businesses that thrived on soldiers' paychecks if they continued to cooperate with hookers. Prostitutes who were apprehended had two options: a jail term and a fine or enlistment in a Civilian Conservation Corps camp for alternative vocational education.

Ness considered his role on a par with that of a military commander, as detailed in this article he penned for the April 1943 edition of *Public Welfare*, the Journal of the American Public Welfare Association:

> Our nation is engaged in total war. Such a conflict is one in which "manpower"—its mobilization, its intelligent distribution, and its conservation—will be a deciding factor in determining the potency of our efforts. We must keep men behind the guns,

in the tanks, piloting the planes, manning the ships. Further, we must maintain the production front on which the fighting strength of the nation depends—the men and women on factory assembly lines and in the munition plants, who fashion the implements of war, the uniforms and the equipment. Any condition threatening the full realization of this objective is intolerable. Yet 100,000 of the first two million men given physical examinations under Selective Service were found unfit for military service because of venereal disease. In war industries 1,200,000 men and women are regularly having to take time off from their work to be treated for syphilis.

Ness boasted of the Social Protection Division's closing down some 350 "red-light districts" across the country. He called for a crackdown by local police, coupled with public education and a variety of social programs for prostitutes, from psychiatric treatment and health care to housing and employment training. "We cannot expect to attack the problem of prostitution intelligently and effectively unless we take action to eliminate the sources of prostitution," he wrote. "The social and economic conditions responsible for the 'social swamps' which breed prostitution must be studied and ameliorated whenever possible. The amount of prostitution in a community reflects to a large degree the lack of constructive opportunities a town has to offer. These include recreation, vocational training, effective employment services and other civic services. Stamping out prostitution is a broad community enterprise, involving all of the community's services—public, voluntary and private."

Ness's work put him on a collision course with J. Edgar Hoover once again. Hoover sent an emissary to a U.S. Army Air Corps conference where Ness was speaking in January 1943 to refute every suggestion that any agency other than the FBI was responsible for success in the fight against prostitution and venereal disease.

"I took occasion constantly to emphasize the Bureau's work and successful cooperative relations with police," the emissary, R. F. Cartwright, wrote in a memo to Hoover. "This was done to counteract the efforts of Ness. . . . I pointed out that suppression of prostitution from a law enforcement angle was a matter of concentration and persistence, rather than one of inspiration."

Hoover's attitude was further demonstrated in a letter he sent to Norfolk (Va.) police chief John Woods, who was concerned that his relationship with Ness might jeopardize his relationship with the FBI. "I would be most cautious of anything Ness offers," Hoover wrote. "There is no advice I would give except to beware of Ness."

Later, when the Federal Social Protection Program sought photographs of prostitutes from the FBI for a crime prevention exhibit, one of Hoover's subordinates suggested that the bureau "label them 'FBI Photograph' to chill the Ness group's administration and carry the impression of the bureau's participation." Hoover went one step further, prohibiting any agency involvement. "If this is Eliot Ness's outfit, I am opposed to any cooperation," he wrote.

Navy officials gave Ness high marks for his work, presenting him with their meritorious service citation in 1943. His personnel files show that Ness also earned consistently high marks from his superiors for resourcefulness, organizational skills, and initiative. The public, however, took little notice of Ness's work, because attention was focused more on developments overseas, plus venereal disease was not a topic people tended to discuss.

Even Ness had difficulty discussing specifics, Dan Moore recalled. "He always had trouble with the word *whore* and—this is so typical of Eliot—he would look for ways to avoid saying it. One time, he came up with 'women who have a low threshold of sexual approachability' to describe them. He had a lot of fun with descriptions like that."

Meanwhile, trouble was brewing once again for Ness on the home front.

"Eliot liked the job quite a bit and I did, too," Evaline told an interviewer in 1976. "We'd go to all these towns and he'd advise them how to get rid of their red-light districts. It was funny, in a way. We met a lot of funny people in those towns, believe me, but after a while it wasn't as enjoyable. It wasn't what I wanted to do with my life. Eliot realized that."

Evaline also grew uncomfortable in the role of socialite. Whenever Ness returned to Washington for extended stays, he insisted on hosting dinner parties for wealthy friends. The guests at these affairs were people Evaline hardly knew and with whom she had little in common; she had her own circle of artistic friends by that time and yearned to pursue her own career.

In 1944 she left her husband under circumstances that neither was inclined to discuss. Evaline rented an apartment in New York City, where she resumed her career as an artist and fashion designer. She was employed full-time as a fashion illustrator for Saks Fifth Avenue. Communication between Eliot and Evaline was infrequent, at best. More than a year passed before the paperwork was completed to officially bring their marriage to an end on November 17, 1945. Ness, who moved into a house on Lakeshore Boulevard in the posh Cleveland suburb of Bratenahl, filed for the divorce, citing gross neglect and extreme cruelty. Details are lacking because the supporting papers disappeared from the Cuyahoga County Clerk of Court's office without explanation.

With World War II winding down and the Federal Social Protection Agency being phased out, Ness began looking for new opportunities. Among friends he had made while cutting his convivial swath through Cleveland's social scene was Jane Rex, daughter of the late Ralph Rex, a major shareholder of the Diebold Safe and Lock Company from Canton, Ohio. Impressed by Ness's reputation and his business degree from the University of Chicago, Rex made him an offer he could not refuse: step in and manage the family's business interests.

Diebold had a long history of innovative security measures, which may have made the opportunity all the more attractive to Ness. Diebold and the Lake Erie Chemical Company developed a system to discharge tear gas into bank lobbies. Their goal was to stop the bank-robbing spree of John Dillinger and his gang. Later, wartime government contracts for armor plating had helped Diebold become the nation's third largest safe and vault manufacturer. In May 1944 the Rexes installed Ness as chairman of the board of directors and ordered him to restructure the administratively waterlogged firm.

Ness sorted through personnel files and consulted with a handful of trusted, experienced executives. He eliminated duplication up and down the corporate ladder, building resentments among some of the more entrenched employees. Ness also steered Diebold down a path of diversification. He saw the potential for using plastic, still in its infancy as an industry, in many of Diebold's products. In addition, Ness opened a separate division for the production and marketing of microfilm equipment. This became known as the Visible Records Company, a Diebold subsidiary.

During his off-hours, a new romance helped soften the emotional sting of a second failed marriage. His companion was Elisabeth Andersen Seaver, a petite and pretty brunette with dark eyes and a pleasant smile. A native of Sioux Falls, South Dakota, Betty studied at the Cranbrook Academy of Art in Bloomfield Hills, Michigan, and graduated from the Cleveland School of Art. She became an accomplished sculptress, studying under the renowned Carl Mittes. Her prizewinning work was featured in many prominent Cleveland art exhibits. A bas-relief she created still hangs over the entrance of city hall in Sioux Falls. During World War II, Betty served as a camouflage expert at the Glenn L. Martin Aircraft Plant in Baltimore. When she met Ness she had been living in New York, working on several commissions.

Like Ness, Betty was pleasant but withdrawn. She remained depressed over a strained relationship with her first husband, architect Hugh Seaver, who left her a widow at an early age, and vowed that she would never marry again. Betty and Ness met through their mutual friendship with Dan Moore, the colorful Ohio securities commissioner.

"She was very attractive—a raving beauty as far as I was concerned—and Eliot was a real likable guy and single again, so I just brought them together and it clicked," Moore said. "Betty was sweet and outgoing, a real pleasure to talk to, and seemed to like the same things Eliot did."

In late 1945 Ness led Diebold's approach to a major competitor, York Safe and Lock Company of York, Pennsylvania, with a merger proposal. That deal was consummated in January 1946, with Ness becoming chiefly responsible for the York firm's thriving safe and vault business, as well as its sales force and branch offices.

To the outside world, Ness was a dynamic business leader destined for wealth and prominence. Behind the scenes, there were disenchantment with his lack of attention to detail and lingering resentment by a small but powerful group of midlevel executives who had disliked him from the start. Some of Ness's friends, both inside and outside of the company, warned him that he was a marked man. Among those who could see what was happening was Dan Moore.

Dan Tyler Moore Jr. had returned to his native Cleveland in 1937 with a physics degree from Yale and a wealth of experience in foreign affairs, politics, and economics. Moore had directed the new Securities and Exchange Commission (SEC) under Joseph P. Kennedy. Upon his return to Ohio, he handed out patronage jobs for President Franklin Roosevelt and was tabbed to head the state's securities division. His main target was Cleveland, the "fraud capital of the United States" at that time. Moore admired the work Ness had done in Cleveland, even though the two were at opposite ends of the political spectrum.

Moore went on to direct Cleveland's regional office of the SEC and Civil Defense, then served as a civilian major with the new Office of Strategic Services, forerunner of the Central Intelligence Agency. Among Moore's duties was to sort out the respective responsibilities of the OSS and Hoover's Federal Bureau of Investigation. He was later dispatched to Egypt, ostensibly as an assistant to the Middle East's economic ministry, but in reality as a spy. As chief of the region's counterintelligence during World War II, he helped to foil an assassination attempt on King George of Greece and barely escaped snipers' fire in Cairo after his cover was blown.

In Egypt, and later in Turkey, Moore was closely associated with James Landis, former dean of Harvard Law School, commissioner of the Federal Trade Commission, chairman of the Securities and Exchange Commission, and national director of the Office of Civil Defense. Landis had powerful influence on Middle East economic matters during the war, directing the movement of goods, the raising of crops, and the issuance of loans in connection with the U.S. war effort.

Moore and Landis parlayed their close contacts with Middle East government and business leaders into a private export-import business, the Middle East Company, and brought Ness aboard as a partner.

"This business had real possibilities," Moore explained. "Naturally, I was eager to let some of my good friends in on it, and I was probably Eliot's best friend at that time. Our troops had dropped millions of dollars in the Middle East during the war and all of that money had to be repatriated. We had an opportunity to cash in on that. Eliot jumped at the chance, which was a wise move, because his days at Diebold were numbered."

Ness became vice president and treasurer of the Middle East Company, while holding on to his position at Diebold, at least in title. Looking out over New York from a Middle East Company office he occupied part-time in Rockefeller Center, Ness was seen as a rising star in business circles. The January 1946 edition of *Fortune* magazine featured a story entitled, "There Goes Eliot Ness," excerpted as follows:

> The headwaiters at such Cleveland night spots as the Hotel Hollenden's Vogue Room and the Hotel Cleveland's Bronze Room all have tables reserved for a slimly handsome young man who may show up only a few evenings a month, but who instantly commands much attention from both sexes. He is Eliot Ness, a lakeside business headliner as the Board Chairman of Diebold, Inc. (safes, locks and office equipment) and VP of James M. Landis' Middle East Company. His table is invariably situated near the exit. Ever since his days as a special Chicago Prohibition agent in the Capone era, he has preferred to appear in a place rather than to enter it. Ness could probably be elected Mayor of Cleveland in a walkaway. Last summer, indeed, he turned down a firm offer of the Republican nomination. One unannounced reason was that he is too absorbed in his $24,000-a-year business role with Diebold to exchange it for the $15,000 political job. Ness likes to use high-flown management engineering terms in discussing what he has done at Diebold; others might say simply that he has an excellent intuitive judgment of people, plus administrative ability. At Diebold, his principal contributions thus far have been the elimination of management deadwood, the discovery and promotion of buried talent, and the revival of a discarded reorganization program. When Ness moved in, Diebold was warring with itself over what to do when the war was over. It was also having renegotiation trouble as a result of consistent overcharging. Ness promptly put through a policy of voluntary price reductions, which boosted net profits. All the new officers filling the ranks are sold on modern administrative methods and Diebold's expansion into a dozen new lines of office equipment. Most competent observers

agree Ness has made an excellent start. Some of them suspend judgment on what may happen to Ness and Diebold in the tough world of the office equipment business. Ness himself says, "I may fall flat on my face, but I'm sure having fun."

Eliot's romance with Betty blossomed, and the two were married in a quiet civil ceremony on January 31, 1946, in Baltimore, Maryland. They honeymooned in New York.

"We talked about a big wedding, with all our friends and family members there for a big celebration, but we both decided that we didn't want all the fuss," Ness told friends in announcing the nuptials. "We're just eager to get on with our lives."

CHAPTER TWENTY-TWO

What Might
Have Been . . .

I N THE MIDST OF juggling his business responsibilities with a new marriage, Eliot Ness became acquainted with an internationally recognized hero, Claire Lee Chennault. The two hit it off from the start.

A tall Texan with rugged features and a commanding voice, Chennault earned a reputation as a daring pilot and a serious student of air tactics. He retired from the U.S. Army Air Corps in 1937 due to physical disability and became an adviser on aeronautical affairs to the Chinese national government. In 1941 he organized and trained the famous Flying Tigers, a group of American pilots recruited to fight for the Chinese against their Japanese aggressors, especially in defense of the Burma Road.

At age fifty-one, Chennault returned to active duty with the U.S. Army Air Forces as a brigadier general. His leadership and superior tactics helped greatly to overcome the inferiority of his airmen in numbers and equipment, and at the same time, Chennault became a national legend in China. Upon his retirement as a major general in 1945, he was anxious to capitalize on his relationships with China's government and its military and industrial leaders. To help accomplish this goal, he turned to Ness.

Chennault convinced Ness that the Middle East Company could profit by importing silk and other Chinese goods. He was also optimistic that, through a new air freight service, Chennault Airlines, Ness's group could deliver a variety of American goods to China. Transportation was the major impediment. Air travel was restricted to the mostly government-owned Chinese National Airways, which was inefficient and congested with passenger traffic. Due to the prolonged war with Japan, China's railways and roads had been largely obliterated. River transportation was slow and of limited usefulness. The movement of commodities from the main arteries to the interior villages was accomplished by slow, arduous sampan or pack train.

China's demand for goods from abroad was sharpened by eight years of war with Japan. Many export-import firms, however, had shied away from China because of economic uncertainties, volatile political affairs, customs duties, taxes, and tolls imposed by provincial and city officials. Chennault believed he could overcome these obstacles through his connections in China, combined with strong U.S. government support for businesses helping China to strengthen itself against the Soviet Union. Ness shared the general's enthusiasm, but his optimism did not rub off on Dan Moore and James Landis. They reluctantly agreed to serve as directors, at least in a limited capacity, and provide financial support to get the new business started. In collaboration with Chennault, they formed the Far East Company and a subsidiary, the Far East Textile Company, to deal exclusively with the China trade.

Among the seven others they persuaded to buy stock were James C. Gruener, a prominent attorney with offices in Cleveland and Washington; Gen. Benedict Crowell, former assistant secretary of war and a director of the Nickel Plate Railroad; James W. Huffman, a U.S. senator from Ohio; and Dan Maggin, a New York financier, director of the American Window Glass Company, and a major Diebold stockholder.

The Far East Company was doomed from the start. China, trying to protect its economy against outside domination, kept firm control over international trade and industry. Private imports were subject to stiff, sometimes arbitrarily imposed, duties. In addition, the Far East Company faced intense competition. By July 1946 more than one hundred American firms and numerous British companies were operating export-import businesses in Shanghai.

In an attempt to capitalize on a new national law requiring that the majority of stockholders in all companies be residents of China, Chennault fell back on his connections to form the Sino-American Industrial and Development Company. Many of the other officers were current or former Chinese military leaders and successful businessmen. Gen. Shen Yu, former field commander of the Ninth War Zone in China, was elected chairman of the board. In a speech presented during the first organizational meeting, Yu told of the great esteem in which he held Chennault and his U.S. associates for their humanitarian gestures.

"On his departure for the United States from Shanghai, the general emphasized to me that he would reject any offers made with the sole purpose of making profit," Yu said, according to an English translation of his remarks. "In other words, Americans who invest in this undertaking must also be willing, as the general himself is, to assist the Chinese people and to help us in the task of reconstruction. . . . Now that the general is ready to lend a hand in improving our living conditions or environment, we are only too glad to take a part in the work for the interest of our country."

A letter from Chennault to Ness from Shanghai that same month made no mention of such lofty goals. "Despite pessimistic reports, I am convinced the time is ripe for action," Chennault wrote. "The Chinese need trade desperately and will work out problems and establish firm contacts with someone else if we don't take advantage of the opportunity offered."

Whatever his motivations, Chennault presented his detailed plans for Chennault Airlines to the Chinese government then began laying the groundwork for establishing bus service in Chengtu, a Chinese cultural and academic center. Back in the United States, Ness obtained quotes from a Detroit firm for the purchase of fifty Ford buses. He also lined up buyers for silk and other fabrics Chennault had secured at a fraction of the amount those goods would bring from the Macy's organization and other U.S. buyers.

For the first few months, the Far East Company imported Chinese silk, musk, and dye, generating modest profits. Chennault, however, soon found it difficult to obtain export permits. More silk eventually did arrive in New York, but the material was of such poor quality that the U.S. buyers Ness had found, including Macy's, rejected it.

Chennault created an uproar in China when he negotiated a $3 million loan from the Chinese Relief and Rehabilitation Administration for the purchase of twelve huge transport planes. Some saw the plan as a ploy to set up a private American air service in China under the guise of a relief operation. The loan was eventually approved, but with two important stipulations: the planes would not carry commercial cargo and any empty space on return trips would be taken up by government nonmilitary materials and official passengers. Chennault would still be entitled to a "reasonable profit," but the prospect of capitalizing on the relief missions was eliminated.

With the Communist takeover in 1947, the government assumed responsibility for all aspects of trade in China, including the operation of a new Soviet-backed, state-controlled civil airline. Within a year, the U.S. government banned all trade with mainland China, effectively bankrupting the Far East Company.

When the venture with Chennault collapsed, Ness concentrated on the struggling Middle East Company. Thomas Dunn, a skilled businessman, was brought aboard as a full-time general manager. Moore and Landis had made inroads in Turkey, Egypt, Lebanon, Syria, Greece, Iran, Iraq, and Ethiopia. Yet the Middle East Company earned commissions of barely twenty-five thousand dollars during its first year. Export licenses were difficult to obtain. At the same time, the Office of Price Administration (OPA) limited the Middle East Company's ability to bring goods into the United States, since other countries were purchasing commodities at higher prices than the OPA allowed American firms to pay.

Despite these obstacles, the Middle East Company remained afloat, due in large part to the officers' willingness to defer their salaries until economic conditions improved. A contract with the Charles Pfizer Company to send pharmaceuticals to Portugal, Turkey, Lebanon, and Egypt gave the company a quick infusion of cash. The Middle East Company represented a West Virginia company selling electric fans and appliances to European nations and helped a Tennessee firm sell hosiery in Cuba. The company also landed contracts for importing ponderosa pine from Mexico for resale to several Cleveland-area lumberyards. This was arranged through Fermin F. Nunez, a businessman whose close government ties landed him the bulk of export permits issued in Mexico.

Directors of the Middle East Company saw Turkey as the most promising long-term market for American goods. There was an increasing demand for steel products, automotive and railroad supplies, industrial equipment, and consumer goods. Moore was dispatched to Turkey to fall back on his contacts there and devise a marketing plan to lure new investors.

Moore persuaded the government leaders to approve construction of a massive hotel in Istanbul, then sold the idea to Pan American Airlines. Pan Am agreed to pay the Middle East Company one hundred thousand dollars as "founder and promoter" of the hotel. Although Moore kept his partners back home apprised of developments, Ness and the others appeared to be preoccupied with their own affairs, which left Moore feeling angry, isolated, and betrayed.

"I don't hold it against Eliot or any of the others personally," Moore said many years later. "I just never considered Eliot a very effective businessman, and he had a lot going on at the time. In fact, I'd have to say he was no businessman at all. He had no instinct for it and it was obvious to everyone except Eliot. He was pleasant and delightful, but too boyish, in a way, to be a good businessman. He used to constantly say, when things weren't going well, 'What we need here is a break.' Well, he sure didn't get too many breaks."

Despite a fondness for children, Ness had none of his own. In late January 1948, he and Betty adopted a three-year-old boy, whom they named Robert Warren Ness. "Parenthood was a new experience for Eliot and he enjoyed it immensely, when he could find the time," said a friend of the Nesses. "He was very frustrated that he had to travel to New York and Washington so frequently on business. He was spread too thin. He wanted to spend more time with Betty and Bobby, and they missed him, too. Betty tried to be understanding, but she felt abandoned at times."

Ness felt a growing restlessness and an unshakable desire to return to public service. He missed the challenges and excitement.

Nevertheless, it was a shock to even his closest friends when Ness announced that he was putting his business career on hold to run in the 1947 election for mayor of Cleveland. A number of prominent Cleveland Republicans had practically camped on the former public safety director's doorstep, urging him to do so. Other popular Republicans had steered clear of the race because they considered the incumbent to be unbeatable.

No one was more appalled by Ness's decision than Dan Moore, who had just returned from Turkey when he heard the news. "He sat right here in my parlor and said, 'I'm going to give it a try,' with a smile on his face," Moore recalled. "I told him he was crazy. I knew he couldn't win and I told him that, but he didn't want to believe it."

Ralph Kelly, a political reporter for the *Cleveland Plain Dealer,* was among those who convinced Ness he had a chance. Kelly believed Ness's achievements as safety director carried more weight with the voters than the problems he had with labor unions and the negative publicity stemming from the car crash and his social activities. The popular Bob Chamberlin agreed to serve as Ness's campaign chairman.

In the time since Ness had been away from Cleveland politics, Frank Lausche had resigned as mayor to seek Ohio's gubernatorial nomination. He was succeeded by Thomas A. Burke, a popular Democrat who had been a friend of Ness's.

Industrial leaders welcomed the return of Ness, whose earlier battles against organized crime and racketeering in the city had benefited them immeasurably. Donations from the business community and generous publicity from the Cleveland newspapers boosted the campaign. Republicans on the city council also gave him a strong endorsement. On the other hand, his support from prominent and privileged Republicans prompted Burke's forces to brand Ness as a candidate of the moneyed establishment.

Anyone who thought Ness had any chance to win failed to recognize the power of organized labor, the apathy and short memories of Cleveland voters, and Ness's exceedingly dull style. In press accounts, he was a vibrant, larger-than-life hero riding back into the city to rescue citizens from the forces of evil. In reality, he was a soft-spoken, middle-aged man who was obviously uncomfortable in the role of politician. Many voters resented the fact that Ness had been away from city hall for weeks at a time while safety director. He had dropped almost completely out of sight for a half-decade.

Charismatic in his early Cleveland days, Ness was now showing the effects of stress and an unhealthy lifestyle, with deep lines cutting through his face, slouching shoulders, and a noticeable paunch. During his speeches, he appeared nervous, stiff, and uninspiring. He paid little attention to current political issues, relying instead on broad principles and his faded fame as a crimefighter.

In one speech, he made a token reference to what he perceived as the issues of the day and took a slap at Burke in the process: "I left a Cleveland that was a vibrant, spirited city interested in accomplishment and improvement. . . . I returned to find it, by comparison, a tired and listless town; its air filled with soot and smoke; its streets dirty and in a most deplorable condition; its transportation system noisy, inadequate and approaching insolvency. The equipment of its police and fire department is poorly maintained. Its traffic moves painstakingly and with confusion. Newspapers indicate that Cleveland streets are unsafe after dark. Cleveland is going backward instead of forward."

Despite the pitch, at times Ness appeared to take his candidacy only half seriously. Al Sutton tried to impress upon Ness that he should avoid fraternizing with his political opponents during the campaign.

"He'd come up to my office," Sutton recalled, "and I'd say to him, 'What are you doing here? You're running for mayor and I'm working for Burke as safety director. He's liable to think I'm a double agent or something. He's about fifty feet from here. Why don't you come back after work, so we can have a drink or something?' It didn't seem to faze Eliot. I think he was just innocent and unaware of the political realities."

Sutton, who was safety director from 1946 to 1952, agreed that Ness was no politician. Still Sutton marveled at his predecessor's early years in office: "He was big in Cleveland because he cooperated with the press, plus he was youthful-looking, intelligent, and soft-spoken. But he was tough when he had to be. He sent about a dozen cops to the penitentiary back in the days when that was practically unheard of. The guy had class, is what it boils down to. You can't teach that. You're just born with it, and Eliot had it."

Even Ness's friends in the press couldn't help him win the election. Ness used most of his modest savings to help counter Burke's heavy campaign donations from organized labor. Ernest Molnar also raised thousands of dollars to help his former boss. With the support of the Republican Party itself, Ness's campaign war chest totaled more than twice that of Burke's.

Volunteers walked through each precinct distributing *The Ness News*, a tabloid that recalled Ness's accomplishments and promised changes in city government. The candidate embarked on a series of handshaking tours of city streets. One pundit said he looked like an ex-athlete trying to relive his glory as he boasted of his accomplishments as safety director. Posters, billboards, and full-page newspaper advertisements implored Clevelanders to "Vote Yes for Ness."

"He thought he could win by standing on the street corner with Betty and shaking hands," Dan Moore remembered. "One time I took out my pen and showed him the math, how he could shake hundreds of hands every day and still not ever see 90 percent of Cleveland's voters. Eliot didn't realize that he had to get himself some fresh publicity, and get the right people to work for him. Let's face it, politics wasn't his game."

Ness launched a series of speeches and advertisements portraying his opponent as ineffective. He also suggested Burke was beholden to union interests and party loyalties. Burke could have retaliated by citing Ness's shortcomings, but he resisted. He also refused to debate Ness before a live radio audience. "The best politics is good government," Burke said in response to Ness's campaign. "My record speaks for itself."

Ness hit harder in the final weeks of the campaign, accusing Burke of resisting rent-control legislation because of political pressure, of bankrupting the city transit system by overpaying unionized employees, and of refusing to offend local industrial powers by cracking down on air pollution.

Just a few days before the election, Ness and Burke made a joint appearance before the Cleveland City Club, a civic organization. Burke, who spoke first after losing a coin toss, defended himself against Ness's verbal assaults by producing a thick stenographic book that he said contained every word Ness had uttered in the campaign. Waving this book within inches of Ness's nose, Burke declared with vehemence, "You have made many charges in this campaign and I challenge you, as an ace investigator, to produce even one scrap of evidence to substantiate the charges."

Ness responded weakly that Burke had shown poor judgment by accepting the endorsement of a wing of the Council of Industrial Organizations known to be sympathetic to communist interests.

The voters sent a loud and clear message on November 4, when Burke won by a margin of almost two to one: 168,412 votes to 85,990. Ness, although disappointed by the outcome, tried to demonstrate that he could take defeat in stride. He telephoned Burke with congratulations and was invited to attend a victory party at the mayor's home. Ness accepted, graciously joining in on the festivities. As the night progressed, he stunned many of those present by toasting Burke with a snide remark, "Who'd want an honest politician anyway?"

"How sad it was to see Eliot Ness, once the toast of the city, now a humbled also-ran," wrote one Cleveland newspaper columnist. A postmortem on the Ness candidacy came from Cleveland reporter John Patrick Martin, who observed that the former safety director had missed the boat by declining to run for mayor in 1941, during the peak of his popularity.

"We all like Eliot, and we all admired him as an honest, thorough expert in the field of law enforcement," Martin wrote in the *Plain Dealer*. "There was never anybody like him in Cleveland. He really captured the imagination of the public in his early years, and he was given a hero's worship unlike that given any city official within my recollection."

After sacrificing his financial security and part of his reputation, Ness felt rejected, humiliated, and betrayed. The political campaign also greatly weakened his status in the business world at the same time the Middle East Company continued to self-destruct.

Fermin F. Nunez suddenly had trouble securing the Mexican lumber supplies he had promised. The few shipments he could deliver cost more than the Cleveland-area buyers were willing to pay.

Adding insult to injury, Chinese business owners who had provided flour and silk to the now-defunct Far East Company brought suit against Ness, Chennault, and the Middle East Company.

The company's only hope of survival was Turkey. But before Dan Moore returned to Istanbul in a desperate attempt to save the company, he tried one last time to help his good friend.

CHAPTER TWENTY-THREE

The Beginning of the End

Dan Moore had friends in high places, including Detroit. Hearing that the city was seeking a new police administrator, Moore had just the man. "Eliot was a natural for the job, a guy with all the credentials anyone could ask for, and he would have jumped at the chance," Moore said. "But no matter how much talking I did, they wouldn't bend. They said they didn't want anyone with political ambitions, since he might upset the political machinery, and Eliot had that damned mayoral campaign in his background. They wouldn't even consider him."

Ness's life had become mired in uncertainty. His responsibilities for both Diebold and the Middle East Company were sporadic and sometimes unclear. Executives at Diebold were plotting a takeover. They were resentful of Ness's managerial style and grumbled over his frequent absences and inconsistency.

In late 1948 Betty and he rented a house in Cleveland, from which Ness commuted the forty miles to Diebold in Canton and pursued his Middle East Company responsibilities—such as they were. Much of his time was spent on the road, including occasional stops in the community of Kent, where he befriended Jack Foyle, a young car dealer. "He was a very lonesome man looking for a friend," Foyle told author Laurence Bergreen. "He was depressed by his defeat in Cleveland for mayor."

Although his financial problems were deepening, Ness paid Foyle two thousand dollars in cash for a new Mercury coupe, dark green, with all the extras. Almost every day, Ness stopped on his way home from work, usually around four in the afternoon, and traveled with Foyle to the Kent Hotel for cocktails and small talk. Ness would occasionally "forget his wallet," Foyle said, but at other times he would flash twenty-dollar bills, buy a round or two of drinks, and insist that the bartender keep the change. At the hotel lounge, Ness passed the hours reminiscing about his days in Chicago, especially about Capone. He complained about his treatment by Diebold and lamented the lost opportunities of his life—his unsuccessful efforts to become an FBI agent, his car crash, his failed marriages, and the humiliating election loss.

Corinne Lawson, the Nesses' housekeeper, recalled the couple's struggles in 1949 and beyond. Lawson said that Ness often joked about his battles with Capone, once telling her that "Old Scarface" had shot at him a few times, "but I outran the bullets." She remembered the time she went to buy meat for the Nesses, only to be told by the butcher that their credit had been shut off for nonpayment of a large balance. "It reached the point where some men did not like him and talked about him [behind his back], but he was liked by the ladies because he was witty. As far as I'm concerned, he was a gentleman. Eliot and Betty were both very nice people."

The Nesses paid Lawson almost twice the going rate because they appreciated her cooking, her cleaning, and her company. When the Nesses were not entertaining, Lawson said, Eliot would often sit by himself, deep in thought, sometimes sipping Cutty Sark and water. "When he noticed I was present, he would 'turn on the sunshine.' He didn't want to burden others with his troubles." And she confirmed his meat-and-potatoes eating habits. "I once asked him, 'How about a tossed salad?' He said, 'Well, you go ahead and mix it up and I'll toss it out the window.'"

By that time, Ness's closest friend and most stabilizing influence, Dan Moore, had moved with his wife and children to Istanbul to work on the hotel deal and other business prospects. Moore persuaded a Turkish company to accept U.S. shipments of pharmaceuticals for repackaging and resale in Turkey. He also arranged for the importation of buses to give Istanbul its first public transportation system.

On the U.S. end, Tom Dunn put together another optimistic report to convince potential stockholders great things were in store for the Middle East Company: "In Turkey, the company affiliated with the Middle East Company is composed of very rich Turks who have unusual influence with the Turkish government. They can influence the granting of import licenses with reference to goods imported into Turkey for which payment must be made in American dollars. In this period of dollar shortages, this is extremely important because no business can be done without the obtaining of import licenses granting the payment in dollars."

With Dunn aboard as a full-time general manager, the primary reason Ness remained affiliated was his potential to bring the company additional business from Diebold. Moore even invited him to sever his ties with Diebold and join him in Turkey. He was confident that the Turkish officials would hire Ness as a consultant to work out solutions to their traffic problems in several major cities, including Istanbul. Betty Ness, however, had no interest in moving to Turkey, and Eliot never pressed the issue with her.

The Middle East directors dispatched Ness to Washington to line up political support for the company. He met with administrators of the Export-Import Bank and lunched with Drew Pearson, an influential newspaper columnist whose interest in the Middle East Company could be traced to the fact that he was married to Dan Moore's sister.

On the other side of the world, Moore began to feel alienated and uneasy. When his letters to his Middle East Company colleagues went unanswered, Moore feared that Dunn, Ness, and the others were allowing the company to collapse. Correspondence from that era, found among hundreds of personal business papers Ness left in an obscure filing cabinet at the time of his death, suggest that Moore's concerns were justified. The Middle East Company directors failed to follow up on business leads and refused to send Moore financial statements that would have informed him of the company's sorry financial state.

The collapse of the pharmaceutical contract was particularly frustrating to Moore. He had found an eager buyer, negotiated a price that would bring the Middle East Company considerable profit, and obtained the necessary permits to bring the materials to Turkey in exchange for American dollars. No one back in the United States hooked up with a provider—although many were available—and the Turkish buyer eventually turned elsewhere.

Moore eventually signed on as a full-time employee of Pan Am's Intercontinental Hotels and resigned as an officer of the Middle East Company. He rarely saw Eliot Ness after that, but Moore's memories remained sharp almost a half-century later:

> He was a delightful man—humorous, interesting, charming, and very easy to like. People naturally gravitated toward him. He was a terrific police administrator, but he ended up trying to be something that he wasn't. I think there's a lesson in all this: If you have a tremendous gift in one area, you should abandon it with great caution. Eliot abandoned something that he was the best in the world at doing, and he suffered the consequences.

The Middle East Company continued its steady march toward insolvency. Mexico placed a steep export tax on lumber and other products for which the company had found buyers. The once-lucrative pharmaceutical trade with Portugal was eliminated when the Portuguese Red Cross intervened with a direct purchase arrangement. Ness, while officially listed as vice president of the Middle East Company, had little to do with the company after Moore's resignation.

At the same time, the Rexes sold their stock and, on April 2, 1951, Ness was voted off the Diebold board. Despite his celebrity status and his legitimate contributions to Diebold during a critical time in that company's history, Ness rates only one brief line in the corporate archives. "There's very little information about him in the company records," said John Kristoff, director of public relations at Diebold. "It's almost as if he came in, did nothing of significance, and left."

One man who had dealings with Diebold during the 1940s agreed to share his observations on the condition that he remain anonymous:

> Eliot got a raw deal. There were people there who resented the fact that Jane Rex had brought him in, out of nowhere really, and

installed him as chairman of the board. It wouldn't be fair to the families for me to name any names at this point. Eliot didn't play favorites at Diebold. He just expected people to do their jobs. That went against the philosophy of a select few who were trying to milk the company for all it was worth. The fundamental difference between Eliot and the rest of them was that he really cared about Diebold and wasn't just out for himself, at least in the early stages, before he got shafted. That's why some of them were out to get him—he wouldn't "go along to get along." And they did get him.

Raymond Koontz, who served as vice president and treasurer of Diebold during a portion of Ness's tenure there, added that Ness's remoteness was what eventually cost him his job at Diebold. "He never really worked here [in Canton]," Koontz said. "He didn't have an office here. He would come here [from Cleveland] a couple of times a week, then maybe miss a week. He didn't really fraternize too much down here and, as time went on, he wasn't really involved in the executive decision-making—he just represented those ladies' stock interests."

Desperate for employment, Ness called on several old friends in Cleveland, expressing a willingness to accept even a low-paying, menial job to support his wife and son. He took a sales position with an electronics wholesaler for a brief period of time. Still interested in law enforcement, Ness tried to interest the Cleveland Police Department in promoting the use of a personal alarm device, sold under the brand name Help Call, for people who were being attacked. He stood to receive a substantial commission on each unit sold, but Ness was too far ahead of his time. These alarms are now commonplace in most American cities.

When the electronics company relocated to Chicago, Ness decided to remain in Cleveland and seek other work. He spent a few months as a clerk in a downtown bookstore, then landed a job selling frozen hamburger patties to restaurants. In time, the frozen-foods business would turn many people, including the Stouffer family, into millionaires but, as with Help Call, Ness was involved too early to enjoy the industry's financial rewards.

Not much has been written about Ness's activities in the early 1950s. People who knew Eliot and Betty during this period say their marriage remained strong even as their financial plight worsened. Eliot probably spent as much time between jobs as he did employed, while Betty continued to pursue her interest in sculpture. Both of them grew close to Robert, a quiet but seemingly well-adjusted boy. Despite their financial difficulties, both Eliot and Betty believed strongly enough in the value of a good education to enroll Robert in a private school and keep close tabs on his academic progress.

In June 1952 Ness landed a job as a trust officer and investment adviser for a Cleveland bank. One of the bank's clients was courting a Cincinnati manufacturer, and Ness was assigned to represent the bank's interests during negotiations. This job brought him to Mark Lehman's house in Cincinnati for meetings with Mark's father.

"Mr. Ness liked kids, and quickly became a favorite at our house," said Lehman, who was eight years old at the time. "He fascinated me and my younger sister with his repertoire of magic tricks. He would discover a quarter in my sister's ear, or close his hand on a golf pencil which then magically disappeared."

Based on outward appearances, Ness was content, but people who were close to him knew better.

"Eliot was very depressed and felt victimized," said a close family acquaintance. "He went out of his way not to let others see it. Deep down inside, he felt guilty and ashamed for failing to adequately provide for his wife and son. But he also believed that he had been the victim of circumstances that were beyond his control—just plain bad luck."

CHAPTER TWENTY-FOUR

"You Should Write a Book"

G. FRANK SHAMPANORE HAD A dream. A short, stocky wheeler-dealer who had drifted through a series of mostly ill-fated business ventures since the early 1930s, Shampanore was sure he had a winner this time. On his drawing board was a Cleveland-based business that he claimed would earn hundreds of thousands of dollars for investors who were lucky enough to get in on the action early.

Shampanore tried to patent a process he developed to watermark checks and other important documents as protection against counterfeiting. Coupled with the watermarking were personal and commercial checks that bore a unique front-endorsement feature. Shampanore believed banks and other financial institutions would jump at the chance to market checks that were attractive, a time-saver for tellers, and most important, difficult to counterfeit.

Among those who came on board was Joseph Phelps, a tall, outgoing former semiprofessional baseball player with New Jersey roots. In the early 1950s, Phelps had promoted natural gas wells and, in the words of a colleague, "made a lot of money for a lot of people in northern Pennsylvania." Phelps was a natural salesman, hale and hearty, with a fixed smile.

Mining interests brought Phelps and Shampanore together in Coudersport, a small village tucked in the rolling hills of northcentral Pennsylvania. Also joining the team was Shampanore's young nephew, William J. Ayers, of Hackettstown, New Jersey, a mechanical designer and printer who was directed to adapt Shampanore's product to the marketplace.

"The watermarking idea looked great," Ayers said during a 1999 interview. "Frank had a lot of people convinced he had a wonderful thing and I bought the whole nine yards."

Shampanore and Phelps sought an identifiable figure to convince investors that these businesses would be profitable. They shared their plan with Eliot Ness, believing that he could attract investors among his former business associates in Cleveland and give the company an air of legitimacy. The idea appealed to Ness, who was not in a position to be choosy. A $150 weekly salary was enough to support Eliot, Betty, and Bobby Ness, and stock options made the position even more enticing.

Shampanore established North Ridge Industrial Corporation as a holding company for two subsidiaries that would conduct the business: Guaranty Paper Corporation, for the watermarking and printing processes, and Fidelity Check Corporation, to produce commercial and personal checks. Although he invested little of his own money, Shampanore became chairman of the board and majority stockholder of North Ridge. Joe Phelps was named vice president, and Ness served as president of the two subsidiaries.

Phelps and Ness were bubbling with enthusiasm as they began a series of meetings with potential investors. William Ayers, however, had a different perspective after his first trip to Cleveland to begin working for North Ridge in 1955.

"Frank took me to a little room with a dinky, hand-cranked printing machine, and said, 'This is what we have to start with.' I was supposed to design and build the machines to take the watermarking process out of the laboratory and make it commercially successful. Then Frank took me to the Terminal Building, where North Ridge had an entire suite of offices, lavishly furnished with six people on staff for marketing and promoting.

"I was appalled. I said, 'You better back off until we have something to sell! It's going to take about two years to build the equipment and perfect the production.' Frank didn't want to hear any of that. He said, 'That won't do. We have to show progress if we're going to get more investors.' I decided to give it my best shot."

Phelps returned to Coudersport, accompanied by Ness, and visited many of the same investors who had benefited so handsomely from his gas well speculation just a few years earlier. Phelps erased many skeptics' apprehensions by promising to buy back all North Ridge stock if the company failed. Meanwhile, he negotiated personal bank loans to cover some of the company's expenses.

During a trip to New York City in late 1955, Phelps and Ness met with one of Phelps's childhood friends, Oscar Fraley, a United Press Associations sportswriter. After hearing the men's sales pitch during a meeting at the Waldorf-Astoria, the lanky, easygoing Fraley said he was not in any financial position to invest in North Ridge.

After the three enjoyed several cocktails, Phelps and Fraley reminisced about their younger days. Ness dozed on a couch. Close to midnight, Phelps told Fraley, "You'll have to get Eliot to tell you about his experiences as a Prohibition agent in Chicago. He's the guy who dried up Al Capone. It's real gangbuster stuff: killings, raids, the whole works. It was pretty dangerous stuff."

Fraley found it difficult to believe the soft-spoken man with the pleasant smile had been such a dynamic crimefighter. For the next five hours, Ness told him of stakeouts and wiretaps, death threats and dum-dum bullets, crashes through brewery doors and the extraordinary teamwork that helped bring down Capone.

"Eliot could talk with entertaining ease in private," Fraley recalled in a story he wrote for *Coronet* magazine. "Something about the relaxed atmosphere and the way we had been gabbing started him off. The next thing I knew, it was six in the morning. For hours I had listened, wide-eyed and wordlessly, as Eliot talked of those deadly days in Chicago. 'Let's knock off and get some breakfast,' Eliot said, stretching and getting up from the floor, where he had been sitting with his back against the edge of a couch. 'Someday,' I suggested, 'you should write a book on your experiences. You might make some money with it.' Eliot looked up over the shoelace he was tying and it seemed to me I could detect a certain bitterness in his voice. 'I could use it,' he said."

In fact, Ness had attempted to recruit Chicago journalists to help him write a book about his Chicago experiences many years earlier, but he found no takers.

Just before Christmas, Ness and Phelps returned to New York seeking additional investors and accepted Fraley's invitation to dine with him at a fashionable downtown restaurant. Fraley repeated his offer to collaborate on a book, but this time he found Ness to be reluctant. "It was a long time ago, and a lot of things happened in a short amount of time," he explained. "I'm not sure I could sort it all out."

"Listen, you've got the newspaper clippings and the souvenirs, don't you?" Fraley inquired.

"I've got a whole locker full of stuff, but you'd have a real problem trying to figure out what it all means. I've never taken the time to organize it."

"Just send me what you have," Fraley insisted. "I'll sort through it, get an outline together, and then the thing will start to flow. At least let me see what you've got. This could really be a seller if we do it right."

Ness agreed to pile his material in a box and mail it to Fraley. He also began writing his own version of his Chicago activities, or at least as much as he could recall. His twenty-two-page typewritten version was disjointed, poorly written, and brief.

Inside the box Fraley found a veritable gold mine: case files, personal financial records, handwritten wiretap reports, newspaper and magazine articles, photographs, personal notations, and more. After assuring Ness that an outline would be forthcoming in a couple of weeks, Fraley took a leave of absence from United Press Associations and began to put the material in some order.

Back in Cleveland, Bill Ayers was working feverishly to develop the North Ridge equipment, and Shampanore and his associates continued to spend money faster than it was coming in. Hoping to generate business with the federal government, they opened a branch office in Washington. Ness called upon his former Cleveland connections but with little success.

"I hadn't seen Eliot in a while, and I kind of felt sorry for him," said David Kerr, a former bodyguard, who was approached by Ness as a potential investor in 1956. "It was pretty obvious to me that he was hurting for money and, quite frankly, I don't think anybody was paying much attention to him when he was out here talking about this great check watermark business he was in. To my knowledge, he didn't sell much stock when he was out here. I didn't buy any."

"It was obvious that we were in a lot of trouble," Ayers remembered. "We still didn't know our capacity or what our cost was going to be, and yet we were advertising in bank publications and printing journals. We were getting people all excited, and we basically had nothing to sell."

Ayers wasn't the only one trying to persuade Shampanore to slow down. Ness, after several months of being a good soldier, confronted the company president about poor management of the business. Angered by what he perceived as insubordination, Shampanore wanted Ness out of the picture.

In July 1956, desperate to cut expenses, the officers of North Ridge Industrial Corporation moved their headquarters from Cleveland to Coudersport. The costs of maintaining offices and a fledgling production facility in Cleveland were far too high. Coudersport offered cheaper labor, lower rent, and closer proximity to many of the North Ridge investors. The company made a token down payment on the former Gates Grocery Store at the corner of Main and Oak Streets in the center of town. Business offices were established above a Western Auto Store on Main Street and over another business a half-block away on Second Street.

Eliot, Betty, and Bobby Ness moved into the lower floor of a modest two-story home on Third Street, near the banks of the Allegheny River. Shampanore, Phelps, and Ayers also moved with their families to Coudersport, as did their advertising manager, Rube Pollan. Ayers immediately went to work setting up a production plant, while Phelps and Ness resumed their pursuit of new investors. The stock was attractive to doctors, business owners, and a handful of government officeholders. Many of these investors were motivated by a desire to support a venture that could benefit the community.

"We really wanted to help promote some economic activity in Coudersport," said George C. Mosch, who with his brother, Herman C. Mosch, invested thirteen hundred dollars in the North Ridge Industrial Corporation and Guaranty Paper Corporation. "It also looked like it might be a good investment. However, some of us felt that they were spending money rather foolishly. We wondered how a company that was just getting started could spend that kind of money on expensive office furnishings and things that weren't necessary."

Frank Shampanore painted a rosy picture of the business in a letter to stockholders. "We carried advertising in the October issues of the *Bankers Monthly* and *Banking,* the two leading banking magazines. The response was so great that we withdrew subsequent advertising until such time as our plants were ready for full production. Paper dealers and printers in Switzerland, West Germany, France, Belgium, Sweden, England, and Canada have indicated interest in joining us in the foreign exploitation of our work."

A large spread in the local weekly newspaper, *The Potter Enterprise,* announced the arrival of Ness and his business partners with great fanfare:

> The annual estimated loss of $500 million to banks, depositors, and insurance companies because of check forgery will be substantially reduced, it is claimed, through use of Fidelity watermarked checks now available to individuals and companies by their local bank. Watermarked papers are available through Guaranty franchised printers, department stores and stationers. . . . Ness's background is highly unusual for a top corporate officer. His brilliant career began as a special agent for the Justice Department, when he headed the investigation of the Al Capone and Bugs Moran mobsters that resulted in a sorely-needed cleanup of crime in Chicago.

A four-column photograph accompanying the article featured the smiling faces of the six officers: Shampanore; Ness; Phelps; Carl Reidy, an attorney from Emporium, Pennsylvania; Verne Haight, one of Shampanore's colleagues, who was named executive vice president, and George McKinney, the corporation treasurer.

Coupled with the watermarking process promoted by Guaranty Paper were Fidelity Check Corporation's "four-square" checks, with the front endorsement feature and a colorful pictorial background of the buyer's choice. The watermarking process of Guaranty Paper was said to be unique; it could be used on paper that was already printed or on blank stock. Forgery experts of that era often printed their own checks (usually payroll duplicates), forged signatures, and had them passed by confederates in a neighborhood where many payroll checks of one company were cashed by merchants, tavern owners, and other businesses. Ness and others believed their product would be impossible to duplicate.

Not everyone, however, was convinced that Guaranty Paper was a good investment.

"Eliot saw the watermarking a process as a wonderful opportunity, but I had my doubts, or at least concerns," recalled John J. Rigas, a young Coudersport businessman at the time. Rigas is now chief executive officer and president of Adelphia Communications, one of the nation's largest television cable companies.

"There were times I wanted to avoid Eliot because he kept trying to get me to invest in the company," Rigas continued. "Frankly, I didn't have the money to do it and I didn't believe in it. That wasn't Ness's fault or Joe Phelps' fault. They were both decent men and they never stopped trying to make it a success. Eliot was the kind of person you couldn't help taking a liking to—an articulate man with a kind heart, a friendly smile, and a warm personality. He was the kind of guy you were glad to have living in your community, even though a couple of his business associates and investors were a little suspect in my mind."

Ness's financial plight became evident to Rigas when the personal checks he wrote to pay his television cable bills were returned for insufficient funds. Ness also borrowed small sums of money from Rigas and other Coudersport business owners to meet the payroll at Guaranty Paper Company.

At the same time, the Nesses didn't take long to work themselves into Coudersport's social fabric. Betty joined the First United Presbyterian Church, just a block from their home. Eliot did not become an official member but occasionally attended services. The Presbyterian minister, the Reverend Robert Loughborough, described Ness as "lonely, gracious, and not at all like the blood and thunder character Hollywood would later depict him to be."

Bobby Ness made several friends in the neighborhood, including Bill Grabe, a boy with Down syndrome who lived across the street. Grabe smiles as he thinks back to the excitement he felt when Eliot Ness came home from work at dusk and invited him to play with Bobby and him in the Nesses' backyard.

Betty, who was not as comfortable living in a small town as her husband and son, told one friend that Coudersport reminded her of "a Norman Rockwell painting; as wholesome, and just about as boring." Her attitude toward the community improved, however, when she found others in Coudersport who shared her appreciation of art. Some of her Coudersport acquaintances persuaded Betty to discuss her skills during a program presented to the New Century Club, a women's organization. Those who heard her presentation, entitled "Sculpturing As a Means of Personal Expression," marveled at Betty's expertise and her accomplishments in the field.

Eliot Ness often remarked to acquaintances that he felt welcome in Coudersport, where the relaxed lifestyle and tranquillity were in such stark contrast to his days in Chicago and Cleveland. At home Ness often donned a sweatshirt and gym shorts to exercise or listen to his extensive collection of Eddy Duchin records. He sometimes stretched out on the living room floor and leaned against the furniture, often balancing a drink on his right thigh. Eliot also spent time reading or playing with Bobby in the yard behind their house. A highlight for Bobby was the three-block walk he and his father sometimes took to the Olympic Restaurant, a confectionery featuring homemade chocolates. He also enjoyed cooking snacks for his father, especially fried egg sandwiches.

"Eliot had an instinct about children and understanding of their needs," Betty Ness said. "He enjoyed and loved them. His son had too short a time with his father, but I sometimes feel that he received more love and attention in those years than some boys get in a lifetime."

Sometimes during the day, and many evenings after work, Ness visited Coudersport's taverns. His favorite was the Old Hickory, a large Victorian home converted to a hotel with a bar in the basement.

"He was a down-to-earth, quiet kind of guy," said Fred Anderson, a Coudersport elementary schoolteacher who often saw Ness at the Old Hickory. "He was usually by himself when he came in. We had heard stories about this guy going after Al Capone, so we'd try to get him to open up and start talking about those exploits. He wasn't boasting, but the stories did sound a little exaggerated. We thought, *If he's so important, why is he driving a beat-up old car?* I guess most of us never realized who he was until *The Untouchables* came on television several years later."

Other Coudersport acquaintances reacted with polite skepticism when Ness spoke of his days in Chicago and Cleveland. Ness looked more like the aging businessman he was than the daring federal agent he had been. He was a guest speaker at a meeting of the Coudersport Rotary Club, where he detailed some of his experiences in Chicago. "Widespread public support of a law such as Prohibition is a necessary ingredient of enforceability," he told the group. "Scarcely half the people in the country were in sympathy with the Volstead Act."

"Who the heck does he think he's kidding with a story like that?" was the reaction of a local schoolteacher, Henry Staiger, as he opened the door of a friend's car following the speech, only to discover that Ness was a passenger in the backseat. Ness smiled, taking no apparent offense.

Other things about Ness did not add up to Coudersport residents. They wondered how a person of his reputation could be affiliated with a company such as North Ridge. They also found it odd that Ness showed such a strong distaste for guns, which were as common as automobiles in Coudersport.

What they did not know was that economic problems were eating away at him. North Ridge Industrial Corporation was self-destructing. Shampanore failed in his attempts to market the products in Washington. The front-endorsement idea never did catch on, nor did Fidelity's pictorial backgrounds on personal checks. Ambitious plans to build thirty small printing plants across the country to produce watermarked checks were shelved, due to the company's financial straits.

As the rift between North Ridge officers deepened and the business moved closer to bankruptcy, Shampanore traded most of his stock for a new Lincoln sedan and fled to Odessa, Texas. There he quietly established a small production plant and attracted new investors for another stab at the watermarking business. Shampanore sent letters to North Ridge stockholders, attacking the integrity and commitment of Ness who, ironically, was one of the handful of people holding the company together.

With the company in turmoil, Ayers received a telegram from his uncle demanding his presence in Chicago the following day to meet with Shampanore and Jay E. Burns, an executive with the Franklin-Burns Company. "I was shocked to learn that they had worked out a plan by which we were to sabotage the company and then pick it up in a sheriff's sale for 'ten cents on the dollar,' to use Frank's words," Ayers said. "I was ordered to return to Coudersport and do everything I could to cause the company to go under. I was promised all kinds of rewards for doing it."

Ayers could not bring himself to leave the North Ridge investors holding the bag and staining the reputation of those who, in good faith, had bought into Shampanore's dream.

"I called Frank and said I wanted no part of this," Ayers recalled. "He basically told me to go to hell, and that was that."

Ayers, Ness, and Phelps set about trying to make things work. They vacated the two auxiliary business offices and consolidated operations at the former grocery store. Ness drew up a detailed marketing plan filled with optimism.

"We are all aware of the remarkable improvements made in the process and the product in the last few months," Ness wrote. "As a result, Guaranty is now in a position to rapidly develop its market." He told of new machinery that would watermark checks, stationery, and other papers and with less spoilage. Ness's plan forecasted annual profits of more than $325,000, assuming that banks and corporations would embrace the watermarked checks and other paper products.

"With the market arrangements we have now, I believe we can sell and produce our product in constantly increasing volumes, at relatively low cost," he wrote. "Our operating and overhead expenses are cut to the bone and can be controlled so that they increase only as sales volumes increase. This condition should result in increasing profits as sales volume increases."

Anyone reading the *Potter Enterprise* of November 15, 1956, and not knowing the background of North Ridge had to assume the business was on the verge of great things. Phelps and Ness earned the unqualified support of the Coudersport Chamber of Commerce after they described the company's potential and forecasted as many as 150 new jobs.

"If we can obtain just 1 percent of the nation's check business, our employment problem will be solved," Ness told the business group. "We have something wonderful, I think, but our problem is letting the world know we have it. Tell your friends to ask for our checks and, with local support as the beginning, we can go on in ever-widening circles to reach the four corners of the nation."

Ness and Phelps boasted of the National Sheriffs' Association endorsement their North Ridge products had received, thanks in large part to the promotional work of association member sheriff Harold Holcomb of Coudersport. While Ness and Phelps promoted, Bill Ayers tried to make the pieces fit together. Orders were coming in, but not enough to make the operation profitable. As hard as the trio worked to keep the business alive, Shampanore was doing his best to destroy it. Shampanore's poison-pen letters continued to arrive in the mailboxes of stockholders, community leaders, and eventually, the rank-and-file employees of the Guaranty Paper Company plant in Coudersport.

Despite these long-distance attacks, Ness retained the unswerving loyalty and respect of the plant employees. Each morning, he and Joe Phelps met at the coffee counter in Mackey's Restaurant to discuss business, often interrupted by small talk with local business owners and politicians who filed in and out.

CHAPTER TWENTY-FIVE

A Symbol of Courage and Decency

E LIOT NESS VISITED THE small office of family physician Dr. George C. Mosch in late 1956, not to discuss North Ridge business, but for a physical examination. Mosch found the fifty-three-year-old patient to be in generally good health, but he was concerned about a slight heart murmur and what the physician described as "a degree of nervousness and anxiety." Mosch prescribed a mild tranquilizer and referred Ness to Dr. Kurt Zinter, an internal medicine specialist and cardiologist in Wellsville, New York, about thirty miles away.

Zinter's examination revealed that the former crimefighter was suffering from inactive rheumatic valvular disease. Eliot was cautioned to avoid exertion and continue taking a sedative. He never mentioned the diagnosis to his friends or business partners, and it's possible he never told Betty.

One afternoon, Ness was deeply involved in preparations for an audit when he received a phone call from Oscar Fraley, informing him that the Julian Messner Publishing Company had offered a contract for their book, based on Fraley's outline and some sample chapters. Ness would receive a one-thousand-dollar advance to be followed by royalties from the book sales. The writer agreed to visit Coudersport and work with Ness on the manuscript. While he awaited the writer's arrival, Ness consulted with his wife and several of his Coudersport acquaintances for advice on the book.

"He was actually surprised that the publishing world was interested in his story," said one of those friends, Jack Dorfeld. "I remember him saying that he was a little upset that Fraley insisted on making his Chicago days sound much more thrilling than they really were. That bugged Eliot. The thing is, though, Eliot didn't have a clear recollection of all that did happen way back then. I think he and Fraley were both under a lot of pressure to liven things up, so they could make some quick money. I know that the Eliot Ness I read about in that book wasn't the Eliot Ness I knew."

"I don't believe Eliot actually wanted the book to be published, but he needed the money and I think he wanted to recover some of his forgotten fame," said Bill Ayers. "He was many times on the verge of chucking the whole project because the book was making him out to be a hero, which he honestly didn't consider himself to be. I still get a little upset when he's depicted as the John Wayne type. That wasn't Eliot's style at all. He was very mild-mannered."

Among others assisting in the writing were Walter Taylor, editor of the *Potter Enterprise,* and Dorothy Wilkinson, who faithfully served North Ridge as a combination secretary–silk screen artist. When Ness visited the home of Dorothy and her husband, Lewis Wilkinson, he often had a bottle of vodka in one hand and a stack of Guaranty Paper check registries in the other. He used the back of the registries to scratch out notes for the manuscript.

"He liked to sit and talk about some of the things he'd done and things he'd seen, but he was also interested in what the other guy had to say," Lewis Wilkinson said. "I was in the contracting business and about every day he wanted to know what I was doing. He asked a lot of questions."

Wilkinson said he would sometimes challenge Ness on certain heroic actions detailed in the manuscript. "He would get a little grin on his face and say, 'Well, we've got to embellish those things a little bit to make them interesting,' or some such remark, which is what Fraley wanted him to do. He thought it was funny that someone wouldn't believe him verbatim."

Dorothy Wilkinson told interviewer John Graves that during the informal hours she spent helping Ness with his book, she found him to be literate and intelligent, although he occasionally had difficulty finding the right words. Dorothy assisted in filling in the blanks and typing Ness's drafts.

The initial manuscript was hardly adequate, so Fraley swung into action. He first had to convince the publisher that the title was appropriate. Julian Messner initially balked because "The Untouchables" was the same name given to members of India's lowest social caste.

The intensive work sessions between Ness and Fraley were sometimes exercises in futility. Meeting in Fraley's small room at the Hotel Crittenden or at Mackey's Restaurant, they worked their way through huge piles of materials. Sometimes, when Fraley questioned Ness about inconsistencies or contradictions, a frustrated Ness would pound his head with his palm. The passage of time had dimmed his memory, and he had to struggle with the fact that newspaper accounts of his law enforcement career in Chicago were incomplete.

At times, he would leave for a walk on the snow-covered streets of Coudersport and return with more of the details having fallen into place. Fraley recalled, "He would start out at a half-run and then, in a few minutes, slow to a lazy, sauntering walk which allowed him to inspect anything in his sight. Little escaped him. His eyes probed the contents of a dusty store window, noticed a misspelled word on a billboard, or spotted an acquaintance through the murky window of a restaurant. Quickly noticeable on these monotony-breaking journeys was the friendly warmth that drew people to him. Eliot had not been in Coudersport long, yet it seemed that he knew everybody in town. He was, their attitude said, a welcome neighbor."

Despite Fraley's encouragement, Ness expressed skepticism about the book's sales potential. Fraley, on the other hand, was so optimistic that he tried to persuade Ness to commit to a second book collaboration, focusing on his accomplishments in Cleveland. Neither of them could have known that *The Untouchables* would provide the seed from which the legend of Eliot Ness would grow.

Betty Ness persuaded her husband to remove one of the anecdotes concerning a raid on a brothel and the arrest of several prostitutes. While the paddy wagon was going around a corner, or so the story went, the back doors flew open and several of the women tumbled out onto the street. Betty was strongly opposed to prostitution and did not think it appropriate for Eliot to make light of it.

In his original manuscript, Ness summarized his own Law Enforcement Theory, which didn't survive the book's final cut:

> The trouble with the Prohibition Law was that such a large section of the public did not believe in it; they either were against it in its entirety or figured it was for the other fellow. There is no law in the books for which there is 100 percent enforcement. Even the law against murder is violated from time to time. The general public will violate a law when it is inconvenient for them not to: for instance, take the traffic laws against speeding and parking. Violation of the Prohibition Law was a great deal more serious at the level of manufacture and sale; such a large section of the public illicitly possessed liquor, this part of the law became almost unenforceable. The underworld therefore became very strong in power of wealth so that there were terrific amounts of money with which to corrupt law enforcement officials.

Ness failed to mention to Fraley many important aspects of his life, from his failed marriages to his unsuccessful political campaign. Fraley later told a journalist he never knew of these developments until long after Ness was dead. He did discuss with Fraley his hard-luck career in business, which strengthened Fraley's resolve to help a man for whom he felt a genuine fondness. Ness said he was desperate to complete the book project as an insurance policy against the total collapse of North Ridge Industrial Corporation.

With only a handful of orders for checks arriving, Ayers expanded Guaranty Paper Company's operations to include commercial printing of nonwatermarked products, such as letterheads, envelopes, and post cards for local businesses. For several months, these small print jobs provided income to meet payroll and other expenses. Phelps was drawing no salary, while Ness, Ayers, and Rube Pollan were receiving only modest paychecks. Treasurer Verne Haight was also on hand, secretly keeping Shampanore apprised of developments.

On March 14, 1957, Shampanore sent letters to Ness and Ayers demanding their resignations "in the interest of economy and the welfare of the stockholders" and accusing them of everything from theft and disloyalty to mismanagement and incompetence. Ayers decided the time had come for his uncle to answer for his actions. He sum-

moned everyone who still had an interest in North Ridge Industrial
Corporation for a board of directors meeting.

More than four decades later, Ayers still has the minutes of that
tension-filled meeting.

"This is the first time in my life that I've felt as if I'm on trial," an
angry but controlled Eliot Ness told the directors. "I've been involved
in gathering evidence on gangsters, putting crooked cops and union
thugs behind bars. I thought I had seen everything, but the behavior
and movements of Mr. Shampanore are something new to me. I plan
to sue him for libel, unless it appears that doing so would cause serious damage to this company."

Ness said Shampanore's attacks on him and Ayers were destroying morale, scaring away investors, and causing stockholders to
believe that they had been swindled. "He [Ayers], and no one else,
has made our product saleable. He's the greatest influence for good
that we have. So, if Bill Ayers leaves, I leave, too. It's quite obvious
that Mr. Shampanore is trying to destroy this company."

An appreciative and disillusioned Ayers then stood to drop his
bombshell: Shampanore's application for a patent on the highly touted
watermarking process had been rejected long ago. The U.S. Patent
Office determined that Shampanore's "magic formula" was similar to
products already developed in England and California, but Shampanore had failed to inform stockholders of this critical blow. He
finally came clean in a letter to Ayers, informing his nephew that, with
new partners, he was moving forward with plans to open a watermarking operation in Texas. Ayers read excerpts to the stockholders:

> North Ridge has only three things of value—the formula, the one-
> sided check, and your machine. I can take a pinch of salt and an
> ounce of vanilla and it's a different formula. I assigned the patent
> application to North Ridge, but it has been rejected. I am setting
> up a new company and letting North Ridge go down the drain,
> salvaging what stockholders we see fit to favor.

Directors and other investors in the room sat in stunned silence.
They closed the meeting by reaffirming their support of Ness and
Ayers, even as they acknowledged that the North Ridge company's
future looked dim.

"They say blood is thicker than water and it hurts me to say this, but I put 90 percent of the blame on Frank Shampanore and his grandiose ideas, combined with very poor business management," Ayers said. "By the time Eliot Ness had any real authority to operate the business, it was pretty much destroyed. Spending money before we had anything to produce was wrong."

Meanwhile, Ness's health continued to deteriorate. A week after the directors' meeting, he complained of feeling weak upon arriving as guest speaker at a meeting of the Coudersport Parent-Teacher Association and nearly collapsed. Once he felt better, Ness delivered a well-received speech on the problems of juvenile delinquency. Three days later, while walking up the stairs to attend services at the First United Presbyterian Church, he became dizzy and had to sit. The Reverend Robert Loughborough, who was among those who attended to Ness, jokingly said, "Well, Eliot, I guess you'd go to any extreme to avoid hearing one of my sermons."

On April 16, Ness appeared before Dr. Mosch for another physical examination, which revealed that he was suffering from high blood pressure. At that time, hypertension was usually treated with a tranquilizer, in the belief that reducing a patient's level of stress could lower his blood pressure. Mosch gave Ness another prescription and advised him to return for follow-up examinations.

"He felt a certain degree of frustration and pressure to accomplish certain goals he set for himself when he came to the community," Mosch observed. "He seemed to be under a lot of pressure."

In late April, Fraley supplied Ness with the final proofs for *The Untouchables* and sent a one-thousand-dollar check as Ness's share of an advance. Anxious to derive additional income from the venture as soon as possible, Ness did not want to delay publication any longer than necessary. Still, he fretted about the content.

Virginia Kallenborn, a reporter for the daily newspaper in Olean, New York, interviewed Ness and found him to be troubled by Fraley's elaboration. "He said, 'It makes me out to be too much of a hero when it was the whole team that did the work,'" she recalled. "He wanted the credit to go to all of the men who worked on the Capone case, but he also figured Fraley knew what he had to do to make the book a good seller, and Eliot said he needed the money to send Bobby to college."

Late in the afternoon of Thursday, May 16, 1957, Ness and Phelps were involved in an exhaustive review of financial reports. They stopped after Phelps complained of a slight headache and arranged to resume their work at Ness's home a short time later. Ness slipped on his jacket and gathered his briefcase for the five-minute walk from the office to his home. The two headed down the steps together, pausing briefly to inform Ayers of their plans.

It was an uncommonly muggy day in Coudersport. Ness and Phelps progressed to the center of town, where they separated to run some errands. Ness stopped at the Rexall Drug Store to fill his prescription and at the liquor store, where he bought a bottle of scotch. He hurried along the tall maple trees that lined the sidewalk, removing his coat and folding it over his arm as he walked. Beads of perspiration formed on his forehead, and his pace quickened as he neared his home.

He dabbed his brow with a cloth handkerchief and headed for the kitchen, peering through a doorway at Bobby, who was in the living room. Twisting the cold water faucet, he reached for the latch of a cupboard above the sink, pulled out a glass, and collapsed. The glass shattered in the sink as Ness fell shoulder-first to the floor. Betty, who was out in the yard tending to her flowerbeds, heard the glass breaking and noticed that the water was running for a long time. Receiving no response after calling Eliot's name, she hurried inside to find her husband's lifeless body crumpled on the floor next to the sink.

Bobby stood a few feet away, frightened by the desperate, helpless tone in his mother's voice as she cried out in panic. She felt Eliot's neck, praying that she might detect a pulse, then scrambled for the telephone to summon Dr. Mosch. Betty was just hanging up the phone when Joe Phelps arrived. Choking back tears, he checked Ness's body, then calmly told Betty there was nothing a doctor could do. Betty rested her head on his shoulder, sobbing. Mosch arrived moments later. Eliot Ness was pronounced dead at 5 P.M.

Bobby Ness said that his father appeared to be in pain as he arrived home, an observation also made by two neighbors who spotted Ness as he approached his house.

Walter Taylor, the newspaper editor, was the next to arrive, in his capacity as deputy coroner. After conferring briefly with Mosch, Taylor telephoned Potter County coroner George Grabe, a funeral

director who lived across the street from the Nesses. Both Taylor and
Grabe concurred with Mosch that Ness had, from all appearances,
died of a heart attack. They agreed that no autopsy would be necessary. Taylor then ran the three blocks back to the newspaper office and
placed a call to the Associated Press to tell the world Ness was dead.

On Saturday, May 18, a brief funeral service was held at Grabe
Funeral Home. Several of Ness's business associates were among the
fifty people attending. "Here's the only man I ever met who had no
larceny in his heart," said Joe Phelps, tears welling in his eyes as he
stood over the open casket. "Eliot was in a different league." Ness's
body was cremated.

The sun shone through the blue stained-glass window behind
the pulpit where the Reverend Harry B. Taylor stood for a memorial
service at the Presbyterian Church of the Covenant's Christ Chapel
in Cleveland. White and yellow flowers formed a semicircle in front.
About one hundred former colleagues, friends, and family members
heard Taylor praise Ness for "his community interest, his public service, his courage and integrity, his youthful and vital spirit, his
warmth and understanding, and his concern for people."

Among those paying their respects were Robert W. Chamberlin,
who had recently retired as a decorated brigadier general with the
U.S. Army, and former mayor Edward Blythin, then a common pleas
court judge. A Cleveland City Police Department honor guard stood
in formation outside the church.

In the *Potter Enterprise*, Walter Taylor offered this eulogy from a
Coudersport perspective:

> What kind of man was this amiable, gray-eyed six-footer with the
> soft voice, who walked from side to side as he hurried along the
> street? Eliot Ness was kind of a walking contradiction, an under-
> statement, a giggler, a "man you knew from somewhere," a man
> you'd pick out if you were looking for a fellow elbow-bender, a face
> in the crowd. This nemesis of syndicated crime was a fall guy for
> every small bore rafter who came along. For a wayfarer seeking a
> "quarter for a bite," Ness was the easiest of marks. He was unobtru-
> sive and little known in the community to which he came as a cor-
> poration president. No son had a better father and no wife a better
> husband. They told me so. Few people in town knew the dimen-

sions of the man who had been euchred into taking over direction of a shaky industrial complex. If Ness did nothing to set himself apart from an assortment of men whose luster as self-appointed saviors of an industry-starved town had begun to wear thin, it wasn't because he was unaware of the facts of life. Within a few short months, he found himself in the eyes of many in the community tarred with the same brush. But his unerring talent for getting things done blinded the former federal agent to anything but the job at hand. That the business is coming apart at the seams cannot be attributed to either bad faith or bad management on his part.

Chicago newspapers, however, did not even note the passing of Ness. In Cleveland, obituaries recalled Ness as a committed, effective public servant.

"His death at 54 is untimely and unexpected," reported the *Cleveland Press*. "It will come as a shock both to the countless Clevelanders who knew him personally, and to those to whom he was, as Safety Director, a symbol of courage and decency."

Former Cleveland mayor Harold Burton, then a U.S. Supreme Court justice, was among the dozens of former Ness associates sending telegrams to Betty. "I have lost a great and good friend," he wrote. "The nation has lost a valuable citizen." In a *Cleveland Plain Dealer* story, Burton praised Ness as "a courageous, competent public official with the utmost integrity, completely devoted to duty."

Among the many ironies of Ness's life was the breakdown of his finances at the time of his death. He owned no real estate and left to his widow only a rusty 1952 Ford convertible, valued at roughly $200; approximately $275 in a checking account; thousands of shares of worthless stock in North Ridge Industrial Corporation; and $200 out of the original $1,000 paid out as an advance for the book. In his wallet were two uncashable paychecks from Guaranty Paper.

CHAPTER TWENTY-SIX

The Legend

OSCAR FRALEY WAS ABLE to insert an epilogue in *The Untouchables*, informing readers that Eliot Ness had died just before the book was published in November 1957. The story captured the interest of producers from CBS-TV's Desilu Studios. In April 1959 the exaggerated exploits of Ness were the basis of a two-part dramatization on *Desilu Playhouse*. Mae Capone, her son, Sonny, and Al's sister Mafalda were so incensed about the distortions that they filed a $1 million defamation suit against Desilu and the show's sponsor, Westinghouse Electric. The suit was dismissed, but it did draw attention to the program's shortcomings. Nevertheless, solid ratings convinced the producers that *The Untouchables* could be expanded into a weekly, hour-long network series for the American Broadcast Company.

ABC hired Walter Winchell to provide the authentic-sounding, documentary-style narration for the gritty black-and-white episodes. Each show featured one gun battle after another, pitting Ness and his G-men against the evildoers in any number of settings. The program's theme music was as tough as its premise. Faced with the task of creating a new action-packed installment each week, the writers plunged into pure fantasy. Theirs was the first television show to use blood squibs, taut storytelling, and some big-screen effects.

Few gave *The Untouchables* much chance to survive, but the American television audience was drawn by the show's frequent, sometimes crudely graphic, bursts of violence and bloodshed. Americans believed they were getting an authentic look at the Prohibition Era.

The show was not popular with everyone. Former Untouchable Barney Cloonan, for example, took offense at the gunfire. "There wasn't any shooting during our raids," he said. "Nobody got killed or even wounded."

"It wasn't until *The Untouchables* came out on TV, and my father was mentioned, that I started asking him a few questions," said the agent's son, James Cloonan. "But he kept saying it was just a job."

The Untouchables' Paul Robsky also pooh-poohed the program. "We really weren't in that much danger," he told a reporter. "We were courageous and took some chances but I don't think anyone really expected we would be attacked or killed."

Even after Ness's death, J. Edgar Hoover remained paranoid about the celebrated lawman. He ordered FBI staffers to watch *The Untouchables* each week and summarize every plot, in case the FBI was misrepresented in any way. Hoover also tried, unsuccessfully, to persuade Desi Arnaz, whose Desilu Productions owned the show, to change the plots so that the Prohibition Bureau's role was diminished and the FBI's profile boosted. Hoover fumed when episodes showed Ness solving a crime that fell under the FBI's jurisdiction.

Over a period of four seasons, 114 episodes aired, starring Robert Stack as a Ness character who was all-knowing and always triumphant. Stack's resounding macho voice was a plus, but he wasn't the first choice for the job. Van Heflin and Van Johnson were both approached, but neither was interested. Stack's trim and taciturn rendition of Ness was off-base in some respects, but no one challenged his representation of Ness's intelligence, courage, and honesty. *The Untouchables* was nominated for a half-dozen Emmy Awards in its first season and won four of them.

The program may have lasted longer, but it offended the nation's Italian population, who complained that it reinforced negative stereotypes. That growing outcry and the backlash being heard from local ABC affiliates as a result of viewer complaints about excessive violence forced Desilu to drop the series. The program ended the same away it began—in a hail of bullets. It resurfaced briefly in 1962 as two movies, *The Scarface Mob* and *Alcatraz Express,* which were actually reedited episodes of the television series.

Stack, already a movie star in the late 1950s, catapulted to fame in his role as Eliot Ness. "It looked better on the screen dark, so we shot mostly night scenes," Stack recalled. "I sometimes stumbled home at four or five in the morning. It was a killer schedule, but *The Untouchables* had a special quality, a motion picture technique on TV. I was proud to be associated with it."

The filming itself presented some element of danger. Stack recalled the time a 1930 Buick he was driving lost its brakes and smashed through a wall at the end of the sound stage. He escaped serious injury but was shaken. "We had some crude props and special effects," Stack noted. "Splinters of glass were flying everywhere. The timing devices on explosive charges were out of the nineteenth century. You had to count the seconds and run."

Stack, who never met Ness, won an Emmy Award for his work on *The Untouchables,* but he insisted he never wanted to steal the thunder from the man he portrayed:

> In Paris, they all recognized me as Mr. Ness. It wasn't me they liked, it was the character I played. Why should they know Robert Stack? The character was interesting; who played it didn't mean a darned thing. . . . Capone owned the cops; he owned Chicago. So when Ness and his men made war on him, they were considered dead meat. You had to be pretty brave or at least a little strange to do that. . . . I made up my mind that the man had to be a counterpuncher, as a stark contrast to the gaudy flamboyance of the villains. It was a morality play of the good guys versus the bad guys, the diametric opposite of 'The Godfather,' that glorifies the gangsters.

"Stack's success is particularly remarkable," observed George Eckstein, one of the show's writers. "Because the series was written to showcase the gangsters, Stack's dialogue didn't present him with many dramatic opportunities. In fact, most of his scenes were terribly expositionary—he was always on stakeout or at his desk. But Bob made those scenes work because of the intensity he brought to Eliot Ness. He didn't just 'not like' the bad guys, he had a pathological hatred for them and it was that intensity that drew the audience in every week."

Among Stack's most cherished souvenirs is a 1952 personal check for ten dollars written out to "Cash" by Ness to cover a losing bet on a sports event. The check, given to the actor by a Hollywood acquaintance more than a decade later, had bounced due to insufficient funds. Stack said the check is a symbolic reminder of Ness's integrity.

"Here's a guy who could have been wealthy if he would have accepted the bribes he was offered, but he stood for something greater, and what kind of thanks did he get? He couldn't even cover a ten-dollar check. I consider Ness a hero. Heroes are driven by their own drum to do the things they have to do. I have known brave men in my life, and there is a commonality to the way they do things."

During an episode of *This Is Your Life*, Stack was introduced to Betty Ness.

"She walked out and I took her hand and kissed it," Stack remembered. "After, they asked why, and I said, 'I don't know. I didn't know what to do.' She was a charming woman. She said it was surprising how much of her husband I happened to capture. That meant a lot to me."

Betty Ness confirmed that assessment during a newspaper interview. "I like Robert Stack in Eliot's role on TV, and so does Bobby," she said. "All but one thing—Stack is so grim-faced through it all, and you know Eliot wasn't like that. He had a much more quiet voice and gentle quality. Much of the stuff they have used would have come as a surprise to Eliot. It's pure fabrication. I hope to establish, as time goes on, that he was just a real good guy who did other things besides going around smashing stills and shooting at people. Eliot was a restless man and an innovator. He was concerned about juvenile delinquency and civil rights long before they became headlines in the newspaper. . . . He lived his life with a constant concern for others and a goal of making their lives better. There wasn't a dull moment in my life married to him. I loved every minute of it."

Even Oscar Fraley was taken aback by the television adaptation of the Eliot Ness character he helped to produce. "As a popular TV series, 'The Untouchables' suddenly turned the gentleman I knew, who died a non-entity, into a national figure," Fraley wrote. "Eliot Ness really was two men. In public he was the Ness of television: talking little, but with authority, and using short, terse phrases. In private, with a few close friends, he was the 'other' Eliot Ness, with a bubbling sense of humor and ready smile. At these times, he would kick off his shoes and sprawl casually on the floor. Then the words rushed out in a smooth flood which mixed wit, perception and warmth."

To his dying day, Fraley made no apologies for his role in creating the Eliot Ness myth. "Any personal and possibly selfish reasons aside, it makes for a warm feeling to know that the man who was nobody in his final years finally came into his own through the publication of our book."

Other Hollywood adaptations have further distorted Ness's image. In the summer of 1987, Paramount Pictures released a $25 million movie, *The Untouchables,* directed by Brian De Palma and starring Kevin Costner as Ness. Scriptwriter David Mamet was careful to specify that the movie was "inspired" by the book written by Fraley and Ness, and even that was a stretch. Incidents such as a hotel lobby confrontation between Ness and Capone and the baby carriage bouncing down the stairs at the railroad terminal never took place. The film's scene of Ness throwing Frank Nitti off a roof was not only fictional, but illogical. The real Nitti committed suicide not long after learning that he would be serving a second prison term for tax evasion and had been betrayed by surviving members of Capone's organization.

Costner had a sincere desire to emulate Ness's personality and mannerisms, within the confines of the script. For advice, he turned to Al "Wallpaper" Wolff.

"They wanted me to be an adviser when they did *The Untouchables* TV series, but I didn't want to, because I knew it would be phony," Wolff explained. "I told Costner that Ness was passive. I told him how to walk like Ness. Ness walked slowly. When I watched the TV show, I just laughed at how phony it was, but parts of the movie were pretty real, even though there was a lot of Hollywood thrown in. Costner did a good job—I was a good teacher."

After the 1987 movie made Ness famous among a new generation of Americans, Robert Stack resurrected his Eliot Ness character in a fictional made-for-television movie for CBS, entitled *Eliot Ness: Welcome to Detroit*. He followed that with another two-hour television movie, *The Return of Eliot Ness*, which aired on NBC in 1991. Stack also narrated an episode of the NBC show *Unsolved Mysteries*, which focused on the inability of Ness and other Cleveland law enforcement authorities to solve the serial killings by the Mad Butcher.

In 1993 a syndicated television show, also titled *The Untouchables*, allowed another generation to follow the legendary figure of Eliot Ness as he battled it out against the Capone outfit. Tony Amandes played the role of Ness during the two-year run of the series, which was carried by about fifty stations nationwide.

Betty Ness received some modest royalties from sales of *The Untouchables*, but the checks, usually for less than fifty dollars, were not nearly enough to support herself and Bobby. In late 1957 they returned to the Cleveland area and visited Corinne Lawson, the former housekeeper. Lawson agreed to let them live in her home while Betty looked for a job. Their stay with Lawson lasted for more than a year, during which time Betty's depression became apparent to Corinne Lawson.

"I would find empty booze bottles under her bed and she was frequently very sad," Lawson said. "But she and Mr. Ness had done so much for me and had been so nice that I didn't care about that."

Betty eventually went to work as a clerk for a clothing boutique on Cleveland's Carnegie Avenue then as a medical records specialist for a Cleveland hospital. She later was a clerk at an art gallery on Seventeenth Street, where old friend Viktor Schreckengost happened upon her one day in 1960.

"I had known Betty before she met Eliot, when we went to art school and then we both worked at the Cowan Pottery Studios," Schreckengost said. "She and Eliot always seemed so happy together and very much in love. It was so sad to see that he had apparently left her with no money, so there she was selling jewelry and pottery and glass, and still looking so elegant and smiling so nicely. I just felt bad that things hadn't worked out better."

Occasionally sought out by reporters for interviews, Betty tried to live a quiet, private life. Eventually, she and Bobby moved into an apartment at Cleveland Heights, just east of the city, and Betty was hired to teach pottery making. Some of the pieces she produced early in her career are showcased as part of the Cowan Pottery Studios collection, which is on display at the Rocky River Public Library near Cleveland. Others are owned by the Cleveland Museum of Art.

After Bobby was grown and married, Betty moved to San Juan Capistrano, California, to live with relatives and continue her work in sculpture.

Robert Warren Ness served in the U.S. Army, then worked at Christie Labs of Cleveland. He kept the ashes of his father at his Cleveland Heights home. He and his wife, Sharon, who were childless, became avid car racing fans and occasionally volunteered as pit workers for their favorite drivers. Robert was studying electrical engineering at Cleveland State University when he became ill. He was eventually diagnosed with leukemia, which claimed his life on August 31, 1976.

Elisabeth Andersen Ness never remarried. She died on November 4, 1977, at her California home at the age of seventy-one. An obituary in the *Cleveland Plain Dealer* stated that she had been suffering from cancer for the past several years. In a letter to an old friend back in Cleveland, sent just a few weeks before her death, she wrote, "I spent too long in cancer research to want the heroic measures that go for the young. I've enjoyed life so much that I can't feel bad. Whatever happens, it's all fine."

For many years, there were no markers to memorialize Eliot, Betty, or Robert Ness. Their ashes remained with Robert's widow in her suburban Cleveland home. In 1997 Rebecca McFarland, a research librarian and officer of the Cleveland Police Historical Society, and Cleveland police commander Robert L. Cermak persuaded the former Sharon Ness to release the cremains to the historical society. On September 10, 1997, some forty years after Eliot Ness died, his wish to have his ashes spread over water was granted.

The ceremony was preceded by a memorial service during which a large granite marker bearing the names of Eliot, Elisabeth, and Robert Ness was unveiled. "Eliot's integrity was pure and his sense of justice inflexible," Rebecca McFarland said.

With six hundred people surrounding Wade Lagoon at Cleveland's prestigious Lake View Cemetery and the eyes of the world looking on via Cable News Network, the ashes of Eliot, Elisabeth, and Robert Ness were poured onto the water as a lone bagpiper played "Amazing Grace." Two police helicopters swept down from the sky and crisscrossed just above the tree line, stirring a current that scattered the ashes before soaring back into the sky and disappearing behind the clouds.

Epilogue

SOUVENIRS OF ELIOT NESS are everywhere, from the Cleveland Police Historical Society Museum, where the public can view his Smith and Wesson revolver and countless photos and newspaper clippings, to liquor store manager Larry Del Grosso's closet, where a pair of Ness's gym trunks, picked up at a yard sale, hang as a reminder of Del Grosso's conversations with a man who became a celebrity.

Large framed posters from the 1987 movie *The Untouchables* hang in many offices of the U.S. Treasury Department's Bureau of Alcohol, Tobacco and Firearms. Still the agency has resisted calls to use Ness's photo and widespread name recognition to promote the bureau, but assistant treasurer Francis Keating believes Ness's screen image has attracted hundreds of recruits. "Generic money laundering and narcotics violations are what the Eliot Ness of today would be investigating," Keating said, "and that's just as stimulating and just as potentially lethal as the challenges of yesteryear."

Rebecca McFarland tries to preserve Ness's memory with a slide show and well-researched speech about his Cleveland days. The Historical Society in 1997 established the Eliot Ness Memorial Educational Fund to bring law enforcement information and history to Cleveland-area schools.

Four death masks remain on display at the Cleveland Police Historical Society Museum, today more of a novelty or a memorial to the Mad Butcher's unidentified victims than an attempt to bring the killer to justice.

Arts & Entertainment, the History Channel, Discovery, and other television networks have produced documentaries about Ness in recent years. Although they have their faults, these programs capture much more of the true story of Ness's life and career than the fiction-alized programs.

Eliot Ness . . . In Cleveland, described by its promoters as "a musical historical fantasy" developed by the Harold Prince Musical Theatre Program in New York City, debuted in 1998. Much of its focus is on Ness's search for the Mad Butcher serial killer.

Oscar Fraley, who receives the credit or the blame for making Ness a household name, depending on who is doing the evaluating, died in Fort Lauderdale, Florida, on January 6, 1994, at the age of seventy-nine. He had been hospitalized with complications from hernia and stomach surgery. During a thirty-eight-year career, the Philadelphia native wrote more than thirty books, many of them focusing on crimefighters and sports figures. He also helped celebri-ties—Jimmy Hoffa among them—write their autobiographies, sometimes as a ghostwriter, and was senior editor of a golf magazine. "He never intended to be a great literary writer—you don't make money doing that," said Anita Diamant, his literary agent. "He was a solid writer who knew how to tell a story." Fraley took offense at reporters who jumped to the conclusion that Ness was an alcoholic or even that he had a drinking problem: "He was a nice guy and a hell of a lawman, but he was not a heavy drinker, despite what people have written. He had a couple of scotches now and then, but he didn't drink very much. Some reporters couldn't resist the idea of reporting that a former Prohibition agent turned out to be a drunk. It might have made a nice story, but they got it wrong."

Fraley knew a good thing when he saw it. After he profited so handsomely from *The Untouchables,* he joined forces with Paul Robsky to produce a sequel, *The Last of the Untouchables,* that featured similar stories with a different hero and scant mention of Robsky's boss, Ness.

George Emmerson Q. Johnson, in the wake of Al Capone's tax evasion conviction, was appointed by President Herbert Hoover to a federal district court judgeship. A year later, he opted for a private law practice that prospered. Johnson died in 1949, so he never knew that his efforts to heap praise on Ness and the Untouchables paid such bizarre dividends a quarter-century later. "My father was proud of his work, but overall a very humble man," George Johnson Jr.

said. "He lived by the philosophy that money is not as important as serving the public."

Al "Wallpaper" Wolff surprised family members and friends when the news media told of his work with Kevin Costner for *The Untouchables* since he had not mentioned that aspect of his career to them. "Stories about my government work were between me and Uncle Sam, and some of them still are," he told a National Public Radio interviewer in 1987. "I don't want to mention names, 'cause they have children and grandchildren and I don't want to put a tag on 'em." When Wolff died on March 21, 1998, at the age of ninety-five, newspaper headlines proclaimed him as "the last of the Untouchables."

Lt. Ernest Molnar's Cleveland numbers racket finally caught up to him in 1949, when he was sentenced to a four-year prison term.

Al Capone died in Florida on January 25, 1947, of complications from a brain hemorrhage and bronchial pneumonia, his legacy much broader than his self-declared "giving the public what the public wants." Five days earlier Andrew Volstead died at Granite Falls, Minnesota, his faith unshaken to the end that "the law does regulate morality." The Prohibition Party remains in existence today, buoyed by a 1999 poll showing that 40 percent of Americans identify themselves as alcohol abstainers—up from 28 percent in 1978.

Eliot's oldest sister, Effie, died on October 30, 1950, in Hazelcrest, Illinois. An obituary described her as "a highly respected teacher."

Edna M. Ness died in a nursing home at Saint Petersburg, Florida, on November 19, 1994, at the age of eighty-eight. "She had been alone for many years," said her longtime friend, Maxine Huntington. "Her greatest wish was not to be known. She was eighty-eight and still wished that. She lived incognito." Edna had come to Saint Petersburg from Miami in 1976, having retired from her job as a typist with a greeting card company. An obituary said that she never remarried, had no known survivors, and there would be no funeral service.

Evaline Ness Bayard died of a heart attack in Kingston, New York, in August 1986 at the age of seventy-five. She was survived by her husband, Arnold A. Bayard of Philadelphia, and a sister. Evaline's career prospered after she left Cleveland, and she remained active as a book illustrator throughout her life, distinguishable for her sweeping lines and soft colors. Her most famous title, *Sam, Bangs and Moonshine,* focusing on a fisherman's daughter, won the 1967 Randolph J. Calde-cott Medal of the American Library Association for the "most distin-guished American picture book." It can still be found on many library shelves. Evaline's final work was *The Hand-Me-Down Doll,* published in 1984. She had moved from New York to Palm Beach, Florida, after she remarried and maintained residences in both locations.

Dan Moore, who died in 1998, saw his friend Eliot Ness as a tragic figure because of his unfulfilled potential: "How would I sum-marize Eliot? His relationships with people were the most important thing to him. He liked to have his friends around him. He was great with anything involving personal relationships and he had a very high moral code. He would have made a wonderful minister. He approached life from the standpoint that human relationships are more important than anything else, and people are delightful. . . . He was probably guilty of being too good at what he did. It's seldom that a person in public life doesn't eventually run into all sorts of traps that are generated by the fact that he has done a good job. You can't do a good job in public life without making enemies. After Chicago and Cleveland, what in the heck could he do for an encore?"

Within weeks of Ness's death, sheriff Harold Holcomb posted a foreclosure notice on the door at the Guaranty Paper Company. Internal Revenue Service field officers seized the company's checking account at Citizens Safe Deposit and Trust Company, and Couder-sport's First National Bank foreclosed on loans made for equipment. Fact and rumor have always mingled freely in what is said of North Ridge, Guaranty, Fidelity, and the whole cast of characters. A planned federal investigation of the corporation's failure was either abandoned or quashed. Joe Phelps sued North Ridge on behalf of the betrayed stockholders, but there was never a trial. After paying off his personal guarantees of the North Ridge stock to his friends, Phelps left Coudersport in October 1957 and became an industrial real estate salesman in southern New Jersey.

Shampanore's watermarking company operating in Texas col-lapsed, and he retired from the business world with little to show for all of his ventures.

Bill Ayers stayed in Coudersport to clean up the mess. Taking over payments on a printing press the bank was about to seize and securing small loans from friends, he opened up Tool Craft, a small print shop and mail-order business for his own tools, just across Main Street from the old Guaranty Paper shop. "I was not going to leave Coudersport under a cloud," he said. "I was the only one left to take the blame, and I had nothing to be ashamed of. No one set out to intentionally beat anybody else out of money. We honestly thought we had a good product. We were probably all guilty of being gullible and overenthusiastic." Ayers's new business struggled until John Rigas, the cable television pioneer, approached him with a plan to produce coupon booklets for customers to use in paying their cable bills. A quarter-century later, when Ayers sold his T-C Specialties (short for Tool Craft) printing business, it was the world's largest producer of coupon payment books.

Eastern State Penitentiary in Philadelphia, which closed in 1970, is now a National Historic Site, attracting ten thousand visitors a year. Al Capone's former cell, minus the carpet, fine furniture, and other special accommodations, remains the most popular stop on the tour.

The Chicago Crime Commission, today a 240-member law enforcement education organization, still rightfully boasts of its origins in the battle against Capone's outfit. "Knowledge is power," the commission's executive director pointed out in a recent crime report. "A well-informed public can organize its resources to protect itself and, ultimately, diminish the impact of criminal groups."

Joe Phelps, visiting Coudersport in 1965, sat at a front table of Mackey's Restaurant and noticed a newspaper story stating that Capone's son, Sonny, had been arrested for shoplifting two bottles of aspirin and a package of batteries from a Miami Beach convenience store. "Everybody has a little larceny in them," was the quote from Sonny Capone, who had changed his name to Albert Francis.

"Not everybody, Sonny," Phelps said after reading the blurb aloud to his lunch partner. Phelps went on to tell his acquaintance about the man with whom he had spent so many mornings at the same counter almost a decade earlier.

Ness himself sometimes looked back incredulously at his own life. "Hell, I'm just like anyone else," he once said. "There were certain things I had to do and I did them. Of course, I'll admit that when there was action at hand I did feel a certain sense of exhilaration;

maybe even exultation. But, many a time after it was over and I realized what had happened or how close a call it had been, I broke out in
a cold sweat."

Bill Ayers, who knew Eliot Ness better than anybody alive today,
wrote:

> The real test of a man's moral fiber is to be found in his everyday
> life. Eliot Ness attacked every menial problem with the same zeal
> that he must have used to attack the overwhelming odds facing
> him in battles against crime. He refused to accept defeat in situa-
> tions where a lesser man would give in. I have never known an
> individual who lived by a stricter code. Eliot was uncompromising
> in his principles, both in his crime-fighting days and in his business
> dealings, even to his own personal loss. They say all men have a
> price. Well, whatever his price was, it was so high that nobody
> could pay it. Eliot Ness was a man to talk and laugh with, to drink
> with, and share the joys and sorrows that make up life. In his place,
> he left a legend that, like most legends, is an unfit memorial.

Bibliography

Books

Allen, F. L. *Only Yesterday: An Informal History of the 1920s in America.* New York and London: Harper & Brothers, 1931. Reprint, New York: Perennial Classics, 2000.

Allsop, Kenneth. *The Bootleggers: The Story of Chicago's Prohibition Era.* New Rochelle, N.J.: Arlington House, 1970.

Asbury, Herbert. *Gem of the Prairie: An Informal History of the Chicago Underworld.* New York: Knopf, 1940.

Bayer, Oliver Weld, ed. *Cleveland Murders.* New York: Duell, Sloan and Pearce, 1947.

Behr, Edward. *Prohibition: Thirteen Years That Changed America.* Boston: Little, Brown and Co., 1996.

Bergreen, Laurence. *Capone: The Man and the Era.* New York: Simon & Schuster, 1994.

Brown, Dorothy M. *Mabel Walker Willedrandt: A Study of Power, Loyalty, and Law.* Knoxville: University of Tennessee Press, 1984.

Condon, George E. *Cleveland: The Best Kept Secret.* Garden City, N.Y.: Doubleday, 1967.

Dobyns, Fletcher. *The Underworld of American Politics.* N.p.p.: Fletcher Dobyns Publishing, 1932.

Fraley, Oscar. *Four Against the Mob.* New York: Popular Library, 1961.

Franklin, Fabian. *What Prohibition Has Done to America.* New York: Harcourt, Brace and Co., 1922.

Hoffman, Dennis. *Scarface Al and the Crime Crusaders: Chicago's Private War Against Capone.* Carbondale: Southern Illinois University Press, 1993.

Horan, James D. *The Mob's Man.* New York: Crown, 1959.

Irey, Elmer L., and William J. Slocum. *The Tax Dodgers: The Whole Story of T-Men's War with America's Political and Underworld Hoodlums.* New York: Greenberg, 1948.

Kobler, John. *Ardent Spirits: The Rise and Fall of Prohibition*. New York: Putnam, 1973.

———. *Capone: The Life and World of Al Capone*. New York: Putnam, 1971.

Liebling, A. J. *Chicago: The Second City*. New York: Knopf, 1952.

Lyle, John H. *The Dry and Lawless Years*. Englewood Cliffs, N.J.: Prentice-Hall, 1960.

Martin, John Bartlow. *Butcher's Dozen and Other Murders*. New York: Harper, 1950.

Meyers, Richard. *TV Detectives*. San Diego: A. S. Barnes, 1981.

Ness, Eliot, with Oscar Fraley. *The Untouchables*. New York: Messner, 1957.

Nickel, Steven. *Torso: The Story of Eliot Ness and the Search for a Psychopathic Killer*. Winston-Salem, N.C.: J. F. Blair, 1989.

Pasley, Fred D. *Al Capone: The Biography of a Self-Made Man*. New York: I. Washburn, 1930.

Peterson, Virgil W. *Barbarians in Our Midst: A History of Chicago Crime and Politics*. Boston: Little, Brown, 1952.

Porrello, Rick. *The Rise and Fall of the Cleveland Mafia: Corn, Sugar, and Blood*. New York: Barricade Books, 1995.

Porter, Phillip W. *Cleveland: Confused City on a Seesaw*. Columbus: Ohio State University Press, 1976.

Robsky, Paul, and Oscar Fraley. *The Last of the Untouchables*. New York: Popular Library, 1962.

Sann, Paul. *The Lawless Decade: A Pictorial History of a Great American Transition*. New York: Crown Publishers, 1957.

Schoenberg, Robert J. *Mr. Capone: The Real and Complete Story of Al Capone*. New York: Morrow, 1992.

Sondern, Frederic. *Brotherhood of Evil: The Mafia*. New York: Farrar, Straus, and Cudahy, 1959.

Thrasher, Frederic M. *The Gang: A Study of 1,313 Gangs in Chicago*. Chicago: University of Chicago, 1927.

Turkus, Burton B., and Sid Feder. *Murder, Inc.: The Story of "the Syndicate."* London: Gollancz, 1952.

Vizzard, William J. *In the Crossfire: A Political History of the Bureau of Alcohol, Tobacco and Firearms*. Boulder: Lynne Rienner, 1997.

Wendt, Lloyd, and Herman Koga. *Big Bill of Chicago*. Indianapolis: Bobbs-Merrill, 1953.

Whitehead, Don. *The FBI Story: A Report to the People.* New York: Random House, 1957.

Wicker, Elmus. *The Banking Panics of the Great Depression.* Cambridge and New York: Cambridge University Press, 1996.

Windle, Charles A. *The Case Against Prohibition.* Chicago: Iconoclast Publishing Co., 1927.

Zorbaugh, Harvey W. *The Gold Coast and the Slum: A Sociological Study of Chicago's Near North Side.* Chicago: University of Chicago, 1929.

Periodicals

"Al Capone: Chicago's Untouchable Mobster." *American History Illustrated,* October 1987.

Arruda, George, FBI Special Agent. "Eliot Ness Revisited." *The Investigator,* May 1988.

Ayers, William J. "As I Knew Eliot Ness." *Potter Enterprise,* 24 November 1971.

Badal, Dr. James. "The Kingsbury Run Torso Murders." *Cleveland Police Historical Society Newsletter,* Summer 1997.

Barrett, William P. "The FBI's TV Files." *Rolling Stone,* 21 April 1988.

Bergstrom, Bill. "Al Capone's Luxury Lockup on Display." Associated Press, 30 October 1998.

Brennan, Ray. "The Capone I Knew." *True Detective,* June 1947.

Carlson, Timothy. "Stack Is Back as Mr. Untouchable." *TV Guide,* 9 November 1991.

"Cleveland Versus the Crooks." *Reader's Digest,* Feburary 1939.

"Crime in Cleveland." *Newsweek,* 21 March 1938.

Epstein, Joseph. "Browsing in Gangland." *Commentary,* January 1972.

"Evaline Ness, Rising Star in the Illustration Firmament." *American Artist,* January 1956.

"Faced Many Perils in Capone Round-Up." *New York Times,* 17 June 1931.

Fraley, Oscar. "The Real Eliot Ness." *Coronet,* January 1972.

Graves, John H. "Meet the Real Gangbuster: Eliot Ness." *Potter County Leader,* 24 June 1987.

High, Stanley. "Cleveland vs. the Crooks." *Reader's Digest,* February 1939.

Jedick, Peter. "Eliot Ness." *Cleveland Magazine,* April 1976.

Kurian, George T., ed. "A Historical Guide to the U.S. Government." Oxford University Press, 1998.

Mathews, Tom. "The Mob at the Movies." *Newsweek,* 22 June 1987.

Merten, Bob. "Eliot Ness in Coudersport." (transcript of speech presented to Coudersport, Pa., Rotary Club on May 10, 1993).

Mitchell, John G. "What the Public Wanted." *American Heritage,* February 1979.

"Ness the Safe Man." *Newsweek,* 7 January 1946.

Ness, Eliot. "The National Program of Social Protection." *Journal of the American Public Welfare Association,* April 1943.

———. "Radio-Directed Mobile Police." *American City,* November 1939.

Nickel, Steven. "The Real Eliot Ness." *American History Illustrated,* October 1987.

Phillips, James Henry. "1929: Prohibition and the Crash." (essay), 1998.

"Reliving a Massacre." *Newsweek,* 29 January 1979.

Robertson, Ed. "The Untouchables." *Television Chronicles,* 1996

Savell, Taris. "Eliot Ness to Millions." *Grit,* 9 July 199?8.

Schickel, Richard. "In the American Grain." *Time,* 8 June 1987.

Shapiro, Laura, and Ray Sawhill. "The First Untouchable of Them All." *Newsweek,* 26 June 1987.

Tamarkin, Civia. "The Last Untouchable: A New Movie Flushes Out An Old Eliot Ness G-Man From Undercover." *People Weekly,* 18 July 1987.

Taylor, Walter. "Eliot Ness's Last Days." *Potter Enterprise,* 22 March 1961.

"There Goes Eliot Ness." *Fortune,* January 1946.

"Turkey: Outpost in the Cold War." *U.S. News and World Report,* 16 July 1948.

"Turkey: Today's Economic Picture in Key Country of Near East." *Foreign Commerce Weekly,* 19 June 1948.

"When Eliot Ness Ran Diebold." *ATM Magazine,* 13 November 1998.

Wilder, Jesse Bryant. "The Last Untouchable." *Northern Ohio Live,* March 1993.

Wolff, Al, and Civia Tarmarkin. "The Last Untouchable." *People Weekly,* 13 July 1987.

Various articles appearing in the following newspapers: *Chicago Tribune, Chicago Evening American, Chicago Daily News, Chicago Herald-Examiner,*

Cleveland Plain Dealer, Cleveland Press, Cleveland News, Cincinnati Inquirer, Wall Street Journal, New York Times, New York Daily News, New York Journal, San Francisco Examiner, Miami Herald, Baltimore Sun, New Castle News, Potter Enterprise, Chattanooga News-Free Press, Olean Times Herald.

Also, files, archives, and souvenirs appearing in the Cleveland Police Historical Museum, Cleveland Public Library, Western Reserve Historical Society, Chicago Public Library, Potter County (Pa.) Historical Society, U.S. Government Printing Office, U.S. Justice Department, Federal Bureau of Investigation, Bureau of Alcohol, Tobacco and Firearms, the collection of F. D. Bruce Cahilly, the collection of Karl Bretz, and other private collections.

Index

PAUL W. HEIMEL has more than twenty years' experience as a
professional writer. His articles have appeared in dozens of
magazines, and he has worked as a stringer for the Associated Press
since the mid-1970s. Heimel has also served as managing editor of
two newspapers. His previous books include *No Longer Any Danger,*
which focused on a nationally publicized double-murder case
involving attorney F. Lee Bailey; *Always a Danger,* a follow-up to the
first book; *Shattered Dreams,* which traced the life of Norwegian
violin virtuoso Ole Bull and his efforts to establish a colony in
northern Pennsylvania; and *High Wire Angel,* an authorized
biography of aerialist Angel Wallenda. Heimel was born and raised
in Coudersport, Pennsylvania, the small community where Eliot
Ness spent the final two years of his life.